CW01023835

A Naval Life

The Edited Diaries and Papers of
Admiral John Locke Marx
1852-1939

isca

Mary Jones is a historian whose chief interest is in the Victorian and Edwardian Navy. She has an MA from Exeter University centring on the Victorian Australia Station, and a doctorate from Exeter centring on the Victorian and Edwardian Naval Officer Corps. She has written about Captain Francis Clayton on the Australian Station, 1884–1888, for the Navy Records Society, and Admiral Sir William May for *Mariner's Mirror*. She has given papers at the Maritime Museum in Greenwich and King's College in London. She has written on various aspects of local history.

She came to naval history somewhat late, as a retired teacher, and admits to having trouble with the hardware, but insists that it is the software of the personnel that is responsible for the quality of the Service.

A Naval Life

The Edited Diaries and Papers of Admiral John Locke Marx
1852-1939

Edited by Mary Jones

PERSONA
PRESS

Copyright © Mary Jones 2007
First published in 2007 by Persona Press
Bridge House, Brushford
Dulverton, Somerset TA22 9AQ

Distributed by Gazelle Book Services Limited
Hightown, White Cross Mills, South Rd, Lancaster, England LA1 4XS

The right of Mary Jones to be identified as the editor of the work has been
asserted herein in accordance with the Copyright, Designs and Patents Act 1988.

All rights reserved. This book is sold subject to the condition that it shall not, by
way of trade or otherwise, be lent, resold, hired out or otherwise circulated
without the publisher's prior consent in any form of binding or cover other than
that in which it is published and without a similar condition including this
condition being imposed on the subsequent purchaser.

British Library Cataloguing in Publication Data
A catalogue record for this book is available from the British Library.

ISBN 978-0-9553095-0-2

Typeset by Amolibros, Milverton, Somerset
This book production has been managed by Amolibros
Printed and bound by T J International Ltd, Padstow, Cornwall, UK

Acknowledgements

My thanks must go first to Commander Andrew Marx, who so helpfully provided me with access to his grandfather's papers, and to his wife Amanda for her delightful hospitality. Admiral John Locke Marx may not have come from a naval family, but he did start one. His son and a grandson both had careers in the Navy. Both became Commanders. His son, George, saw service in two world wars and grandson Andrew saw varied service in the Royal Navy for over thirty years, retiring in 1984. Andrew's help with family research and his enthusiasm for the project have been greatly appreciated. I am also grateful to him for the provision of most of the photographs in this book.

I only hope this academic approach to such a character as his grandfather has done him justice. I would simply say what Trollope said about his characters: 'If I have not made the strength and virtues predominant over the faults and vices, I have not painted the picture as I intended.'[1]

At the academic level, I must particularly thank Professor Nicholas Rodger for his erudition in respect of the content, and his encouragement in respect of the project. I am also indebted to the help of Dr Steven Smith at the National Archives, and the never failing good offices of Plymouth Naval Library. My husband bore with my enthusiasm when all was going well, and my anguish when computers, research, etc. failed. He provided a keen and much appreciated eye for proofreading.

With acknowledgements come apologies for any errors that I may have made in this recording of such a long and remarkable 'Naval Life'.

Note

John Locke Marx never mastered the art of punctuation. The obscurity of some of his sentences is notable even in an age that used fewer commas. His spelling was suspect and his knowledge of the names of places and persons haphazard. In quoting from his own writing I have deciphered his handwriting as best I can and been scrupulous in using his own words wherever possible. However, I have found it necessary to add punctuation in order to ease readability.

Ranks given to naval officers in the references are those at which officers retired.

Contents

List of Illustrations

Facing page 146

1 Francis J Marx, John's father.

2 John Marx with older brother, George.

3 The young Midshipman Marx.

4 HMS *Swinger,* Marx's first ship as Lieutenant and Commanding Officer.

5 The young Lily Heath.

6 Lily as John's Marx's wife.

7 Breech Farm, the Marxes' first house.

8 Commander John Locke Marx.

9 Admiral John Locke Marx.

10 Clatford Lodge, Marx's house from 1906–1939.

11 *HMS Dominion,* Marx's last battleship, courtesy of Walker Archive.

12 Marx with his beloved horse, Stilton.

13 Almost the last outing with the Tedworth Hunt, picture from *Tatler.*

14 Marx by the bunker he built at the beginning of WWII to resist German occupation. It is still there!

15 Kapitan Leutnant Ziemer, the German Commander of *UB 23.*

16 The 'Grand Old Man'.

For Andrew and Amanda Marx who made this
project both possible and pleasurable.

Foreword

Anyone familiar with the life of the Victorian Royal Navy will be familiar with admirals' memoirs. All too many of them give the impression of a service whose only professional interest was seamanship, and whose only intellectual recreation was snipe-shooting. This is not a fair picture of the real Navy. Published memoirs, then as now, represented what the writers wanted to remember, and what the publishers thought the public wanted to buy. Remote and difficult subjects like tactics, strategy and naval technology did not sell books to a general audience, and those officers who were minded to write about them tended to publish elsewhere. What the public was offered, and expected to be offered, were genial reminiscences of travel and adventure, untroubled by self-doubt and unrevealing of private feelings (except in some cases religious feelings). They are good sources of anecdotes, and a valuable guide to late-Victorian attitudes to the recent past, but they are no more a reliable record of historical fact than any other memoirs. Nor, of course, do they reveal anything disreputable or shameful about the authors or their Service. Most admirals' memoirs could safely be left upon the dressing-table of a maiden aunt (at least, a maiden aunt interested in snipe-shooting).

John Locke Marx's candid private journals provide a striking contrast to all this. His career was successful, as far as the public was concerned, but his private writings reveal a discontented and even embittered man, critical of his fellow-officers and of the Navy. His unflattering character sketches of his shipmates are as libellous as those of James Anthony Gardner's late eighteenth-century memoir, but lack Gardner's cheerful good humour. Marx never seems to have found real personal stability in his career. His numerous visits to brothels and consequent bouts of venereal disease, something which he reveals to have been commonplace among junior officers, went on to remarkably late in life.

Marx belonged to a lucky generation, carried effortlessly to high rank by the rapid expansion of the late-Victorian Navy. We may guess that in another generation, faced with more intense competition, he would not have risen so far. There is little to suggest that he found the Navy intellectually stimulating, or even personally satisfying. It may well be that such attitudes were more common than we realise. There must have been others who thought and acted as he did, but they did not often write journals, and they certainly did not often leave them for posterity to read. For the historian this is all the more valuable. Mary Jones has brought to light a vivid and revealing private view of the inner life of the Victorian Royal Navy as it definitely did not wish to be seen.

N. A. M. Rodger

---

1 A Trollope, *The Prime Minister*, p388.

Chronology

John Locke Marx

Ships	Rank	From	To
Britannia	Cadet	January 1866	April 1867
Phoebe	Midshipman	May 1867	November 1870
Caledonia	Midshipman	January 1870	June 1872
Excellent	Sub Lieutenant	June 1872	November 1872
Excellent	Sub Lieutenant	January 1873	April 1874
Lord Warden	Sub Lieutenant	April 1874	November 1874
Invincible	Second Lieutenant	December 1874	January 1875
Achilles	Second Lieutenant	May 1877	August 1880
Fawn	First Lieutenant	December 1880	April 1883
Vernon	Lieutenant	April 1883	June 1883
Excellent	Lieutenant	June 1883	June 1883
Swinger	Lieutenant + Commander	October 1883	August 1887
Vernon	Lieutenant	April 1888	
Mersey	Commander	July 1889	September 1889
Belleisle	Commander	November 1890	November 1892
Royal Naval College, Greenwich	Commander	April 1893	July 1893
Blanche	Commander	August 1893	August 1894
Barossa	Captain	August 1894	June 1895
Gunnery, Torpedo, Signals courses	Captain	June 1895	September 1896

Ships	Rank	From	To
Terpsichore (manoeuvres)	Captain	June 1897	September 1897
Royal Naval College, Greenwich	Captain	September 1897	September 1898
Proserpine	Captain	September 1898	October 1900
Sick leave	Captain	October 1900	October 1901
Grafton and Warspite	Captain	October 1901	November 1902
Hogue	Captain	November 1902	May 1904
Suffolk	Captain	May 1904	October 1904
Mars	Captain (ADC)	October 1904	August 1905
Dominion	Captain	August 1905	April 1906
War course, Portsmouth	Rear Admiral	October 1906	January 1907
Signal course, Portsmouth	Rear Admiral	September 1907	
Retired	Rear Admiral	September 1909	
Retired	Vice Admiral	July 1910	
Retired	Admiral	June 1913	
Agatha	Temp Commander RNR	November 1914	January 1915
Stephen Furness	Temp Captain RNR	January 1915	June 1915
Iolanda	Captain RNR	June 1915	May 1916
Q 13, renamed *Aubretia*	Captain RNR	August 1916	May 1917
(DSO)	Captain RNR	March 1917	
(CB, military)	Captain RNR		
ACS *Bayano*	Admiral, Flag Officer Escort	August 1917	August 1918

Reverted to Retired List, December 1918

Introduction

John Locke Marx joined the Royal Navy as a diffident, young cadet in 1866. He retired as a redoubtable old admiral in 1918.

When the young Marx joined the Royal Navy it was in the doldrums of the 'sixties. There was little activity, and promotion was slow. By the time he became a lieutenant and commanding officer, the old Victorian Navy was at its height, with its dispersed squadrons of sailing ships, naval brigades, and independent captains. They operated in scattered fleets of men of war, armoured cruisers, corvettes, sloops, schooners and gunboats. They kept the peace of the far-flung British Empire, treading a wary path between action and diplomacy, safeguarding the Queen's Pax Britannica. Marx was a captain in the New Navy when the dispersed fleets of the Pax Britannica were being brought home by the powerful First Lord, John Fisher[1] and amalgamated into the great home fleets of the Edwardian Navy, with its powerful battleships and professional, homogeneous Officer Corps. Not everybody approved. Fisher's rival, Lord Beresford, steeped in Old Navy tradition, thought it the great betrayal.[2]

Captains serving in the New Navy had to operate differently from Old Navy captains. The handling of the new Dreadnoughts, cruisers, steam / turbine battleships, the torpedo drills and director-spotting gunnery, required different skills. For those who were young, the changes were easy to assimilate, but for those who had been brought up in earlier days, it was hard.[3] Certainly Marx found it so. He had not had enough experience of big-fleet work. His temperament flourished in the autonomy and freedom of the dispersed

1

fleets of the Old Navy, it was less happy in the restriction of the large fleets of the New Navy and the requirements of conforming, bureaucratic professionalism. The New Navy did not demand the small-scale diplomacy, empiricism and proactive leadership of the independently operating captains of the Pax Britannica, which Marx exemplified. In a centralised Navy devoted to 'grid iron' tactics and the strategy of a big-steam battle fleet, there was little room for individual action. Marx might well have agreed with the young New Navy officer,

> There was a young man who said, 'D-n!
> I suddenly see that I am
> Only able to move in a predestined groove;
> I'm not ev'n a bus – I'm a tram.[4]

Marx retired in 1909, and although becoming Rear Admiral in 1906, he never flew his flag at sea.

But Admiral Marx had enjoyed his naval life and when there was an opportunity to return to it and do something heroic for the service and the country, he took it with both hands. At the age of sixty-seven, he camped out on the steps of Whitehall till he persuaded an initially reluctant Admiralty to allow him to return to the Navy to serve as a Captain Royal Naval Reserve (RNR) in the auxiliary patrols of the First World War. Here, his combative personality again caused problems. Their Lordships decided he would be better off out of the way, and gave him the autonomous command of a 'mystery' Q ship, chasing German U-boats. This independent and dangerous work was much more to Marx's liking. His bravery resulted in his being awarded the Distinguished Service Order (DSO). In the last year of the war, Admiralty decided it preferred convoys to Q ships and at last Marx got the chance to fly his flag as an active admiral, in charge of merchant convoys on the west coast. Admiralty recorded its appreciation of the 'arduous, responsible and valuable' work of this courageous old admiral. When peace eventually came, Marx took final retirement and returned home to Clatford Lodge at Alresford, Hampshire, where he died at the age of eighty-seven, still riding to hounds, albeit with a glass eye, and building a bunker for the Second World War.

Marx's long career spanned the important development of the Royal Navy from 1866 to 1918, from the Old Navy to the New. Because of this, his journals, memoirs and papers give us a valuable and unique window into this changing naval world. He left behind three detailed journals and various short diaries, letters, memoirs and papers, covering the period from 1866 when he joined the Officers' Training Ship, *Britannia*, to his death in 1939. Such extensive papers give us an inimitable account of a naval life, an intimate personal insight into a naval career. For these papers were not written and kept for public consumption. The Victorian and Edwardian Navy was a period particularly rich in public memoirs. Retired admirals, looking back with affection and nostalgia over the years of their successful careers in the Navy, were great autobiographers. Without an autobiography one was hardly validated as a member of the naval elite. If retired officers did not write their own story, there was usually someone around who would. Biographies abounded. But the need to write for public consumption vitiated the truth. The value of Marx's diaries is that they were written for himself alone and are to be trusted. Hence the emotional ups and downs of the early years; the candid emphasis on physical health, particularly in relation to sexual matters, the details of shipboard living and naval personnel as he saw it and the preoccupations of his social life. It is from such revealing individual accounts that we build up a picture of naval life as a whole. It is necessary that they should be brought into the public arena. They are the small pieces of a jigsaw that make up the whole picture.

Marx's diaries reveal a basically unassuming and ordinary naval officer looking, as all good officers did, to advancement, but not unduly ambitious. When he jumped into the sea to save a drowning man, it was with an eye to promotion, when he led a naval brigade detachment it was for excitement, when he took his Q ship into action it was to allay boredom, as well as to win the war. It made him none the less deserving of his decorations, none the less a hero. It was a heroism borne of the training and culture of the Old Navy: a training for endurance and duty; a culture of individual initiative and bravery. 'So were they all, all ordinary heroes.'[5]

Marx was a popular officer who always enjoyed the social life and 'camaraderie' of the Old Navy. He was never short of good company at the dinner table and appreciated the presence of an attractive woman. His promotional career was much like that of any other ordinary naval officer: a combination of merit, some little interest and the quicker promotion provided by a fast growing Navy. Like many of his contemporaries, Marx was intelligent but not a man of intellectual reflection. His writings show little imagination, he had no desire to record anything above the obvious. But intelligence and literary expertise were not highly rated or considered much of an advantage at that time. Any overt display of intellect was discouraged in junior officers. First Lieutenant K. Dewar withdrew a report on the gunlayer's test on Admiral May's advice. He was told he was *'now in the promotion zone and that in [his] own interests it would be better not to forward [his] report to Admiralty'*.[6] Lieutenant Domvile's Gold Medal essay for the Royal United Services Institution in 1907 obliquely criticising Fisher's dreadnought, nearly lost him his promotion. Admiral Richmond entered into a remarkable relationship of intellectual tutor to the young Lieutenant Stewart but he advised that young officer that his inquiring mind would probably shorten his career.[7] Marx may not have been intellectual but his Old Navy temperament allowed him to be critical. He was always his 'own man'.

---

1 Lord Fisher of Kilverstone, Admiral of the Fleet, OM, KCVO, DSO.

2 Admiral of the Fleet, Lord Charles Beresford, *The Betrayal* (London, 1917).

3 Admiral Sir Reginald Bacon, *A Naval Scrapbook* , p258.

4 Lady Poore, *Recollections of an Admiral's Wife* (London, 1916), p289.

5 With apologies to Mark Antony.

6 Vice Admiral K Dewar, *The Navy Within* , p125.

7 BRNC, unreferenced. Letter from Lieutenant Ross Stewart to Admiral Henderson, 28 May 1917.

One

'...the noble boy...' 1852–1865

At 20 minutes past 3 pm, my dear wife gave birth to a noble boy. She suffered severely but is doing well. Mr. Covey attended her and her dear kind sister Louisa was with her.

The 'noble boy' born to the forty-five-year-old mother, Anna Maria Marx, on 23 April 1852 was John Locke Marx. The birth was recorded in Anna's diary by the enthusiastic father, Francis Marx, and two days later Anna herself was recording it:

About half past ten Dr. Butler was here again and with my dearest Sister Louisa remained with me till the birth of my second boy – who came into this probationary world at twenty minutes past three, being born with a caul over his head. He was pronounced to resemble his father – having dark hair and deep blue eyes and being of a brown complexion. At least as compared to his brother whose hair and skin are of the true Jason fairness. My sufferings were shortened by a dose of Ergot of Rye judiciously administered when I was beginning to get exhausted and to feel that the acute pains were in reality not furthering the birth. I have infinite cause for thankfulness, for much as I had dreaded my trial before it came, I had no terror when the struggle really began...my Heavenly father was indeed with me as I walked with heavy groaning through the valley of the shadow of death.

Francis Joseph Marx had married Anna Maria Selina Locke, daughter of wealthy Devizes banker and MP Wadham Locke, in 1848. The Marx family originally came from Germany, probably Bremen, where John's great grandfather Dr M J Marx, who was Jewish, was thought to have been physician to the Elector of Cologne. He wrote several medical books in High German. He died in 1789 at Hanover after which his wife and six children emigrated to the freedom of America. They seem to have done well there since they sold land to the founding fathers of Richmond. On old maps, the southwest corner is marked 'Marx's addition' and the street outside the County Court is called Marx Avenue. However, by about 1835, there was a shortage of money and the family were writing to relations at home, '*I think we will have to sell the slaves!*'

In 1813, Dr Marx's second son, George, had come to England, probably for medical treatment, and finding it to his liking, stayed. He married Selina Chambers, probably a Protestant from Southern Ireland. He then set up as a City merchant in 2 Lime Street Square under the name of Marx and Wheatall. Apparently they prospered since George came to own property in Whitechapel and Mile End. He lived in Bedford Square, and Edgware Road, before finally moving to the prestigious 81 Eaton Square. He died in 1835. The Marx family under George would presumably not have been regarded as Jewish, since to trade in the City up to 1835 one must be a Freeman, and to be a Freeman one must be a Livery man and neither could be Jewish. We do not know when the family converted – early after arrival in England or before leaving America. George's wife Selina died in 1826 and he then made a fortunate second marriage to the wealthy Mrs Johnston of Shaldern, Hants, who brought into the family the large, country-house property of Arlebury at Alresford in Hampshire. George had seven children, of whom the eldest was Francis Joseph Marx.

Francis Joseph Marx, John Locke Marx's father, was born on 16

September 1816. He was educated at Eton and Christchurch, Oxford, as befitted the now gentlemanly status of the family, and was a member of Wyndham's Club. He was an intelligent and enterprising young man. He travelled round Russia and when he came home he wrote a book, *The Serf and the Cossack, A Sketch of the Condition of the Russian People.* In it he perceptively forecast a revolution in the country. In later life he moved down to the family house, Arlebury, where he led the life of a leisured Hampshire country gentleman. At the age of thirty-two he married the older Anna Maria Selina Locke, aged forty-one. It was Anna's second marriage; her first husband was George Purefoy Jervoise of Shalstone, the MP who died in 1847. The age discrepancy and the speed with which Anna married for the second time argues the love match, which it undoubtedly was. At Arlebury Francis became a notable leader in the local gentry of the neighbourhood. He was elected a member of the Hampshire Hunt and in 1852 became its secretary. In 1867 he was a major in the local militia, the 1st Volunteer Battalion, Hants Regiment. He served as a Justice of the Peace, and was a pillar of the local Anglican church at Tichbourne. It was a fine parental example for John to follow. The family grave, which may still be seen at Tichbourne Church in Hampshire, and the family plaques on the church wall, demonstrate the family's full integration into the gentility of English Protestant life.

Anna and Francis Marx were devoted and caring parents. John was Anna's second son, her first was George Francis Marx, born in 1849. There were no other children. George and John had a free and happy childhood, with all the attention of their parents, in the beautiful, rambling house at Arlebury with its spacious grounds and elegant verandas. John enjoyed the company of his older brother George and his family life with his father and mother, despite what might seem an excess of Victorian piety on the part of Anna Maria, judging from the many entries detailing her own religious life:

1 January 1865
I desire humbly and heartily to begin the year with fervent

prayer…oh that it [life] may end in the Eternal City, where I shall behold his face.

Oh God what would mother's do, did they not know that thou art everywhere!

4 December 1870
We went to church and the Father Mother and both their sons partook for the first time of the blessed symbols of the Body and Blood of Christ.

15 October
Went into Winchester…service in the nave of the Cathedral – very long, but the sermon by the Bishop of Peterborough banished all sense of fatigue…

Anna Maria's entries also show the more formidable side of her character:

9 April 1854
To church, Mr Brodie preached an excellent sermon in aid of the school building fund. He wanted £14 or £16 – he got £9 6s more shame for card playing and back biting Alresford!

July
Terrible and disgusting news – Mrs. Benham informs me that Eliza is six or seven months gone with child…

Apart from religion, hunting was the main preoccupation of Anna Maria's diary. Her entries were often headed by the name of the current horse, which her 'dear Francis' was riding – Battle Axe, Stilton. An ability to hunt and ride was an early requirement for the Marx boys, as for their peers. Anna recorded in her diary of her twelve-year-old son:

21 December 1864

...a long and weary morning in covert. The boys rode like bricks. Johnny took seventeen jumps...

30 January 1865

Francis and Johnny rode over to Dean House. The little mare was being very fresh and it sent the blood to my heart to see her rear – but Johnny sat firmly and well...

As Secretary of the Hampshire Hunt, Francis kept a hunting diary with meticulous accounts of each day's run. In October 1851, he was the proud owner of five horses, 'Bay Mare, Quaker, Shamrock, Cornet & Midnight', though on 9 March 1852, 'Mare put her foot in a rabbit hole and rolled me over... '. Sadly, he was to be more than 'rolled over' by one of his beloved horses. It was a throw from his horse that caused his death in 1876.

It was a busy household of servants, friends, relations and animals. John and George grew up in an atmosphere of sentimental, though nonetheless, genuine love. It was always 'darling Johnny' and 'dear George'. Francis was 'father cat', Anna was 'mother cat' and John's friend Munday was a 'kitten'. Johnny's first pair of shoes, dated 1853, and a lock of hair dated 1860, carefully kept by his mother, can still be seen.[1] It seems to have been a life typical of the best Victorian gentry, ordered, leisurely, dutiful, careful of the welfare of servants (except the unfortunate Eliza, perhaps), and full of the small joys of ordinary social life, the dances, the visitations, the churchgoing. The Marxes moved in prestigious society. They numbered among their friends at this time several important naval officers: Rear Admiral Geoffrey Phipps Hornby,[2] Captain Charles Shadwell, soon to be Rear Admiral,[3] Vice Admiral Seymour,[4] and politicians like Sclater-Booth, Conservative member for Hampshire. A diary entry for November 1870 declared, 'the house was full of company – Sclaters – Bentinks, etc.'. Anna Maria had been used to political company in her father's house. Disraeli had been a visitor. It is interesting to note that Anna Maria and her sister feature in George MacDonald Fraser's *Flash For Freedom*, when in 1848 Flashman stayed a few days with Wadham Locke at Devizes. Disraeli and Lord George Bentink were also there. Flashman seduces Anna Maria's sister Fanny but is resisted by Anna!

Anna's sister, Fanny Duberly, had made a name for herself by following her soldier husband, Captain Henry Duberly, to the Crimea and riding round the camp regularly, giving her opinions on matters to all and sundry. She recorded them in a book she wrote, *Duberly's Journal of the Russian War*. When he was six, John's mother presented him with a copy inscribed, 'This record of his aunt's courage and endurance is given him by his mother.' There is a photograph taken by Roger Fenton, in the British Library, of Fanny on her horse with her riding habit spread round her, 'to hide the mange spots about the saddle'. Her husband stands by looking less than enthusiastic. John always had a good relationship with what he called his 'festive aunt'.

John's first prep school, Hinds, was part of his happy childhood experience. At the age of nine, he wrote to his mother, '*It is very Joly at scooll*,' and took cakes that his mother gave him to his school friends. But the jolly days had to come to an end. John was intended for HMS *Britannia*, the Royal Naval training ship, and like most boys intended for *Britannia*, he had to attend a crammer to be prepared for its entrance exam. At first, when the exam was easy crammers were not used. Fisher and men of his era (Fisher entered the Navy on board *Victory* in 1854 and was only required to write out the Lord's Prayer),[5] joined from the normal varied education of the time; the schoolroom at home, an outside tutor, or a dame school or preparatory suited to a standard upper / middle-class education. But by 1865, in view of the now 'moderate' examination required, further specialised education was needed and coaching for the naval officer entry exam was offered to would-be candidates by individual instructors who were either retired naval instructors or who took time off from teaching in order to instruct their pupils. As a result of these early initiatives by individuals, three main cramming schools developed: Burneys, Stubbington and Eastmans. Dr Burney's Naval Academy was at Gosport, Stubbington House School and Eastman's were at Southsea. The crammer chosen by John's parents was Grove House, also at Southsea, though less prestigious and probably less expensive than the former. The average cost of a crammer seems to have been in the region of £40 to £45 a year, which compared favourably with the best private / public schools, Marlborough costing £72 a year, Haileybury £80 and Charterhouse £90 to £110.[6]

The necessity for specialised education meant that 'darling, darling Johnny' had to leave the comfort and security of home for North Grove, the crammer at Southsea, where he had to learn the harsher facts of life. Admiral George King Hall, who entered *Britannia* in 1864, and was also prepared at Grove, remembered Mr W Johnson, the retired naval instructor from HMS *Calcutta*. He noted Johnson was 'a great believer in the cane' – King Hall was 'generally caned on Monday mornings'.[7] No wonder an advertisement for the crammer, Ravenswood House, later declared 'Great pains bestowed on backward pupils'.[8] John also encountered other hazards at Grove House. He wrote to his mother:

From North Grove, Southsea, 30 November 1865
Football match cancelled...their has been a great row...I don't quite know what it is but is something about the seniors who wrote a letter to one of the masters because he had done something to them.... . I think that I shall be fit to have my nomination in June.

Nomination was an issue for the Marx family. It was the first hurdle in a naval career. Before a boy could become a naval cadet, he had to apply to the Board of Admiralty for a nomination and in order to receive one, he had to show that he was a 'gentleman'. In Victorian society, no man could be 'altogether successful unless he be esteemed a gentleman'.[9] The Victorian naval officer corps was essentially a body of men 'esteemed to be gentlemen': 'gentlemen' possessed an innate sense of honour and devotion to duty, 'gentlemen' had an inbred ability to lead and command. 'Gentlemen', it was thought, possessed all the qualities essential to the naval officer corps. As a gentleman, the aspiring young officer would not only share an attribute of God – 'that Gentleman of the most sacred and strictest honour'[10] – but he would also promise 'the fine and governing qualities of his class':[11] that class of persons described in a contemporary dictionary as having independent means, e.g. men of superior position in society, or having the habits of life indicative of this.[12] 'Whatever else they are, they are certainly "gentlemen",' said Captain Francis Clayton, of his officers in 1885.

Applications for nomination had to be made to the Board of Admiralty on behalf of the aspiring cadet by influential patrons, or sponsors, who thus guaranteed the social status of the boy. Between half and two-thirds of all nominations were held by the First Lord himself (in John's case the Duke of Somerset), and the remaining number by members of the Admiralty Board. The process of nomination was generally speaking based on the regulations standardised by Admiralty in 1857.[13] Every flag officer, on appointment, might make two applications for cadets of his choice, every captain on commissioning a ship might make one. Six cadetships were given annually to sons of gentlemen in the colonies on the recommendation of the Secretary of State for the Colonies. Seven service cadetships were also given annually to 'sons of officers of the Army, Navy or Marines who have been killed in action, or lost at sea on active service, or killed on duty, or who have died of wounds received in action or injuries received on duty within six months of the date of such action or injury'. One 'young gentleman' was appointed annually from the training ships *Conway* and *Worcester*. Applications for nomination could also come from other suitably influential patrons – a naval captain or above, a member of the aristocracy, a Member of Parliament – and were entered in the First Lord's Patronage Book to be accepted or rejected as the case may be.

Lord Somerset's Patronage Book seems to indicate that in John's time it was not too difficult to get into the Royal Navy. Almost every one of the 153 applicants in Somerset's book (1859–1867) appears to have received a nomination, though only 81 candidates appear to have ended up as cadets. This would seem to indicate an ease of nomination in the middle 'sixties that bears out this time as a low point in naval recruiting. Poor promotion prospects and insufficient employment discouraged prospective entrants. But as the Navy increased in popularity and prestige, so did demand. By the late 'seventies, the involvement of the Royal Princes Albert and George had upgraded the social desirability of a naval career. As William King Hall said, when in 1869 the Prince took his young sons to *Warspite*, dressed as naval cadets, 'Your Royal Highness is lifting us up. We have been too long in the mud.'[14] The process of nomination, fairly simple in 1860, became more complicated during the late 'sixties and almost frenzied by the late 'seventies and early 'eighties as the number of applicants increased and refusals multiplied. Action in the Crimea or the Indian Mutiny was adduced to support application; heroism at Waterloo was remembered: H J L Clarke's father had commanded the Scots Greys and had had three horses shot from under him and his leg smashed at Waterloo.[15] H H Brown's uncle, Sir W Bellairs, had two horses killed under him and Robert D'Arcy's grandfather had been 'shot in three places'. Nor was it only the Crimea and Waterloo that were remembered. C E Greenway's grandfather had been 'severely wounded by a 14lb shot in the American War, 1812 and the shot was still in possession of the family...'(!)[16] Social class became ever more important and the patronage system became a fierce filter, manipulated by the government to control numbers and quality of entrants. Those with important social connections, backed by earls, dukes, viscounts, duchesses, etc. had no trouble obtaining nominations, the right political connections would also usually secure a nomination, and good naval or military connections. But it could be a difficult and anxious time:

> We Scot Skirvings had no naval influence...various strings were pulled, most of them ineffectual and time passed.... In the end I got an absolute promise of a nomination from Lord Goschen and that through the good influence of Lord Elcho, the eldest son of the Earl of Wemyss, who was a lifelong friend of my father's. When I actually had the nomination...I was 21 days too old.[17]

John had no such anxiety. He was fortunate. His father was an independent gentleman, he knew several senior naval men capable of applying for nominations and on 10 October 1865, the influential Rear Admiral Phipps-Hornby wrote to his mother:

> To say the time has come for him to apply for Johnny's nomination. Wrote to thank him and invited him and Mrs Hornby to come to us on 24th.

Marx's name does not appear in Somerset's Patronage Book so we do not know which member of the Admiralty Board gave him his nomination, possibly Sir Alexander Milne, since Marx mentions his name again later. However, John's successful nomination was undoubtedly due to the influence of Admiral Phipps Hornby.

But before John could become a naval cadet, there was still the matter of the entrance exam to be negotiated. In 1865, the Royal Navy had introduced its first 'moderate' examination. Until then the entrance examination consisted of no more than an indication of ability to take limited dictation, to perform a simple sum and to recite the Lord's Prayer. The medical appears to have been little more than an indication of tolerable fitness on sight.18 But by the time John took the examination, the candidate was required:

1 To write English correctly from dictation, and in a legible hand.
2 To read, translate, and parse a passage from French, or from some other Foreign Living Language. [A dictionary was allowed.]

And to have a satisfactory knowledge of:

3 The leading facts of Scripture and English History.
4 Modern Geography, in so far as relates to a knowledge of the principle Countries, Capitals, Mountains and Rivers. To be able to point out the

position of a place on a map when its Latitude and Longitude are given.

5 Arithmetic, including Proportion, and a fair knowledge of Vulgar and Decimal fractions.

6 A knowledge of the Definitions and Axioms of the First Book of Euclid.

Should a candidate be able to speak French or any other Foreign living Language, it will be noted in his favour, and as drawing is a most useful qualification for Naval Officers, it is recommended that Candidates for the Service should be instructed therein.[19]

In this examination, in the use of history, geography and the abandonment of Latin in favour of foreign languages, the Navy was at the forefront of contemporary education. It represented the use of a 'modern side' well before other public schools, with the possible exception of Rugby. Naval educational thinking was fuelled by what was regarded as good for the Navy, not for society generally. It could afford to abandon the accepted classical tradition.

Most boys struggled to get through this entrance exam and John was no scholar. He was a boy who liked an active, outdoor life and found the restriction of study difficult, as his letters show. His mother was 'not sanguine of his passing'. Yet to everyone's delight, pass he did, and in January of 1866 the 'noble boy' John Locke Marx left the comforts of Arlebury and the devotion of his parents, for the rigours of life on *Britannia*, the officers' training ship lying in the estuary at Dartmouth. He was now embarked on his long and colourful career as an officer in the Royal Navy.

---

1 In the possession of Andrew Marx, grandson.

2 Admiral of the Fleet, Sir Geoffrey Thomas Phipps Hornby KCB, GCB.

3 Vice Admiral Sir Charles F A Shadwell.

4 Probably Vice Admiral George Henry Seymour.

5 Admiral of the Fleet Lord Fisher of Kilverstone GCB, OM, GCVO (1842–1920) who entered the Navy in 1841 and was First Sea Lord from October 1904 to January 1910.

6 M Jones, *The Making of the Royal Naval Officer Corps, 1860–1914*, vol 1, ch3, PhD Thesis, University of Exeter, 1964.

7 L King Hall, ed. *Sea Saga* (London, 1935), p265.

8 *The Times*, 1 November 1890, p3, column 5.

9 A Trollope, *The Prime Minister* (London, 1876), p2.

10 Schapera (ed), *Livingstone's African Journal, 1853–1856* (London, 1963), vol 2, p374.

11 Matthew Arnold quoted in H Perkin, *The Rise of Professional Society* (London, 1989), p119.

12 *Oxford English Dictionary*, vol 6, pp452–54a.

13 Admiralty, 12 May 1857, Navy List, 1868, p311.

14 King Hall, *Saga*, p260.

15 Clarke's father was a commander. The boy received a nomination in Hunt's Patronage Book, held at BRNC Dartmouth.

16 C Greenway in Hunt's *Patronage Book*. He had only his mother as recorded patron and appears not to have been successful.

17 R Skirving, *Eastman's Royal Academy*, MM 77 (191) pp379–87.

18 Fisher, *Memories*, p261.

19 Regulations for the Entry and Examination of Naval Candidates, 6 February 1865, Navy List.

Two

The Training Ship (1866–1867)

'I wish someone would kick up a row about it...'

HMS *Britannia*, the officer's training ship situated on the Dartmouth estuary, was a relatively new departure for the Royal Navy. In 1729 a naval academy had been set up in Portsmouth dockyard for forty young boys entering between the ages of thirteen and sixteen. In 1806 it became known as the Royal Naval College and in 1816, it took boys at the younger age of twelve and a half to fourteen. The course lasted for two years and then the cadets went to sea. It was not popular! Since naval education was regarded as education for seamanship, most officers and admirals of the time thought the boys were wasting their time ashore. They should be in training ships with instructors at sea. So the college closed in 1837. But there was still a lobby for something more systematic in the way of the education and training of naval officers and in 1857, cadets were sent to the jury-rigged stationary ship *Illustrious* at Portsmouth. But by 1859 this was not big enough and it was considered necessary to have a single, stationary three-decker ship for the training of officer cadets and the *Britannia*, the fifth ship to bear the famous name, was appropriated for the task. Moved to Portland in 1862, she was further moved to Dartmouth in September 1863 as Portsmouth and Portland were considered unhealthy and lacking in surrounding amenities for recreation. No doubt little Dartmouth was delighted to have this addition of over 500 naval personnel permanently encamped in her harbour with all its implications of economic and social status.[1] A year later, in 1864, with increasing numbers of cadets, Admiralty decided they needed an additional ship and the *Hindustan*[2] was moored ahead of *Britannia* with a covered-over bridge joining the two ships from the bow of one to the stern of the other. They were both old wooden line-of-battle ships and retained one mast between them. This was the foremast of the *Britannia*, which was used, fully rigged, for teaching the cadets elementary seamanship. It was to this two-ship officer training school, with its unique accommodation, that John Marx came in 1866.

John Marx was not one of those boys like Admiral Beresford,[3] for whom 'the neatness and order of the stately ships, the taut rigging, the snowy sails, the ropes coiled neatly on deck…left an abiding impression upon my youthful mind'. Marx's youthful mind was concerned with the pleasures of home, of hunting with his well-loved father and brother, of caring for favourite animals, of fun with friends and family. Marx did not join the Navy because he was fired with enthusiasm for the service. He joined the Navy because it was expected of him and he had a desire to see the world and a willingness to become a naval officer in order to do so. If that meant *Britannia*, so be it.

In his often misspelt and totally unpunctuated letters home, with their careless handwriting and hurried, slap-dash style, John Marx tells us what it was like to be a naval cadet at *Britannia* in 1866 and 1867. He had come from a happy, pious, sheltered family life and was no young 'man of the world' as some other cadets were. In many ways he was immature. Nor was he an intellectual. He was just an average, likeable, fair-minded young cadet, willing to make the best of any situation; ideal malleable material for the Royal Navy to train up as a naval officer.

23 January 1866
Father brought me on board today. I like it pretty well. We slept at the railway hotel at Exeter last night I know a good

many fellows on board my chest came this evening...I went on shore this afternoon and played football in the field instead of going out in the gigs I am at the seven port table.

John Marx's first day on board *Britannia* seems to have gone well. His father was *'pleased with the arrangements for the ship'* and Marx, as we shall now call him, was excited at the novelty of the new naval school on the water. He enjoyed meeting up with chaps he knew. He felt important in his cadet's uniform with its waistcoat and its jacket with three brass buttons on the sleeve and its little, close-fitting cap with the peak a half-turn down. It was impressive to be received by the Master-at-Arms and introduced to his marine servant. It was fun to go ashore in a ship's boat and find a field to play football in. It was fun to eat at port table and sleep in a hammock. He was looking forward to all the new experiences.

Two days later things were not so good. He wrote to his father, *'I like this place only [twice underlined] pretty well...'* and four days later he confessed to his mother, *'I was not alright the first two or three days...'*. John Marx was probably not the only one who was 'not all right' for the first few days on the training ship. Although it was no worse than other public schools and certainly better than some, it was still a daunting initiation, even for those used to the rigours of crammers and the harshness of other contemporary schools. The great wooden hulk of *Britannia*, with its lofty mast and three rows of portholes, towered over the apprehensive newcomer as he came up a gangway crowded with older cadets, some with their caps pushed to the back of their heads as a sign of rank, and shouts of 'New! Name? Class? Date?' and other more ribald inquiries. Various initiations followed for 'the cheeky news' as the first term was known. One was to inquire if the newcomer had been weighed. Of course not, so the poor 'new' was hurried off to the model bowsprit and seated in the bight of the crupper chain, given a good swing, and at the psychological moment the chain was slipped. The victim either got badly hurt or was given a nasty bump. Or an innocent 'new' lying in his hammock with his face exposed would find himself 'eyeslapped' as some older fellow passed by and took a swipe at his eyeball with the heel of his hand or a slipper. Before the dazed 'new' could come round, the perpetrator had disappeared. Or he might be walking on the deck to find himself suddenly faced by a horde of older cadets, arms linked and springing from nowhere, rushing towards him down the deck and knocking down everyone who happened to be in their way. This favourite game was known as 'humbugging'. Older cadets would also dispose of 'sundry of their articles, such as soap', etc.[4] Members of the 'swagger' terms, the two senior terms, were allowed to carry 'togies', short lengths of cord with large knots on the end for the purpose of administering punishment on the juniors. They were privileged to 'ask names and make other personal inquiries'.[5] During these interrogations certain words were not allowed. Despite progressive Admiralty efforts to control it, bullying and riotous behaviour was endemic since cadets were left mostly to themselves and their own devices apart from study times. Tupper,[6] a later cadet, recorded that they hardly saw an officer unless in connection with punishment.

However, as the days proceeded Marx came to terms with his new school: '*I like the ship better than I did,*' he wrote to his father a few days later. The comforting camaraderie of friendship asserted itself. He '*knew a good many fellows on board...Trott is a very fat fellow and is rather an ass. I found him out.... Jones who was at Hinds is a chum of mine.*' Munday, 'the kitten' to Marx's parents, was also a fellow-cadet. Marx liked sleeping in a hammock. He liked having his own chest, the personal domain of his three-foot-six by two by two-foot-three wooden box with its polished brass nameplate, to keep all his possessions in, with its compartments for clothes and books and a place for his washbowl and a small lockable tray for cash: '*my chest is very good and I think my books are alright... *'. He took his place in the mess at number-seven port table and scrambled noisily with the others for his share of the food served. He learned to climb the rigging, although he was never one of those cadets who climbed over the futtock shrouds. (The futtock shrouds were the short, stiff standing ropes or chains played out from the edge of the 'top'. To climb over them meant climbing more or less upside down.) He later declared that he *was very sorry that I never did*. He even became blasé: *we go on shore everyday but already it is rather stale*. On cold days when the wet deck became one mass of ice, there was the fun of slides. He enjoyed the novelty of hearing a band play on board on Sunday evenings, and learned early the naval skill of dancing. His boyish optimism grew. He asked his parents for five shillings and *bought a jolly compass*. In his free time he enjoyed *a jolly walk* and found some *jolly crystals*. It was *very jolly being in the sailing cutter as you learn something besides pleasure.* He was impressed by the novelty of having his own servant. Grandly he told his father towards the end of his first term, *I gave my servant 2s.* By the end of the term he was quite *one of our fellows*. He wanted to make sure friends and family had the photographs taken of him as a cadet: *send her [Aunt Fanny] a phis-gogue*. A photograph was sent to Mr Bell, his old teacher at North Grove, and Marx received one in return. He seems to have suffered no separation anxiety.[7] Perhaps he had found life at home a little claustrophobic.

Certainly Marx would have felt comfortable in the company of the 'fellows'. A survey of cadets from 1860–1880 shows that about thirty per cent came from an Army background, then almost equally about sixteen per cent came from Church, Navy or his own, 'independent' background.[8] Over eighty per cent lived in average upper-class homes like Arlebury and came from his own area of the South East of England.[9]

Cadets were entered in groups every three months and known as terms. The first and second terms had their hammocks and chests on the gloomy, lower deck of *Hindustan*. The third and fourth terms were promoted to the main deck of *Britannia*. *Britannia* had three gun decks, main, middle and lower. Below the lower gun deck was the orlop or cockpit deck. This was always very dark, being lit by small scuttles, sealed windows that were under water in a fully loaded ship. In the early days all cadets had slept here with their hammocks slung in rows and their chests beneath. At the stern of the lower deck were four studies and a larger space, which formed the cadets' mess room. Forward of this was the 'galley' and a small mess room for a ship's company which only needed enough men to keep the ship in order and provide seamen instructors. The after end of the middle deck held the officers' wardroom and the French study. Sunday service was held on this deck and seamanship taught there. The awesome captain's quarters were on the after part of the main deck with a small study adjacent. The sickbay was at the fore end. There was a drawing study and two others under the poop. This was where evening recreation was held, under the supposedly watchful eye of a cadet captain. There were additional classrooms and studies on *Hindustan*.

The syllabus for cadets once arrived in the *Britannia* was daunting for all but the most able. Apart from instruction in seamanship it was heavily oriented towards mathematics and Marx was no young mathematician: '*I believe we have to pass out of the first instruction of seamanship in a week. We do trigonometry Euclid & Algebra and lograthims which are nearly all new to me… .*'At the beginning of the course each boy was told his placing in his term according to how well he had done in the naval entrance exam. Thereafter, he was told his placing at the end of each term, and his placing when he finally passed out. The course lasted four terms and at the end Their Lordships expected cadets to have a competent knowledge of arithmetic, algebra, Euclid, trigonometry, and have had some elementary instruction in the principles of surveying and construction and have some knowledge of English, French, geography, history and drawing. Marx promised his father that he would '*try and sweat though it is very hard but one good thing is that fellows let a chap sweat if he likes and you can go in the studies…*'.

There were also the practical skills of seamanship to be acquired. This was more enjoyable. Marx had fun learning to sail *Britannia*'s boats, and going out with the other fellows in the blue gigs. He mastered the intricacies of knotting and splicing, the manipulation of ropes, anchors, and cables. He was more wary of having to climb the rigging in order to acquire the skills of the yardarm. One can understand his caution in the matter of the futtocks, '*the gap at the end of the ship or the cross trees*' as he referred to it. He described what happened to one cadet:

he only slipped his footing and by great good fortune caught by
his arms instead of going overboard, caught by his arms in the
hole through which the topgallant mast's head goes and his name
was Risk.

And another:

a fellow was up on the cross trees and he slipped through but
luckily he caught by his armpit and fainted he was lifted out by
two cadets and three bluejackets where sent up to help him down
he recovered and as he was going down the topmast rigging he
fainted again and fell but the two bluejackets who went down
before him caught him he is alright directly he came on deck
today…

For Marx it was enough to go through 'the lubber's hole', an easier opening at the top of the masts, and climb the ordinary rigging, *'I have been in bed since Thursday with contusians or some rot on my legs…I got it by falling on the rattlings and barking my shins…'*

The academic subjects were classed as study, the boat work was seamanship. French and drawing were 'out of study'. 'Study' was always given more weight than 'seamanship'. Admiralty recognised the importance of navigational brainwork, for example 2,000 marks for 'study' and 1,000 for 'seamanship'. A cadet's final passing-out place depended on his final term's exams. Those who passed out at the top got 'sea time', that is to say they were promoted to midshipmen earlier. At the fourth-term examination cadets were classified according to their merits in seamanship, study, and conduct, and were given sea time accordingly:

	Study	Seamanship	Conduct
First Class	six months	three months	three months
Second Class	three months	none	three months
Third Class	none	none	three months

At the end of his first term's examinations, Marx felt that he was *'getting on pretty well, both in study (7th) and seamanship, (4th)'*. He sent his father his first-term examination papers to look at. But when all the marks were added up, he was disappointed to find *'I have taken a third with 402 marks. I hope I shall do better next time.'* He was comforted by the thought that *'there are a lot of fellows plucked [failed]'*.

The end of the examinations meant the beginning of the Easter holiday. The young Marx could not wait to meet up with brother George again, to hunt with his father, to see all his favourite animals and friends. His mother too was delighted at the thought of seeing him again. But when he arrived, she was shocked to see how pale and thin he had become. The stocky young lad that she had sent away to *Britannia* had changed:

> 17 April – darling Johnny back from Britannia – He looks very pale and brings a letter from the Staff Surgeon recommending tonics.

It is not surprising that his mother was worried about his health. There was always the risk of an outbreak of infection on board the insanitary *Britannia* and Marx had previously told his mother that there were *'twenty three fellows at sick bay and in hospital with measles'*. He had said he was glad not to be aboard the *Bristol* where they had yellow fever. Admiralty tried later to combat disease on *Britannia* with a process of fumigation. Cadets were shut up in a small cabin that was burning sulphur. There were voice pipes in the sidewall through which fresh air could be breathed, but when one boy too many was shut in and no notice taken of his efforts to get out and he nearly died, fumigation was abolished. Also food at this time was barely adequate in *Britannia* and 'the extraordinarily hard conditions' spoken of by Marx's compatriot, Admiral Cresswell, did not make for strong, healthy young cadets. [10]

To the young Marx, a fellow being 'sent away' and not returning from holiday was nothing unusual but to Admiralty the number of boys being sent away was a matter of growing concern. Some japes were merely the ordinary fun of schoolboys, '*somebody put some oil into some ink...and if the fellow is caught he will be sent away, there was one sent away the other day,*' but Their Lordships felt that too many cadets were being sent away from *Britannia* for bad behaviour. A look at the punishment records of the time is revealing. Offences ranged from spirited misbehaviour to moral undesirability, from 'skylarking and scrambling for biscuit to gambling and purchasing Rum for other Cadets'. There were offences of 'obscene language and indecent writing'. Dismissal offences ranged from 'cribbing in final exam', being 'undesirable Cadet...basically difficult and impertinent' to 'inducing two ship's boys to purchase Rum for himself and other Cadets.' There were many offences of bullying, 'bullying new Cadets, bullying Cadets when aloft, bullying Mr Sadler, bullying Mr Talbot'.[11] Marx was anxious to reassure his parents but also to alert them to the possibility of his being in trouble. '*You must not be surprised if I come only I have not got into any rows yet...*'

In order to remedy the situation, Their Lordships decided to appoint to the training ship a new captain with a reputation for severity. George Granville Randolph had previously been in command of the frigate *Orlando,* 'a marvel of smartness'.[12] Captain Powell, the current captain, had made some effort previously to reform the training ship, but it was felt that Randolph, with his reputation for severity, would be more effective. His brief was to instil discipline into the training ship and improve its academic performance. Rumour was rife among the cadets. '*There is a new captain coming named Randolph. I hope he is a jolly fellow but I believe he is not,*' wrote Marx, and with trepidation, '*Skipper Randolph comes on the first of May.*'

Captain Randolph made his presence felt straightaway:

> *There are great changes in the ship captain Randolph is rather strict there was a jaw about pocket money but nothing much. I expect you will get a letter about it a lot of new captains were made up.*

There are three fellows going to be bunked [birched]. We had a whole holiday on Queens Birthday but it was not very jolly as we were not allowed to go above the anchor stone and were not allowed below Kingswear in gigs or shore dinghys.

(Perhaps Randolph had heard how one of the cadets nearly got trapped in the mud down river, while trying to catch a duck!)

Randolph was the typical Victorian martinet: a man of integrity and genuine care for his cadets, but any leniency was to him a sign of weakness and a dereliction of duty. A deputation of cadets went to see him to complain about meat left from the previous day being served up as poor quality hash for the next breakfast. Randolph listened and replied, 'You are quite right, boys, it shall be stopped.' The delighted boys were then told, 'But you will have nothing in its place.'[13] Marx was unhappy with the growing severity:

I said the ship was very strict 3 fellows having been sent away this half and another threatened.... I hope if you say anything to Mr. Baring you will not mention my name as I shall be spited and also I know of nothing really wrong except that it is very much stricter than last half...

In fairness he pointed out to his parents that Captain Randolph was very jolly off duty. But the 'jolliness' did not compensate for the increasing hardship of the new regime.

I wish somebody would only kick up a row about the Britannia its getting very strict and a lot of fellows got second class for trespassing and the senior captain did not get anything who was with the same fellows because the commander believed his word against all the witnesses but the other fellows said he was among them. The same fellow Thomson is the greatest cad immaginable...

And again,

> *There are three fellows going to be bunked…Jones…got birched*
> *very unfairly it being a very great shame…*

So long as Marx thought it was fair he took it in the nature of things.

Unbeknown to Marx, however, some people *were* beginning to take an interest in the increasing severity of birching at *Britannia* and were about to 'kick up a row' about the regime. But it was not until John Marx had left that Mr Bass, the Liberal member for Derby, asked questions in Parliament. On 25 July 1867, he tackled the First Lord, Mr Corry, on the question of excessive punishment at *Britannia* and asked Mr Bass whether

> when a cadet was punished his arms and legs were tied to ring
> bolts so that he could not move and that he was flogged with
> a birch broom which had previously been steeped in water to
> make it more pliant, that fifteen cuts were inflicted with it on
> the back and that doctors invariably attended.

Mr Corry declared that this was not so, that he had ordered an investigation and that punishment at *Britannia* paralleled that of other schools.

> Mr Bass: The arms are not tied to ringbolts?
> Mr Corry: Certainly not.[14]

Here is Marx's account of procedure under Randolph:

> *May 1866….two fellows were birched yesterday for buying*
> *biscuits at a turnpike. The way it is done the fellows are all*
> *drawn up on the lower deck the culprit has his briches taken down*
> *by two corporals a table is lashed in a port forward on the*
> *Starboard side and the fellos mattress is lashed down to it then a*
> *fellow is lashed to four ringbolts by the two corporals hands and*
> *legs across the table and the Commander says doe your duty und*

then it commences one fellow bore his dozen with out a word the
other fellow howled at half a dozen it was not very hard I was
told by some fellows as I did not see them a fellow was bunked
the other day for going up in the model room and cutting some
very jolly rattling on one of the cadets models.

Although, as Corry said in the debate, birching was commonplace in schools and the young Marx, so long as he felt it was fair, accepted it in the nature of things, contemporary opinion did start to turn against the use of excessive corporal punishment in schools. The 1860s were the years when public disquiet at bullying and official brutality in schools first made itself felt. Hence the publication of *Tom Brown's Schooldays*, and the concern expressed in the House of Commons. There were still unregenerates like Percy Scott[15] who continued to advocate a good birching even into the 'enlightenment', but in the September of 1867, five months after John Marx had left the training ship, Admiralty had Captain Randolph superseded by Captain John Corbett.

Marx managed to avoid painful punishment, but it was difficult to '*keep out of a row*', and also remain one of the fellows. He told his concerned parents, '*I have got into a good many rows for skylarking which I meant to keep out of... .*' But how could a fellow hold his own if he was not to indulge in a bit of skylarking? Marx's conduct and punishment sheet records that he made a 'noise at Messroom door after being sent out, disobeyed orders of Lord G Campbell, Cadet Capt.', and was guilty of 'Disorderly conduct at table;' enough to keep him in the good books of the other fellows. The socialising of a like-minded community in the unwritten ethos of *Britannia* was an essential element in the training of young naval officers. Marx was also in the good books of the main naval instructor, the Reverend Job Inskip. His mother, always careful about her son's religious instruction, had asked Inskip to take him into his Bible class. He replied,

Dartmouth 15 September 1866 — My dear Madam, I shall be
very happy to admit your son into the Bible Class and to prepare

him in due time for confirmation. He is a good boy and I
therefore have the more pleasure in doing what I can for his
welfare. Job M Inskip.

Meanwhile Randolph was also trying to improve academic performance: *'if you do not make progress two weeks running you get sent...'* Marx wrote anxiously. He was relieved to report in July,

I have taken a 2cnd in Study and a third in seamanship my
character will be
Study satisfactory
Seamanship fair
French unsatisfactory
Conduct good
Attention much

Randolph encouraged academic effort: *'the new rule has just come out that the fellows who pass first class are to have a gold stripe on their arm those who take a first in seamanship and study are to have a broader one and at each exam a first is taken a stripe is added.'* Passing marks for exams were increased and new monthly exams in seamanship were started. It was the *'Hardest exam for the third term they ever had...many fellows will be plucked.'*

Randolph not only endeavoured to lift the academic progress of cadets, but he instituted other practical improvements: *'the lower deck studies have been thrown into the messroom there is lots of room now'* (room for 150 boys). *'The ship is nothing but whitewash and paint.'* Not only was the ship painted and a new racket court added, but an attempt to improve the damp and insanitary ship was made when a donkey engine was installed on deck to pump up water from below.

However, the undesirable behaviour of cadets still caused concern.

...two fellows were arrested for stealing, I expect they will get
bunked they bagged a bunch of keys of a fellow named Berkley

*and the fellow found it out by one fellow confessing and it came
to the commanders ears and he took them and crossquestioned
them and one fellow confessed but the other declared he did not
do it though lots of fellows can witness they did...*

Randolph used all the various means at his disposal: birching; second-class punishment; lower deck or cockpit mess; disrating of cadet captains who had failed in their duties. Second-class punishment meant that a boy had to wear a white stripe on his sleeve and follow a separate regime:

*Get up at 6 am in winter, 5 am in summer, fall in and drill until
prayer time (8 am)
Stand apart from other cadets at all musters
One and a quarter hour's drill every afternoon: leave stopped,
except one hour on shore under charge of a corporal.
Stand on the middle deck one hour after evening prayers.
Kneel apart at prayers.
Eat at 2cnd class table in the messroom with no soup, beer or
second course.*

Lower-deck mess, also known as cockpit mess, was the same as second class but with bread and water, only, eaten down below under the eye of a marine sentry: '*two fellows got cockpit mess for being troublesome on study and a captain got disrated for bullying...* '. One can only feel for boys who must remain physically active on such a reduced diet! Even so, the severe punishment did not succeed in eliminating the misbehaviour and the bullying at *Britannia* though no doubt it alleviated it. The severe punishment did, however, help to toughen the cadets and inure them to the hardship and privations that they would find in their later lives at sea. Admiralty deliberately approved of a regime at *Britannia* that would cater for,

> a supply of young officers...their habits and mode of thought
> yet unformed, [that could] be more easily inured to the peculiar
> habits of a sea life, be more accustomed to its unavoidable

privations, and occasional hardships, be trained up in attachment to their profession, and be induced to adopt it heartily, as their vocation in life.[16]

It has always been, and still is, a problem for Admiralty to 'inure to the necessary hardship' boys who have come from comfortable and secure home backgrounds. It is hard to draw the line between legitimate severity and brutality in training. But Marx wanted as little hardship as possible. Again he assured his parents, '*I hope to be able to keep out of rows there has been a row about the blue gigs and no fellows are to mix except the first and second term are to go together and the third and passing out number.*' This separation of terms was another attempt by Randolph to eliminate the bullying between terms. Interestingly, at this stage Marx sent his father a photo of 'his gang'. The gang consisted of O'Hara, second term, Bennet, third term, Elliot, passing out, Bremer, third term and Springrice, third term.

A gang was useful to a fellow when it came to fights, whether with other cadets or local town 'cads'. The town was full of the local 'cads' and 'cads' needed putting in their place. Sunday was the day set aside for dealing with them. Already a young cadet could feel the buzz of action and leadership, fronting an ambush and acquitting himself well in the latest battle against the cads. Marx sent an enthusiastic account of such a fight to his father, complete with diagram (and total lack of punctuation!),

…when we came to the creek…we met 50 cads and a few fellows started stoning them we went straight through but when we had passed they began blaguarding us and throwing stone's so we met about 15 more fellows we kept them back up a lane marked D while we kept up the hill retreating as we were late they tried to pass us but we would not let them so we had a scrimmage in which several fellows got a little hurt but I got a black eye but I broke my blackthorn stick across his back then we retreated again but had two more stands in the last one a cad hit me on the back

*with a great stone so I got in a wax rushed after him and chivied
him down the lane alone as the skipper was seen and so our
fellows ran I ran and gain on him a little and just as I was going
to hit him in a turn I saw Captain Randolf wife two daughters
and he stood across the road and cried stop and I nearly went into
his arms then he said what you doing what is your name and I
gave it to him and he took the cads name and address he then
asked me to tell him all about it and I told him and he said tell
me some more fellows so I did say Bower (b) Allen (a) and he
sent me to tell them but the cads had all formed inside the hedges
and pepered me as I ran and hit me on the back and nearly knock
me down but when I told the fellows all about they charged down
and captured several and took them to the skipper who took their
names and said he wished we had licked them well and some
fellows chivied them down in to Dartmouth when they caught one
and began to lick him and the people cried shame and hollourd
out Mr. Boyce they are licking your son so he said I wish they
would lick him well.*

Despite Randolph's unofficial support of the 'fellows v cads', there
had to be official punishment. '*They have put the whole ship on an
allowance of bread about 1 and a half pounds per day.*'

Marx was now coming to the end of the first year. '*There have
been a great many rows this half and I expect a great many will be sent
away... .*' He was thankful not to be one of them and was full of
excitement about the Christmas holidays and optimism for the future:
seeing brother George again, hunting with his father, becoming re-
acquainted with his beloved animals. His letters to and from home had
been regular throughout. He had wondered '*who George danced with
at the ball*', he had kept up with all his father's hunting experiences,
he had inquired as to '*whether the Conservatives will get on well...and
whether the Atlantic telegraph will succeed*'. He had thanked his parents
for '*the jolly verses*' they had sent him from *Punch*. (He did not know
that one day he himself would feature in one of *Punch*'s jolly verses.)

The holiday was a chance to catch up with all this life outside the naval school. But it was a short-lived respite. Short-lived, because he and Munday had to go to North Grove House, their earlier naval crammer, to do extra study during the holidays. As his mother said, 'It is hard!'

By the end of January, the all-too-short holiday was over and Marx was on the train back again to Dartmouth for his final term. Some of the cadets had celebrated the holiday by getting drunk on the train home and had caused a nuisance: '*Some names have been sent to the Admiralty for being disorderly in the train by which I came home…the two who got drunk are not coming back…*'

There was all the excitement of a new term: '*the captains have been made, some most awful fools*'. Marx never seems to have envisaged himself being made a term captain or shown any desire for it. He had a modestly realistic assessment of his own potential and a strong awareness of his own inclinations. They did not include overt leadership at this point. He was prepared to acknowledge that some of the new captains were '*very jolly*' but '*some the opposite*'. As schoolboys so often will, he started the new term with the best of intentions: '*I am going to work hard and also at French.*' There were other optimistic signs for the new term. There were rumours of ninepence a week for pocket money and they had meat for breakfast for the first time. The optimism was short-lived. On 8 February Marx wrote, '*I do not know why the pocket money has been stopped,*' and he complained about the increasing birchings, '*there were four birchings and two second class besides because a lot of fellows were marching up and down the middle desk humbuging and shoving fellows out of their way and one of them knocked over a fellow and damaged him about the face and they got birched and second class…. I was very nearly there but did not feel quite well and so did not go.*'

Marx was now nearly fifteen and in his last term. He was 'a niner', 'a passing out', 'a swagger', with all the privileges of seniority. He could lord it over lesser beings, with his cap pushed to the back of his head, its peak turned up as far as possible, his knotted 'togie' swinging threateningly. He showed no tendency to be a bully himself. He expressed sympathy for those in trouble and a fellow feeling for anyone being treated unfairly. He showed concern when he heard of friends or relations in difficulty. When a certain ship's corporal died, '*Bennet and a few of us…got up a subscription.*' Marx asked his father to send one shilling from his bank, a week's pocket money. When he heard of a local family falling into debt and likely to be ruined, he felt sorry for them. There was an unfortunate outbreak of mumps and chickenpox on board *Britannia* at the beginning of his last term and he was upset to hear his friend Munday had been taken to hospital with chickenpox. Marx was lucky to escape it. He was also disturbed to hear that his father had a bad accident to his leg while out hunting. But the main focus of all his thought was now on passing his final exams and getting his first ship.

It was not so much the type of ship that concerned him as to where his first posting would be. He wanted something exciting. His parents were friendly with Admiral Seymour and Marx wrote and received letters from the Admiral while at *Britannia*. He hoped the Admiral would use his influence to get him a good posting. He asked his parents to remind the Admiral of him and ask for a ship. '*Have you any idea what station I shall get on I do not care as long as it is not the West Coast and the Channel Fleet.*' He was looking for excitement and wanted something further afield. He reminded his parents that they must now start the preparations for his new life as a midshipman, '*It will cost about £100 as there will be many more things to be got than for my coming on board here.*'

The excitement of the future, however, had to wait until he had passed his final examinations. They took place in March and Marx told his father about each examination as it arrived: '*Seamanship and navigation exam, Scripture and English History, Euclid, Geography and Dictation, Lower deck…notting and splicing.*' He sent him some of the examination papers. He had worked hard and done his best and was hopeful of having done well. When the results came out he was not too disappointed. He had taken a creditable second, and added to that had received a good-conduct certificate. His mother was pleased,

Dear J passed out of the Britannia and came home with a very good character. He took a second class. Only 10 took a first.

Did it make a difference to an officer's career, what class of exam he had achieved as a cadet at *Britannia?* Apparently not. The ship a boy was sent to was not necessarily a reflection of his placing at *Britannia*, nor was it crucial to success in the later seamanship examination. Although there was a tendency for those passing out at the top of the class to be sent to large ships, any rule was vitiated by the presence on those ships of cadets who had passed out badly. Although a good placing might provide some 'clout' when getting one's first ship, it was not axiomatic. It would appear then that the young cadet leaving *Britannia* in 1867 had everything to play for.

With relief and anticipation that his new life of exciting adventure was about to begin at last, with school finished and the prospect of a ship that actually sailed before him, the young Marx left *Britannia*. All things considered it had not been a bad start. He could now look forward with confidence to his life as a junior midshipman.

---

1 See H Dickinson, 'Britannia at Portsmouth and Portland', MM, vol 84, no 4, November 1998, p7.

2 Sometimes referred to as *Hindostan*.

3 Admiral of the Fleet, Lord Charles Beresford (1846–1919) KCVO, KCB, GCVO.

4 Admiral of the Fleet, Sir William Henry May GCB, GCVO, *The Life of a Sailor*, p2.

5 Admiral H Fleet, *My Life and a Few Yarns* (London, 1922), ch2.

6 Admiral Sir Reginald Tupper GBE, KCB, CVO.

7 See N Dixon, *On The Psychology of Military Incompetence* (London, 1976), pp296–98.

8 M Jones, *Officer Corps*, ibid, p49.

9 Ibid, p22.

10 Admiral W Creswell, *Close to the Wind*, p2.

11 Record of Conduct Book, BRNC Dartmouth, A 1.

12 P Statham, *The Story of the Britannia* (London, 1905), p74.

13 Idem.

14 Hansard.

15 Admiral Sir Percy Scott, *Fifty Years in the Royal Navy,* Murray (London, 1919).

16 BPP, 1870, XXV, p844.

Three

Junior Middy (1867–1870)

'I hope just to manage…'

Marx was pleased to hear that he was to be appointed to HMS *Phoebe*, awaiting her commission in Plymouth Sound. She was a fine frigate and would probably get a good posting. Travelling down by train he met three fellow-cadets who were also on their way to new ships at Plymouth. They were in a state of great excitement, and very anxious about their chests, which seemed to have got lost and were only found in Plymouth *'after a great deal of trouble'*. However, they had met *'a gentleman who seemed to take an interest in us'* on the train, also travelling down to the docks, and he helped them get their chests into a wherry and even refused to let them pay. It seems even in the naval doldrums of the 'sixties the general public was well disposed towards young men in the service. With mounting excitement the midshipmen made their way to their respective ships. But when Marx arrived on board *Phoebe*, it was all a bit of an anti-climax. Nobody took much notice of him and the young cadet was disappointed to find *'there were very few'* on board. However, it made his first task not too onerous:

21 May
I had to keep the middle watch last night as there was only the first lieutenant on board I lay down on some sails and whent to sleep.

The *Phoebe* was Marx's first experience of a ship at sea and he looked forward to seeing her in action. She seemed to bear little relation to the stationary *Britannia*. She was 280 feet long, with 520 officers and men. Her enormous masts were 160 feet tall, and her yards had a spread of 95 feet. Her bunkers carried 340 tons of coal. She had a flush deck without poop or forecastle and bulwarks that were eight feet high around most of the deck so nothing outboard could be seen except through a gun port or gangway port. She also had, what Marx had not yet seen, a working steam-driven screw propeller that was raised or lowered according to needs. Typical of the transition from sail to steam, *Phoebe* had been cut in half and a new middle piece set in to house the engines. Passages from port to port were generally made under sail, but steam could be used for going in and out of harbour or if the ship was in a hurry or becalmed. On the upper deck were six, muzzle-loading, sixty-four-pounder guns. On the main deck were the four impressive, new, seven-inch, six-and-a-half-ton guns. They were rifled and fired 120-pound projectiles and some double shell weighing 210 pounds. They were mounted on iron or steel carriages, recoiled on slides and were the great show guns of the ship. There were also thirty smaller smooth-bore guns. Marx looked with anticipation to the moment this great, new, exciting ship would put to sea. *Phoebe* was also remarkable for the new device of a bathroom for the gunroom, but there was insufficient fresh water for it, so the midshipmen and subs of the gunroom continued to use the time-honoured method of screen, hose and saltwater from a wash deck pump on deck.[1]

However, it was not the ship herself, but the dark hole of the gunroom that was to become the immediate focus of young Marx's new life. It was about eighteen feet long, partitioned off from the lower deck, and about seven feet wide and about six feet from deck to beams. It had two sliding doors and for ventilation two scuttle ports, circular holes about six inches in diameter, which could only be opened on very calm days. The steward's pantry, about seven feet by three, communicated with the gunroom by a small serving hatch. In the constant semi-darkness, lamps were always lit. The only oils permitted were the foul-smelling colza or whale oil – some might have preferred the darkness!

John Marx's first reaction to his new life in the gunroom was much like his reaction to his first experience of *Britannia* – intimidated but stoical. '*The outfit of the mess is pretty well. I hope just to manage. I will do my best…. Our mess is very crowded.*' From the superiority and prestige of having been a senior cadet at naval college, Marx found himself once again a being of no account – a wart.[2] If he had learned the power and importance of senior cadets at *Britannia*, he now learned what an important personage was the sub-lieutenant in a ship that carried midshipmen: 'he has the very souls of the junior midshipman in his care… '.[3] The care of these souls involved a good deal of physical attention and might involve anything from a single beating, to the daily 'fork in the beam', when the gunroom sub would push his fork up into an overhead beam at the end of a meal and all the junior midshipmen would stampede out, the nearest senior midshipman acting as 'whipper out' with a dirk scabbard….[4] As a new 'wart', Admiral William May remembered being half-dead with sea sickness in his first storm and being urged on deck to reef topsails by a young sub with a hunting crop. Admiral Smith Dorien remembered being cooped up in the gunroom of *Endymion* with drunken subs who brandished broken bottles and a pistol.[5] The initiation in *Phoebe* was equally unpleasant, all new 'Middys' had to have a broad arrow carved into their noses by senior subs whose reputation for bullying the juniors was apparently well known. '*Some fellows cut a broad arrow on mine and two other fellow's noses. It did not hurt but only bled a little.*' This was supposed to indicate that from now on they were government property. A little cayenne pepper was rubbed in for further effect. One of the problems of the bullying subs in gunrooms was that many of them were very much older men who had failed to get promotion in the stagnant promotional lists of the 'sixties and 'seventies and took it out on the youngsters. The regime at *Britannia* had done what it could to stop the use of bad language and swearing but according to Marx's compatriot on *Phoebe*, William Creswell, the language aboard ship came as a painful shock to most of the newly fledged middys. 'I would not mind anything if it was not for the horrible swearing,' one of them declared, but Marx, although from a sheltered, religious background seems to have taken this in his stride. There is no mention of it in his letters. Memoirists castigate the bad gunrooms of the Old Navy,[6] but take it for granted that the gunroom system of cooping up youngsters at the mercy of their seniors should remain unchallenged. It was the way of the Navy. Again, it reflected the attitude of contemporary public schools, which gave its schoolboys similar experiences.[7] In some gunrooms, there was what might euphemistically be termed 'moral laxity'. Certainly the young Chambers 'did not understand…a great deal that went on' but knew that 'things were far other than they should have been'.[8] At its worst, a bad gunroom in the Old Navy was only another form of Eton's 'long chamber'.[9]

However, the young Marx could not concentrate on his troubles in the gunroom, but had to turn his attention to the demanding work of the ship. Apart from classroom lessons and seamanship under First Lieutenant Francis Starkie Clayton, 'a very able seaman, much admired and liked by the Midshipmen',[10] there were all the regular drills of the ship: fire drills, going to quarters, evolutionary (sailing) drills, signalling with flags and lights, drilling with the various guns, target practice and cutlass and rifle exercises, manning and arming boats, drilling landing parties ashore and afloat. At just fifteen a young middy had responsibility for a division of men, responsibility for a boat or top, and a four-hour 'watch and watch'. He had to go aloft with the seamen to make or shorten sail if necessary, tack ship, weigh anchor and work cables. He had to be very smart running aloft in order not to be overtaken and trodden on by the agile and skilled upper yardmen and topmen. He must also always be prepared to produce his 'watch bill', a list of the men under him mustered at any given time, and he had to keep a log illustrated with charts and coastal sketches, which could also be inspected at any time. Many midshipmen's maps and charts were works of art in themselves and Marx was no exception. His later maps and diagrams were beautifully executed though his handwriting left so much to be desired.

The first task of the ship's company was to settle in and prepare for a commissioning inspection. It meant a week's cruise in the Channel: '*We are beginning to shake into our places now…the Commander has joined. His name is Grant and he looks rather strict. Captain Bythesea came on board yesterday… .*' Captain John Bythesea was one of the first group of recipients of the Victoria Cross in 1856. During the Crimean War, as a twenty-seven-year-old lieutenant in HMS *Arrogant*, he offered to intercept important despatches from the Czar. He and a stoker, armed with just one pistol, landed on one of the Aland Islands and after reconnoitring the island for two days, when the despatches arrived, ambushed the five men carrying them. Two of the carriers dropped their bags and ran but the other three surrendered and Bythesea took them back to *Arrogant*: hence the VC. One might have thought that the young Marx would have been very impressed by this. He makes no mention of it. Did he know?

The week's cruise made Marx realise he needed a number of new things. He quickly set about telling his parents what he required, '*My journey and the carriage of my chest cost 40 [shillings], 6d and you gave me £1 10s.*' A week in *Phoebe* made him realise he wanted '*a great many things…which I shall not be able to get with my allowance, viz 2 chest covers of white duck, Watchbill, Workbook, Washingboard…please send my telescope…my gun.*' He suggested they ask Aunt Mary to send him '*a set of studs*'. He also needed a letter of credit so that he could draw his mess money – thirty shillings a month. He sent his father a form of wording to be copied and returned to the Captain,

Mr John Marx naval Cadet or Midshipman is hereby authorized to draw quarterly or half yearly as may be convenient on Messrs. Coutts, Arlebury, Alresford, Hants the sum of £50 sterling per annum.

He could only withdraw money with the consent of the Captain.

Initially, Marx was gratified to find that he had been appointed '*aidedecamps*' (ADC) to the Captain. However, it presented him with a problem when the time came for the dreaded Admiral's commissioning inspection. The inspection was to be carried out by Admiral 'Pincher' Martin. He was known for his severity and exacting standards. After much work and anxiety, much scrubbing and polishing, it was hoped that everything had been done to the Admiral's satisfaction. There was only one snag. As Captain's ADC, Marx had to stand beside the Captain at the commissioning inspection, and as he had just had his nose embellished, the Admiral could not fail to notice it. It caused considerable consternation. As he explained to his mother,

He saw that my nose and two others were slits and has made a row about it but Captain Bythesea was very kind about it and tried his best to get the Admiral not to say anything about it but could not succeed but I hope the fellows will not get anything.

The Admiral would not be mollified by Captain Bythesea's endeavour to play down the incident as acceptable, traditional naval rough-housing. He called all the midshipmen onto the quarterdeck and examined them. He insisted on complaining to Admiralty about the disfiguring of Marx and his thirteen fellow-midshipmen. But such was the unwritten law of the Navy that at the subsequent Board of Enquiry, 'every one of the "mutilated" young gentlemen completely exonerated the culprits from having used any bullying force'. They declared they had all welcomed the embellishment as part of the tradition of the Navy. Such loyalty, seeded at *Britannia*, flourished in the gunroom.

The work of the ship continued and Marx sent his letters home detailing all the small activities of his shipboard life. '*Yesterday we had rifle and heavy gun practice. We had pretty good shooting but the seven inch rifles guns made an immense concussion.*' He told them about the Chief Engineer being landed at Plymouth because '*he became mad that the engines would not work well*' and discussed the excitement over the forthcoming review at Portsmouth for the Queen's Jubilee. He hoped his parents would be able to go, and that he might get some leave to see them. He thanked them for sending his gun and the powder and shot flasks and said that Aunt Mary's studs were very pretty. He hoped his father's leg would get better soon and that all the animals were all right. He told them about '*a jolly bathe*' he had just had. All the ships were preparing and collecting together for the review. It was very exciting: '*there are whole lots of ships going to be there*'. When the review took place, Marx was disappointed because his family had not had a good sight of the illuminations. The limelights had been quenched in the fog and rain.

After the review, in July and August, *Phoebe* travelled to Cork and Queenstown in Ireland. The young Marx was beginning to settle down in his new environment and find his feet, but he was still a schoolboy at heart. At Deal, on the way, they played the 6th Depot Battalion at cricket and were '*most awfully licked as our best players were away... . Another day they went in shore and played cricket under difficulties, when we got to the place we found a whole lot of cadds who tried to keep us out but we soon drove them away.*' In August the ship moored at Queenstown where they were able to go ashore almost every day. The freedom and relaxed atmosphere suited Marx. He made many references to this '*very jolly*'... '*rather jolly*' time. He was delighted that *Phoebe*'s cutters came in first and second in the regatta races. There was excitement over a collision between the *Tamar* and the *Himalaya*. In Marx's still schoolboy style:

> *The Tamer came in here on thursday and when going out yesterday when to close across the bows of the Himalaya and her Fore topgallant studing sail boom caught the Himalaya's Fore topgallant stay and carried away her Fore Topgallant mast close to the cap.*

Accidents could teach young midshipmen the requirements of good sailing as well as proficiency.

After Queenstown the ship returned to Plymouth before leaving for her main commission, which would last for three years. This gave a chance for a brief visit home to the delight of his mother: 'Johnny walked into the library!!! He is grown and so loving and dear.' When he returned to the ship there was great anticipation and some anxiety while the new midshipmen awaited news of her destination. Would it be a tedious home posting or something exotic far away? To the delight of Marx and all the youngsters, they learned that *Phoebe* was to be attached to the North American and West Indian station: excitement and the possibility of action, at last.

Marx wrote his last letters home before leaving. At this point he was still the ingenuous, enthusiastic, optimistic boy of *Britannia*. His chief concern at home was still the state of his father's leg, after his hunting accident. '*I hope…it will get straight without having to break it again.*' He was glad it had not prevented Father from enjoying his latest militia camp and he hoped George would pass his Army exams. His last words were to wish Father and George '*good sport*'. Unfortunately, we have no more first-hand accounts of Marx's life until he starts his journal in 1871. We have to piece together the next three years from other sources. They were significant years in which the experiences of his life would start to change him from a cheerful, untroubled boy to an uneasy young man.

They started well enough. He had passed the initial exam, which turned him from cadet to official midshipman in October of 1867, and with the other newly fledged midshipmen he looked forward to their first destination – Halifax in Nova Scotia. Halifax was renowned for its good fishing and shooting within easy distance of the harbour. After a long and difficult voyage across the Atlantic with mostly unfavourable winds, it was a delight to stretch one's legs in the dockyard on arrival and plan a few days' adventure ashore. But the stay was disappointingly short and they were quickly off for a brief visit to Bermuda and a couple of cruises in the Spanish Main. Trips ashore were limited and shipboard work became the centre of Marx's life.

The midshipmen were divided into four watches. Marx was fortunate in being in a watch with a kindly, easygoing junior lieutenant over them. William Creswell was appointed senior of Marx's watch and referred to Marx as 'one of the very best'. The work of the ship was hard and food scarce but there was a compensating prospect of a good winter at Quebec, where as Creswell said, 'Fishing (salmon, trout, all the very best), shooting grouse, moose even, sleighing, skating, awfully nice people,' would abound. They could not wait! What a blow then to learn that Quebec was not to be! Instead, *Phoebe* was to become part of Admiral Phipps Hornby's so called 'Flying Squadron', a fleet of ships got together for a round-the-world trip to show the British flag and train the younger officers and men in fleet sailing and the ways of the Navy. Not everybody approved of it, some officers complained that it took too many senior men from the service.

Reluctantly then, in 1869, the young midshipmen of *Phoebe* set sail for Bahia to meet the 'Flying Squadron'. But resentment must have changed to excitement when in the harbour they saw against the backdrop of a bright blue sky, the shining white sails of an actual fleet – all of six ships! The *Liverpool*, *Bristol*, *Endymion*, *Liffey*, *Scylla* and *Barrosa*. William Farley, a midshipman in the *Liffey*, recalled their arrival:[11]

> At Bahia next we anchored, remaining but two days
> The Brazilian flag we did salute, the same to us she pays:
> The Bristol here we left behind, bound to Old England's shore,
> The Phoebe joins us in her stead, as was proposed before.

Although William Farley's poem was not of breathtaking quality, it provides a graphic account of the daily life of the Flying Squadron. It was the first experience the new middys of *Phoebe* had of sailing with other ships, and other ships brought the appearance of new cadets. *Phoebe* was assigned six of them from the *Bristol*. It was a mixed blessing. Certainly, it meant Marx and his friends were no longer the *warts*, the most junior and despised of beings, but in the company of the new cadets with their well-fitting clothes, the young middys were embarrassed. They saw how shabby they had become without realising it. None of their clothes fitted any longer. Sleeves were much too short and there were gaps between jackets and trousers.

In this new fleet sailing, Marx and his fellow-middys would be under the command of the remarkable and demanding Admiral Phipps Hornby, one of the most admired Admirals in the Navy but a trial to the young midshipmen,

> ...to do our best, our Admiral for to please
> With might and main and ardent zeal, it is no task of ease.

Phipps Hornby was dedicated to the idea of training the young officers to be familiar with all the exercises of the fleet as the correspondent of the *Sydney Morning Herald* explained:

> Every night some duty had to be carried on, so that every opportunity is given for the young officers to become practically acquainted with all exercises...the Admiral frequently makes signal for the watch on deck to shift jib, spanker or topgallant sail, and by doing so the crews are all being brought into a course of good instruction...the midshipmen and Cadets, by his order, are continually put through a course of instruction, and most stringent examinations are periodically imposed by the naval instructors, and the results are reported to the Commander in Chief...some days were entirely given to squadron evolution sailing... . The heat has been intense and when any sea has been on and the cabin ports closed it has been unbearable. [12]

Creswell remembered the heat engendered by twenty-three men in a gunroom of eighteen feet and no ventilation.

Admiral Smith Dorien, another midshipman of the Flying Squadron, looked back on the demands of its sailing:

> A sailor's life is not devoid of anxiety and little can be comprehended by those who have not had the experience of reefing topsails in a gale of wind, for it was then necessary to hang on to the ropes and yards with a temerity that knows no bounds – not only would the ship be rolling heavily, but the force of the wind whistling through the rigging would be such that the human voice would be lost in the reverberation of the storm... . The arc through which they were swinging was a

very great one... . The nest of ants not human beings on it, would find themselves at one moment almost in the surf of the sea and at the next hanging above the universe... . (On one occasion when no orders could be heard, the spars and rigging came down on the heads of Middys and those aloft)...the terrible language...impossible to imagine so much blasphemy.[13]

The squadron was to visit Buenos Aires, Monte Video, Cape of Good Hope, Australia, New Zealand, Japan, Vancouver, Honolulu, Valpraiso, round the Horn, Bahia and home. Phipps Hornby ordered a continuous programme of evolutions and smart drills. This meant *Phoebe* would have to pick up her paces. According to Marx's later reports, she was rather a slack and somewhat unhappy ship under the Acting Commander Crowle, 'Jerry, the awful',[14] and the surprisingly ineffectual Captain Bythesea (a VC was apparently not always the guarantee of a good captain). She would perforce have to become more purposeful and efficient,

> Of sailing tactics once again, all day our Admiral choosing,
> With skill each Captain works his ship, their courage never loosing!
>
> The Phoebe lets her life-buoy go, from her a man is gone...
>
> The Phoebe with us nearly foul'd, but no damage there was done...

With the departure of Crowle in Australia, for disgracing himself with his incompetence in harbour under the eyes of Phipps Hornby, and with the promotion of 'the beloved first Lieutenant'[15] Clayton to Commander, things improved aboard *Phoebe*.

> The Phoebe took the challenge up, and both ships did their best
> The Phoebe beat and won the race, the truth must be confest [sic].

And at the end of the voyage, after a storm in which *Phoebe* lost her foreyard, and had to fall behind,

> ...as our bell did toll for church, she then came passing by,
> With her fore-tops'l flying set, what better could outvie?
> And soon she took her station up, it pleased us much to see
> That she was able to lead on and join in company.

The lines of W H Farley sadly reveal the incidence of mortality experienced by the fleet. According to him, four men died aboard ship from illness and eleven by accidents on board or drowning. One can imagine the sobering effect of these repeated funerals upon the new midshipmen,

> How sad and solemn too, next day, the bell was mournfully
>   toll'd,
> His hammock served him for a shroud, in which his corpse was
>   rolled
> His lifeless form to the deep we gave, while his funeral rites
>   were read
> Where he now sleeps, until once more the sea gives up her dead.
>
> And three days after his sad fate, another one befell
> To the Scylla in like manner, it grieves us sore to tell...

Perhaps this mortality contributed to what was apparently not a happy time for young Marx. He referred afterwards to the shortcomings of Captain Bythesea and the various troubles and rows on board, but does not explain exactly what they were. Perhaps hunger exacerbated tensions. May, Smith-Dorien and Creswell all recalled difficult times in the gunrooms of the Flying Squadron and severe hunger as supplies ran low. 'We were always so hungry that after the mutton-bone had been scraped clean, we broke it in two to get the marrow out.'[16] They were known to others and themselves as 'The Hungry Six'. Food and fresh water were always scarce and sometimes almost to starvation point. It seems amazing that officers and men who lived on meagre rations of salt beef, bacon and biscuits, with the occasional fresh meat, food that would today be condemned as inedible and unhealthy, should have remained fit enough to perform the physical feats required by the Flying Squadron. Christmas dinner at Hobart, supplied by the Colonial Government, must have seemed wonderful with its ample supply of beef, flour and fruit.

However, despite difficulties, the experience in the Flying Squadron did give the junior midshipmen good training in the elementary knowledge of a naval officer: how to sail a ship, how to manage the men of a watch, how to manage boats and boat stations. It also gave them some time ashore with parties, picnics and visitations, in which to learn the skills of polite society. They also learned some of the less desirable skills as Marx discovered later.

> It is scarcely necessary to say the officers of the fleet are received everywhere with welcomes, and the fashionable world is all excitement with the public and private entertainments which are nightly taking place and to which gentlemen are invited…
>
> On Monday His Excellency gave a grand ball at Toorak, which was attended by a large number of the officers and the elite of Melbourne…
>
> Friday is to be devoted to a picnic at Fern Tree Gully, which is to be a very stupendous affair.[17]

The officers returned these compliments by opening their ships to visitors and entertaining them. Thus the young midshipmen learned the skills of naval hospitality, which have always been a mark of the service.

The squadron left Australia for the second half of its round-the-world trip in December of 1870. There would be nearly another year's sailing before it arrived in England for a spell of much-needed home leave and a chance to relax and eat decently again,

> And now in England safe arrived, one prayer I ask of all,
> May we a kindly welcome meet, good news our minds enthral

> May we have pleasures rich and rare, with friends who waited
> long
> For our return in safety, and with them be among.

By the time they returned home, they would be all of eighteen years old and senior midshipmen. The voyage of the Flying Squadron with all its dangers and excitement, its need for unquestioning obedience, its hardship and at times boredom, its introduction to worldly pleasures, had truly been a rite of passage. The awkward adolescents had become young men. It was time for paying off certificates. Captain Bythesea gave Marx his, and affirmed that he had,

> served, with sobriety and satisfactorily, he promises to become
> a steady good officer.

> Bythesea 16 October 1867–29 November 1870.

The young Marx was pleased. It boded well for his future as a senior midshipman.

---

1 For a full account of *Phoebe* see Creswell, ibid.

2 Fairbairn, *The Narrative of a Naval Nobody*, p61. What is known at a public school as a fag.

3 Commander H Stoker, *Straws in the Wind* (1925), p18.

4 '…a custom clearly dating back to wooden ship days, when the gunroom sub would push his fork up into an overhead beam at the end of a meal, and all the junior Midshipmen would stampede out, the nearest senior Midshipman acting as "whipper out" with a dirk scabbard.' Oswald Frewen, *Sailor's Soliloquy*, p50.

5 Memoirs of Admiral Smith Dorien SMD/1 MM.

6 Admiral B M Chambers, *Salt Junk*, p119.

7 See Frewen at Eton, *Soliloquy*, ch2.

8 Chambers, *Salt Junk*, p67.

9 For description of horrors of 'long chamber', Eton's dormitory, see Gathorne Hardy's graphic description in *The Public School Phenomenon* and H. Lyte's account in *History of Eton College*, pp415–21. For bad gunrooms see Creswell, ibid, p5.

10 Creswell, ibid, p27.

11 W Farley wrote a long undated poem entitled 'The Flying Squadron'.

12 *Sydney Morning Herald*, 2 November 1869.

13 Smith Dorien, ibid.

14 Creswell, ibid, pp94–95.

15 Ibid.

16 May, *The Life of a Sailor*, p17.

17 *Sydney Morning Herald*, 4 December 1869.

Four

Senior Midshipman (1870–1873)

'...that damned b-t-l'.

On 30 November 1870, John Marx arrived home on his first leave since becoming a midshipman. His mother was delighted,

> Our dear son walked in, we were overcome... . He is a fine fellow with a beautiful voice and a most loving manner.

Despite his mother's welcome, Marx was surprised and rather upset to find himself 'hardly recognised...nobody seems to know me'. This was true for many of the returning midshipmen who usually had not seen their families for three years or so. Life at sea had toughened and hardened them. They had left as boys and returned as physically grown and independent young men. Not only did people appear not to know Marx, he hardly knew them. He found his father 'much altered' (the hunting accident had aged him) and although his mother was less so, he also found her changed in that now she seemed to 'complain a great deal'. In fact, she had incipient heart trouble.

But Marx himself had changed. As well as mementoes brought back from his voyage, he also brought with him another souvenir of many a midshipman's life: venereal disease. He was now suffering from an attack of 'the clap'. Somewhere on his voyages he had discovered the delights and hazards of sexual experience. It was to be the '*bête noir*' of his early life. He was under no illusions as to his illness and that it was caused by the inclinations of his own temperament. It was this that made him start his first journal, and it is to this journal kept intermittently over many years that we owe the remarkable story of his life and can read the complex nature of his personality.

Marx opened his journal on 27 December 1870, with a careful and combative introduction:

> I intend to try and keep up this journal which I am commencing today. I have tried this sort of thing before but failed after 6 months but then I had tried too much putting down my own thoughts and actions in such a way that other people might read them and failed because I could not expose the springs which often moved me as they were what the hypocrites of this world call immoral. My experience has been that though most men and women put on a cloak of modesty they are really in thought so often not in deed as bad as the worst. Not in deed because they are cowards being afraid of punishments both at present and hereafter. I am sure that few of the actions which are called good and which in themselves are good come from any true love of doing right for right's sake but from a wish to propitiate some indistinct and misty vision of an almighty being which they are afraid will punish them for all their misdeeds which they have committed.

Typically, after giving vent to his feelings, the young Marx did not dwell on the philosophy of his troubles but cheerfully set about making the best of a spell of life at home. He was now a high-spirited young man of nearly nineteen years and he enjoyed the social life of the neighbourhood; the hunting, the dining, the dancing with 'the jolly girls', especially, the 'very jolly' Flory – 'very jolly though what Haywood would call coarse, though that is not the right name for her as she is pretty and I think quite ladylike'. He became gallantly indignant on Flory's behalf: 'she is run down by the Matronage of the neighbourhood who are about as spiteful a lot as you could pick up headed by Mrs. Benson, whiped in by several other ladies whose names I shall always remember so it is useless putting them on paper'. The weather was notably icy so there was much skating with the 'jolly, laughing, chaffing girls'. He 'skylarked in the long room with the girls. Gertrude looking very nice.' He had trouble deciding which of 'the devillish nice Summers girls' he liked best: 'Effie looks very demure but really has a great deal of fun and humbug about her. Sadly the younger comes out in rather stronger colours in the way of laughing and chaffing though in dress they are always black.' It was a far cry from the rigours of 'The Flying Squadron': there was a touch of Jane Austen in his description of social life. 'The party that had been at Lasham came home. Conny looks very well and is one of the jolliest girls I have the honor of knowing. Edith had grown a good deal.' We shall hear more of Conny and Edith. There were also the regular visits to church and occasionally the reflective young Marx would comment on a good sermon that he had heard.

However, despite his attempts to ignore it, Marx's attack of the *clap* did not improve. It became worse, and his conscience worried him: 'I did not attempt to defend it as of course it is no good and I think those who do are Hypocrites as they do evil and call it good.' No doubt in the religious environment of home, it all seemed particularly bad, but he knew how difficult it was to maintain upright intentions faced with the attractions outside. On New Year's Day 1871, he wrote, 'What a lot of good resolutions made to day will be broken before another comes.'

He explained his current situation to his friend Haywood, who was, 'shocked but took it better than expected…not having been away from home since he was 16 at any place where he could get into mischief [he] does not understand one's temptations'.

We do not know when or where Marx visited his first brothel but it was probably an experience gained towards the end of his time with the Flying Squadron. So sadly, the pleasure of his first holiday as a dashing young midshipman was spoiled by his continually feeling seedy. His testicles swelled and he stayed in bed...: 'not much acute pain, except when they dangle'. He saw the doctor who told him not to eat or drink wine, gave him a pill to take morning and evening and said he should be well in a week. He was not. Mother declared him 'very poorly'. Time was running out and on 9 January, the family doctor, Dr Butler, had to send a sick note to Admiralty saying that Marx would not be able to join his next ship. He got an extension of leave. On 17 January he was taken worse and had to telegraph Dr Butler. Mother now declared 'Johnny alarmingly ill'. It was not until a 'violent perspiration mercifully relieved him' that he recovered. Marx said it was 'the heaviest sweat' he ever remembered.

In fact, at this stage, Marx was probably suffering from acute gonorrhoea (epydidymites) with added infection. A general illness with fever ensued. There were no antibiotics. The most primitive antibiotic (the sulphonamide group) did not get discovered until 1938.[1] Few people and certainly not his mother knew the real cause of his debility. While he was getting better, a number of visitors called to take his mind off the tedium of staying in bed, something he always hated. He amused himself jotting down in his journal some of the funny stories visitors told him, stories not always suited to the drawing room,

> Another. Mr Willie Onslow whom appears to have turned out an utter blackguard was attempting what is called at Eton to spoon a fellow, and felt something warm inserted into his trouser pocket and being quite happy for the time let it remain and did not look till a minute afterwards when it turned out to be the spout of a kettle of hot water which was judiciously poured into the place where his pocket ought to have been.

There were more innocent ones: 'Good story. Brodie preached a sermon and asked the people weather they had ever tasted or smelt a sole, at which some wit replied yes.'

Marx saw more of 'the jolly Flory.... Curious, I can look up or stare anybody out of countenance in the county except that d-d girl and after about 30 seconds, down go my eyes and I begin to feel uncomfortable... .' Flory gave him her photograph, 'expect she will be done for the next time I see her'. He even wrote verses for her but unfortunately,

> my meter and rhyme,
> will not keep time.

Once he was seen to be getting better, his father had a stern talk with him, making it clear that he disapproved of his grown son's way of life,

> I am in very bad odour first my cl-p secondly I am accused of not being frank thirdly I have the misfortune to see absurd things and to laugh at people's weak points but it is not my fault I can not help it.

Then to cap it all, he got excruciating toothache and had to have an extraction and five stoppings. He was miserable and began to think he would 'never get rid of my disease until my dying day which if this goes on is not far away'. The affairs of the service went some way to taking his mind off his troubles. On 30 January he went with his father to the United Services Institution in London and 'heard a very good lecture on torpedoes by Captain Dawson and one on the buoyancy of the naval hammock by Admiral Ryder'. Walking around London with his father, he was able to have a more friendly chat with him and elicit some sympathy as he explained about his life in *Phoebe* and the rows, and why Captain Bythesea got such a bad name. It was a weekend visit and Mother came too. They packed a lot in. Marx took the opportunity of discussing national defences with General Pringle Taylor, who although *rather prosy* seemed to have the right ideas in admiring the Prussian system of tactics and their system for the Commissariat. He went to Burlington House and enjoyed the pictures.

He went to Admiralty to inquire about his future ship. He called on Hobhouse where they discussed the distribution of land: 'if it gets into the hands of a few the millions will rise and redistribute it without something is done by law to prevent it'. He paid other visits and in the evening went to the Prince of Wales Theatre, which he thought beautifully fitted and heard two very good pieces with good acting, 'some very pretty girls'. When they returned to Hampshire, they found Admiral Pincher Martin at one of the local houses. To Marx's embarrassment, his father insisted on thanking him 'about the nose row'.

Marx was now well enough to take up his next appointment as a senior middy in HMS *Caledonia*. This time, he left home 'devillish sorry' and with none of the excitement of his first appointment. He was older and wiser now. He still wanted to make progress in the Navy, but he had fewer illusions about the life and he had enjoyed being at home. He would miss all the 'jolly girls'. After a great deal of trouble his chest was put aboard the *Duke of Wellington* and he travelled in the *Himalaya* to pick up his new ship at Malta, ready for a cruise in the Mediterranean. It was a good posting. *Caledonia* was the first armoured flagship to carry an admiral, Admiral Yelverton, and although she was no longer the Mediterranean flagship (the newer *Lord Warden* was) she was an advance on *Phoebe*; she was a wooden line-of-battle ship that had been converted to a broadside iron clad. She carried ten seven-inch breech-loading rifled guns, eight 100-pounder smooth-bore guns, and twelve 68-pounder smooth-bore guns. She was full-rigged broadside, had a single steam-driven screw propeller and a maximum speed of thirteen knots. Lord Clarence Paget testified to her fighting powers and her ease of manoeuvring. However, despite the feeling of having stepped up in the world, Marx was anxious. He had heard that the Commander and Skipper of *Caledonia* had bad names in the service. He hoped he would get on all right.

Things started well. He was a senior midshipman now and in contrast to the *Phoebe* he found the gunroom messing on *Caledonia* good. At the commissioning inspection, Admiral Yelverton on examining the new midshipman's logs and their watch bills, complimented Marx on his. Afterwards, when Marx asked the Commander, Pringle, for shore leave, he was gratified to find that the Commander refused it 'in the politest manner possible on the grounds of my misfortune'. Marx always responded well to people who treated him well. But now his 'misfortune', which had again bothered him on the *Himalaya* and meant a spell in the sick bay, started to trouble him once more. He had a 'slight return in right testicle though not much'. The doctor sent for him and put him in the sick list. His fear of subsequent illness was made worse by the anxiety of his conscience: 'I often think what the devil will become of me in the end as so many things pass before my mind.'

By March he could no longer ignore his worsening state. Infection in the twenty feet of fine tubing behind the testicle can even hang about a long time today, despite modern medication. In 1871 there was little alleviation. Marx's testicle was so bad that he could 'only crawl'. He had to go to the ship's sick bay. It was 'a fine airy place', but he found it depressing. There was always a 'smell of drugs besides having a lot of men worse than yourself all over the place'. His messmates were good and came up to see him often. Then his general debilitation was made worse by a new trouble. At first he did not know what it was, and found it 'rather odd waking up in the morning smelling a beastly smell not knowing whence it comes'. To his surprise he found that the beastly smell emanated from his smallpox vaccination, which he had 'taken no care of… . Rather odd…smelling a beastly smell not knowing whence it comes and finding that it is your own arm.' Vaccines, being less pure in those days, could give rise to infection and failure. Re-vaccination was common. A sailor being re-vaccinated at the end of that year, 1871, remarked, 'They vaccinate on the wrist now instead of the arm: and do you know what that is for? Why, don't you see, if the place mortifies, they have a chance of saving your life by taking your arm off.'[2] Added to Marx's bad reaction to his vaccination, the pain in his testicles was now so acute he decided reluctantly that he must write home and tell his father of his condition. He was greatly relieved to find his father 'sensible and kind as always'. His father, being older when he married and a much travelled man, was tolerant and doubtless well acquainted, if not personally, with the problem. The doctor insisted that Marx stay in bed: 'Good Lord deliver me... .' Marx never wanted to lose time to sickness, but how much time was lost to the Navy through sailors and officers being incapacitated by venereal disease? A ship in a gale or in trouble needed all its personnel.

At least, it was a chance for Marx to write and receive the letters from home, which meant so much to him. He was particularly interested in receiving cousin Conny's 'good letters' telling him all about events at home. He was much taken with her and wrote often to her though he told her he could not 'say what he meant'. Was this because she was his cousin and it would have been inappropriate, or did he simply feel inarticulate? He procured a box of gloves to send her.

The ship continued to cruise along the coast of Italy and her officers enjoyed the chance to see all the local sights. Marx saw Stromboli from the ship 'which was smoking away like blazes but it does not come out of the top like a sensible mountain but from a hole in its side'. The other midshipmen went to see the Blue Grotto at Capri and a special trip to Rome was arranged for them. Naval captains often provided educational and recreational trips for their midshipmen. They recognised this as part of their training. Marx missed out on all of this. He was frustrated. 'For some time I have been seeing the fruits of having any thing to do with that damned b-t-l.' He blamed himself for his own folly. It wasn't until 6 April that he got up for the first time, feeling rather weak but hoping to be better shortly. On 15 April, the ship came back into Malta and Marx recorded that the doctor had begun to treat him for clap and he might be out in a fortnight. It seems rather late in the day. Had the ship's doctor, Dr Cotton, only just recognised the illness or does it mean that medical treatment was not available until they sailed into the Grand Harbour at Malta? It was not a question of going to hospital. Naval hospitals did not admit personnel suffering venereal disease. But Father, in true parental fashion had embarrassed Marx by writing a letter to the senior surgeon, 'a foolish thing to do', Marx complained. Was it this that procured the late suitable treatment?

This was a troubled time for Marx and his conscience worried him in more ways than one. An incident took place the night before he came out of the invalid list. There was a game of cards and Sub Lieutenant Jago,

> ...called me a cheat and by God I did not hit him. I hardly know wether to be sorry or glad. Was it funk? I think not. I hope not. What was it? I do not know. The facts were I was an ace and 3 and undecided wether to take the next card but as I had decided to take the next card and said so, Jago turned up a 5. As I said another card before he turned up, he said I cheated. By – I should have hit him if I had done right but even now I am cursedly undecided. My right course would be to make him apologise or Q Dk him which I will do if I can only decide. ['Q Dk him' referred to the holding of an official inquiry by the Captain on the quarter deck.]

As a young officer, Marx was increasingly beset by indecision and a lack of confidence, no doubt exacerbated by what he perceived to be his moral and physical weakness in sexual matters. Again, during May, his condition deteriorated. His testicles swelled, became bigger and more painful. In desperation, he went to see the ship's surgeon, Dr Delmege, who said he could do nothing. He simply advised Marx to 'keep quiet'. Not easy, as Marx said, with 'hard drill and getting out boats'. There was fearful pain. He could not sleep. Eventually the pain was relieved by lancing but it was back to bed on doctor's orders. Again he had to amuse himself. He wrote verses to the 'jolly Flory' at home. She had sent him her photograph and he wrote on the envelope,

> This contains of a photo of Miss Flo
> Who although you may not know
> I will tell you in this ditty
> is both good and devilish pretty

There is not a man for 10 miles round
who would not give some 40 pound
If Miss Flory to him would say
I'll be yours just name the day.

Her hair she has enough for two
If it is all hers I never knew
When hunting she rides well and straight
And at the death was never late

Of offers for to marry she's had several
but has told them all to go the devil
She now talks of going and leaving the country
But people say Deacon only wants a bounty.

Now my wishes are these
First Miss Flory to please
Then that Deacon may long have the pounds and hunt them
and that his leaving the country may be all bunkum.

It seems that Deacon was his father's huntsman and a suitor to Flory and that they were to leave the country together. But apparently Deacon stayed on as a hunting official for another £100 a year and we hear no more of Miss Flory. Marx's heart was easily moved by a pretty woman and there were plenty of them.

On 19 May, he started to feel better and Dr Cotton told him he should be out of the list within a week. 'Please God I may never get this sort of thing again.' The next day, Captain Cochrane put his head round the gunroom door and told Marx to 'go to school in future'. Marx felt humiliated; he had never liked the sarcastic Captain and was delighted when he heard that Cochrane was to leave the ship. TC 'gave us a speech saying that he was just leaving us, he hoped the new Captain would be just and all that sort of thing and in fact a lot of twaddle without much sense and a bad delivery'. The new captain, Stanhope, was said to be 'a very good sort indeed' and Marx looked forward to his coming. But when Stanhope arrived, he 'looked ill and thin…appeared a little nervous'. Marx remarked honestly and even-handedly that if he had not known of either man he would certainly have assumed that Cochrane was the finest of the two. He noted that 'the last thing T.C. did was to send a man to Choky and another who had been tried by court martial to 5 yrs penal servitude'. He felt that his dislike of Cochrane was justified when Cochrane gave him what he regarded as a bad certificate,

> …has been in the sick list during the whole period except a few days. His conduct has been satisfactory 30 November 1870– 6 June 1871…

It seems not an unreasonable comment.

The small incidents of the commission continued while Marx was recovering. He was not allowed any leave but given a little light boat work. *Caledonia* enjoyed a successful admiral's inspection, but shortly afterwards her main yard was carried away while hoisting out the first launch and she had to have a new one. In June, she had to go to the aid of the *Lord Warden*, which went on shore coming out of dock. In July the flagship had occasion to return the compliment: *Caledonia* had struck a rock off Santorini,

> When we got on board we found she had struck on a rock while going about 2 knots. The Lord Warden got hold of one of our bower chains and tried to haul us off stern foremost but could not succeed. I went with James [Henry James, Navigating Midshipman], and sounded round the ship then went on board the Lord Warden and told the Admiral, Wise and Brandreth…[3]…the Admiral ordered us to blow out 3 boiler and shift our cable out of the bow all ready to be towed off by the bow. We took the ground about amidship on a detached reef with 28 and a half fathoms under the bow and 3 and three quarters under mainmast, 3 and a quarter under stern from which it gradually deepened. We hefted our cables out of the bow ports. The Flag towed with one cable but the securings

gave way. We then passed in both cables and…having all hands jumping on the FC we began to move which gladdened all our hearts and at last we came off. We then got in boats and began steaming for Malta.

By July Marx was out of the list, 'no ill effects from my balls', and was able to go ashore at last. Unfortunately, the freedom seems to have gone to his head – or another area! Anchored at Malta, he went ashore with fellow-midshipmen, George Wingfield and clerk H Harris. They walked out to Melia at Casilea. They 'had a liquor and then came back to Valetta and remained backing and filling between Borges and Maurice, went down to Florian to have a look round.' It seems that they saw the attractions of the place only too well and his companions, or possibly Marx alone, yielded to temptation. For the first time we see in his journal the diagram that apparently indicated sexual activity: a cross in a field of dots. We can only surmise what it meant, since a similar form of asterisk is used in this connection on other occasions relating to sex.

But it seems that in other ways too Marx was throwing caution to the winds. Perhaps he felt in some way that he might as well be hung for a sheep as a lamb! He took a sailing boat out, was nearly capsized, and got into a row for leaving his watch unattended. He declared he was 'always getting into rows with the Commander. He is down on me at present.' His leave was stopped and he was frustrated that he could not go up Mount Etna with the other fellows. He recovered his spirits when at Corfu he was allowed ashore and had 'a jolly ride, went the rounds, but saw and did not touch, heard of a french lady maid but it turned out a sell'. He also 'dined aboard HMS *Defence* which was well worth seeing as she is in such beautiful order but yet they say he [the Captain] spends nothing but his allowance.' This was a time when many captains spent a great deal of their own money in improving the appearance of their ships.

No sooner had the likeable Captain Stanhope arrived than he was taken to hospital with smallpox. There was sorrow all round when he died in July. He had been 'so much liked and missed in such a short time.' His brief captaincy had a great effect on Marx. His obituary, a letter to the *Army and Navy Gazette* is the only surviving naval obituary found among Marx's papers,

> Pray do not let such a man as Chandos Stanhope pass away without something more than a formal notice of his lamented and untimely death. He was the beau ideal of a British naval officer, the noblest and gentlest of gentlemen, the bravest and smartest of seamen, the best beloved of officers. In him were united energy with modesty, zeal with discretion, intrepidity with coolness, the most joyous cheeriness with the most perfect self respect, Happy those who, having served under his command, make his bright example their guide through life.— I am, &c., ONE WHO KNEW HIM WELL.

Perhaps Marx decided that was the sort of captain he would like to be. He would take Stanhope for his role model. Commander Charles Pringle was promoted to Acting Captain.

Now that Marx was feeling better, he started looking ahead to career prospects and aware that he had no important connexions in the service, he now decided that he needed to do more on the social front. He needed to cultivate some 'interest', some relationships that would advance him in the service. The Salmons at Gibraltar were the first recipients of his new resolve. Captain Nowell Salmon had invited him to visit and Marx found him and his wife 'very jolly…I intend cultivating them'. Indeed as time went by, he did make good relations with the Salmons, particularly Mrs Salmon whom he greatly admired. He also hoped to make some headway with the influential Captain William Codrington when he came on board. He gained an interview with him in Pringle's cabin. Codrington, who knew of the young midshipman's misfortunes, greeted him cheerfully and told him that it served him right. It confirmed Marx's opinion that the Captain seemed a good sort of individual and that he would like to sail with him. He tried to give a good impression, but later Salmon interrupted and started talking and Marx, already diffident, feared he did not appear to advantage. However, Codrington ended up by saying that if ever he could be of any use, he would be only too happy to oblige. Marx met Codrington on further odd occasions and could not have given too bad an impression since his next ship was indeed captained by Codrington.

The Flying Squadron was in at Gibraltar and Marx was delighted to have the opportunity of seeing Creswell and other old friends. They 'went ranging but luckily found nothing'. Then he had to turn his attention to work. On 10 August there were evolutions all day. The sight of so many ships in harbour at once was impressive. Marx grew more enthusiastic; the Channel and reserve fleet had come together, twenty-four vessels in all. He noted with satisfaction that *Caledonia*'s drill was much better, and that the Flying Squadron did very badly. He was also delighted to hear that *Caledonia* was to go to Queenstown. It would be a welcome opportunity for some relaxation after the effort of all the evolutionary drills.

It was at Queenstown that Marx had the good fortune to meet brother George. George was now a captain. Together they visited the family of the Army captain who had sold out, thus enabling George to buy his promotion. George looked well after his attack of fever and they went out walking together. Marx took to smoking a pipe for the first time with 'birds eye' tobacco and found 'I could stand it'. They went sightseeing together and played croquet, which tried Marx's temper 'as the balls would not go where they should'. He was glad for the chance to tell his brother of his problems and sort things out. Afterwards he declared, 'I find I am the fool of the family after all in what has to do with civilised society though I once thought differently... .' When it was time to part company, Marx was 'very sorry to go. George was most hospitable and kind and I hardly liked accepting what I did from him. But I may not see him for years as our paths are so different but by Gad if I can do him a good turn, I shall remember he is not only my brother but as good a fellow as ever stepped.'

George's good advice was, alas, quickly forgotten. No sooner had Marx said goodbye to his brother than he met the assistant surgeon, Alfred Delmege, and fellow-middy, Ewen Domvile, going back to the ship, but, he reported later, 'did not go off like a sensible fellow but stayed ashore and am in for it again'. Then came the anguished resolutions, 'I have made up my mind to try no more dodges but give it up for good with God's help.'

In August he received another certificate, this time from Acting Captain Charles Pringle,[4] 'attention and sobriety'. He was disappointed and noted, 'The certs I have got in my time have not been up to much except from Bythesea... .' Perhaps Marx should not have been too worried by Pringle's minimal certificate. It would seem from a study of midshipmen's certificates that unless the midshipman was outstanding, little was said but much was taken for granted. Sobriety was always attested to and generally the accolade of 'satisfactory' was considered enough.

On Saturday 22 August 1871, Edward Lambert and Henry Stephenson joined the *Caledonia*, as Captain and Commander, respectively, and a new lieutenant, James Gambier, joined whom Marx thought 'a nice sort of man'. Captain Bythesea arrived on board to hold an inquiry on the Chief Engineer Steil for loss of coals. Marx could not resist noting that he was 'hauled over the coals'. Bythesea took the opportunity of solicitously advising the young midshipman to become a life member of the United Services Institution, which Marx thought he would work on. Again, he was puzzled to learn what a poor reputation Bythesea had in most people's eyes. His father had said that he had never heard any good of the man and Captain Salmon agreed, saying he was intensely selfish, 'which I think he was though he was certainly very good to me. I ought not to join in the hue and cry against him.' When the new Captain and Commander came aboard, Marx thought Lambert was 'like an old dog at the last gasp. Stevenson [sic]is strict and I do not know what to make of him.'

The *Caledonia* sailed on for Lisbon and the work of the ship continued with all its various hazards. There were a great many gun salutes to be made as they sailed up the Tagus because Prince Humbert of Italy and the King of Portugal were constantly coming off to see the ships. This caused a tragic incident when a gunner, while firing a royal salute, had both his arms blown off from the back-firing of the gun and explosion of a cartridge, 'a more awful sight it was never my lot to see, one of his arms passed close to me...he was getting on pretty well when we left,' which was more than could be said for 'poor Smith, a 2cnd class painter who got his head knocked in by the hook of the Fly Mast rope block carrying away. He will not recover.' In another tragic incident, a boy, Arthur Martin, was thrown over the wheel and broke both his legs. 'I had seen him a few minutes before and sent him for my rug... . He was then standing and leaning against the middle wheel of the three, the starboard, where 5 minutes afterwards he met his fate. We were not rolling or pitching at all heavily only they stopped the engines and Walters cautioned them to stick to the helm, at which the other men let go...we buried him next day.' Marx also noted that a man named Pinnock fell from aloft, and died from internal injuries. He made no further comment. Young officers could not allow themselves to dwell on the mortality of their profession and these things happened. They had learned that in the Flying Squadron. They did not let it interfere with the optimism of youth, 'some of us were skylarking on the poop when Corby (a Lieutenant) sung out, "Officers, officers, don't you know better..."'

Marx was mate of the forecastle in Lieutenant Henry Walters's watch and was pleased to find himself getting on well with him. It was not always the case. Marx was easily convinced that people didn't like him and then the feeling tended to be mutual. This was a happier time. He enjoyed the sailing in the Mediterranean and the chance of foreign exploration. He wrote extensively in his diary of a trip to Cintra, describing its architecture and attractions. This is a notable feature of Marx's developing mind. His letters and diaries almost invariably hold only brief records of his activities but when it comes to any sightseeing or excursion, he often writes long, enthusiastic, detailed and careful descriptions of geography, archaeology and architecture in his private diary. The world and its people interested him: a characteristic inherited from his travelling father, no doubt. There was little imperial arrogance in the young Marx.

In October the ship returned to Gibraltar, where he met Creswell again, who came on board and said he had been 'unfortunate in his love matters', as were his fellow-midshipmen, George Bosanquet, [5] Arthur Babington and the Assistant Paymaster, Charles Dunbar. They had all caught 'the clap from the same house at Cadiz'. Marx was not alone in his experience. The Commander was not impressed with his middys. 'He said that we were a d-d useless lot but he could not catch us as we did what we were told and nothing else.' Marx seemed to be in hot water a good deal of the time. He recorded one of his interviews with Stephenson:

> Adamson [Henry Adamson, fellow-midshipman] caused me to get reported by young Blunn [James Blunn, instructor] and I was in a funk of losing time or having a serious punishment, but when the Commander called me up the dialogue was as follows,
>   Commdr. You are reported to me by Mr. Blunn for giving him trouble. What the devil do you mean by it? Have you anything to say?
>   I (In a funk) Nothing Sir (looking down)
>   Commdr. I believe you don't care a damn, Sir, for being reported to the Captain. Stop your leave for a week.

Perhaps this defiance reflected not only the young midshipman flexing his muscles into adulthood, but a personality that did not naturally conform. This was true of many of the Old Navy officers who were not natural conformists and grew up in a relatively free atmosphere – not only within the Navy but within society itself. New Navy rigour and restrictive Victorian morality did not make itself felt until later. Marx began to think the grass might be greener elsewhere. When Bythesea came into Gibraltar on the *Lord Clyde*, he thought it would be better to get out of *Caledonia* and return to one of his old skipper's ships, perhaps 'he was not so bad after all'. Marx made several attempts to see him but to no avail.

    Letters continued to be sent to and from home. Family still retained an important hold on Marx's affections. His father was off to militia camp and he wished him well. He was concerned to learn that brother George was cut up about being sent to India. This was understandable when the mortality of soldiers sent to India was so high. Marx continued to write and send gifts to cousin Conny, 'I like that girl very much', though apparently the arrival of 'that blasted box of gloves' caused some family consternation. 'Conny has not written to me lately (the young huzzy).' Again, was this because she was a cousin and any close relationship would be considered inappropriate? Or was she already marked out for George? 'Poor, dear Edith Jervoise is very ill…I pray God she may recover as they are my only relations for whom I really care.'

As winter approached, the thought of the coming examinations for Sub Lieutenant became uppermost in Marx's mind. He was beginning to get 'in a funk' about passing them: 'only six months and three weeks more and then's the <u>day</u>…am trying to work which is devillish hard'. He was also anxious about the forthcoming Christmas celebrations. It was the custom at Christmas to carry officers around the lower deck, ostensibly to foster good will and the bonhomie of the season, but it could also be used as an excuse to get back at officers who were unpopular, without recrimination. The diffident Marx was glad to find that he 'was carried round the lower deck rather against my will but I think it showed I was not much hated as I got round without a missile being slung at me'. In fact he decided that after a jolly evening of 'penny readings', it had really been 'not such a bad Christmas' after all, plenty of 'cake and duff' though not so good as the last one at home.

The months went by and Marx became more and more apprehensive about the forthcoming final exams. During the past two years there had been exams every six months in arithmetic, algebra, Euclid and mechanics, navigation and trigonometry. Marx's marks had been generally adequate and his performance always 'approved', but it was difficult to keep up with the schoolwork when the emphasis was on the practical side of a shipboard life. Marx found the schoolroom sat ill with the excitement of an active sailor's life. And as we have seen, there were other attractions! The practical training at sea culminated, so long as the midshipman had reached the age of nineteen, with the dreaded 'viva voce' seamanship examination to be taken before a board of three captains. For this examination no numerical grading was given, but a class of certificate based on valuations and opinions of the aforesaid captains was given. Presiding captains had the midshipman's papers and logbooks before them, and were to,

> strictly inquire into the...professional knowledge in all the details of an Officer's and Seaman's duty...against each of which we have stated our opinions of his proficiency.[6]

The opinions given were valuations from 'fair' to 'very good'. At the end of the proceedings a final class of seamanship certificate was awarded, from one to three. This method of final examination made the decision appear very arbitrary and dependent on the good will or otherwise of the captains concerned. Personal animosity, favouritism, a bad digestion, could all come into play. It was the way in which the seamanship examination was conducted that exasperated midshipmen. After five years' training, 'The labour of years [was] sifted in a few hours.'[7]

By 1870, the whole educational and training system of the midshipman had proved problematic and it prompted Admiralty to set up a committee of inquiry. The combination of schoolboy, sailor and officer was difficult to manage for the instructing officers as well as the middys themselves. The Shadwell committee, set up in 1871, examined the system. It agreed that 'fair', 'good' and 'very good' were not adequate standards of measurement with which to give a final class of certificate that would be reflected in career promotion. It should be validated by numerical measurement. Witnesses to the committee had pointed out that some examining captains would not give a first class on principle. A new system should obviate such injustice.[8]

Marx realised the importance of this arbitrary examination to his career and viewed it with great trepidation. 'I am working pretty hard but with not much apparent effect. Please God I may take a first but I

70

am afraid it is unlikely though I will try my utmost.' He vowed not to work on Sunday. Marx liked to hedge his bets with God. He retained a Victorian respect for the Almighty and an uncertain, lingering belief in the power of the Deity to affect his life. However, the respect accorded divine authority was not reflected in his attitude to the authority of the naval powers set over him. 'The Captain is a blackguard and the Commander is mad', but he was even-handed enough to admit, 'I like him a little [the Commander] in spite of his eccentricities which are disagreeable as he stopped my leave the first fortnight we are in Malta.'

From March onwards Marx started working seriously. As usual he found it 'devillish hard'. If he was being virtuous in not working on Sundays, he was also being virtuous in other directions. Perhaps remaining virtuous was made easier by the number of balls and dances he was now going to in the company of the proper young ladies of Gibraltar. Always on the lookout for a jolly partner, sometimes he was successful, sometimes not. 'I felt damned bashful but that soon gave way luckily...and I danced a good many dances with different people... .' He liked the Miss Balderstones whose mother 'is as black as one's hat'. He seems to have been popular with the girls, who loved a dashing young midshipman, but less so with his elders. He did not always follow correct etiquette in the matter of introductions and was sensitive enough to know that he often 'made an ass of himself' in polite society, but then life in the Old Navy did not set out to educate young officers in matters of etiquette. That they learned for themselves – or failed to. On one occasion Marx and another midshipman, Middlemas, passed the Balderstone girls sitting in their garden. Middlemas, thinking the girls were 'not quite proper' nodded and winked at them and made what Marx thought were disgusting Masonic signs. The girls looked shocked and Middlemas realised he had made a mistake. He apologised, but too late. When Marx next saw one of the girls she shunned him. He wrote, 'All our fellows have fallen in love here with different girls but they are not nice as a rule.' A touch of jealousy? Did he feel disadvantaged in the presence of nice girls? However, on the whole he thought that his social life was going well. There were theatricals on board ship and he did some acting. He enjoyed it and was surprised to find that he did not feel nervous. In fact, he felt a growing confidence: 'I have been pulling and paddling my own canoe with great success lately. I must retrench if I can as I am shifting into debt.' Letters again from Conny at home no doubt helped to sober him up. Also in addition to Father's quarterly allowance, a £2 tip from Mother 'came in very handy indeed'. But there was a cryptic note on the evening of 16 December: '...lost my M-h- [manhood?] of a months standing, damn it, but then having done it once I can do it again,' and on 27 January the asterisk appears again as Marx 'went on shore out of the way had one * Caravan Bridge'. It was hard to wait for one of the 'nice' girls.

There was another spin-off from the more dissipated side of Marx's life. A number of 'disreputable' persons would keep claiming acquaintance with him at the local 'hops' despite being told to go to hell. He took desperate measures. He decided to avoid dances for the time being and shave off his beard. He was shocked when he saw himself in the mirror, and could not believe the 'miserable object' he presented. Thankfully, the ship was about to sail to for Malta and Smyrna, which was 'a blessing as I made an ass of myself by shaving and not going in for society'.

When the *Caledonia* returned to Malta, Marx had the good fortune to meet George again. George was on the *Euphrates* going out to India. Mother had hoped that the two brothers would have a chance to meet and indeed they did. They went out walking and visited the opera, one of Marx's favourite diversions. It even seems likely that they visited a brothel together. Perhaps George had changed. There is a correspondence between him and his parents which indicates that he too might now have fallen to temptation. His mother said that they had received 'a stunning letter from George' which his father 'appeared to take more lightly' than she did. George had escaped an outbreak of scarlet fever on board *Euphrates*, and knowing the mortality that postings to India implied, perhaps he was making the most of the uncertain time ahead. He relayed to Marx all the family news from home. There was news of the death of a friend, a financial inheritance of

£100 a year in trust for Marx, and young Haywood was to be married to 'a devillish nice girl'. He told all about the animals and servants at home. Not all Victorian life was prudery. George said that 'The mother says that Effie sees too much of her lover and that they will be like children who lick the honey pot... . Moreby has been making a balls of it being found on top of his neighbour's wife... .' They were both evicted and he went to Australia. But there was disturbing news about Mother. She had been unwell and Dr Butler had diagnosed a congested heart valve.

Meanwhile the life of the sea continued with its hazards and accidents. The grounding of sailing ships at the mercy of tides of wind and weather was a fairly common occurrence. On 15 March 1872 the *Lord Clyde* got on shore and the *Lord Warden* and the *Enchantress* had to go to her aid. They got her off after a good tugging match. She was aground from her fore to her mizzen chains and very much damaged. There were other problems. There was always the danger of being lost in fog. Also in March there was the tragic accident in *Ariadne*, when a man fell overboard and boats going to his aid were capsized. Sub Lieutenants Jukes and Talbot were drowned in the rescue attempt and sixteen men died. It may have meant promotion to rescue a man in the sea but it often meant dicing with death to do so. Such promotions were well deserved. Marx himself had dangerously capsized when he went out for a sail with Midshipman Crawford Conybeare.[9] The boat had sunk and in trying to haul it up they pulled up the telegraph cable. Mother was disturbed to hear of this 'narrow escape from death'.

Marx's examination was now fast approaching. Other midshipmen were already being tested. 'Bosanquet and Noel passed. Bosanquet got 3 2s, not bad. I hope I may be lucky. Please God I shall as I must try hard.' Later, Adamson passed with three twos, which surprised Marx and seemed rather unfair since he did not work, some said it was a fluke. 'God grant I may pass as well or by Jove how the heathen will (rage) (chaff).... . I am working pretty hard but with not much apparent effect. Please God I may take a first but I am afraid it is unlikely though I will try my utmost.'

Not working on Sundays wasn't Marx's only virtue:

> I am in 1st cutter as Conybeare has gone sick with c-p buboes and other disagreeables. Babington, Duncombe, Dunbar, Sherrard have been let in at Strada Versevo. Poor Batten has also got an awfully bad dose from the same place. I have been pretty virtuous for some time past and intend to remain so until after my examination.[10]

At length the great day came, or rather two days. On 14 and 15 April 1872, Midshipman John Marx went before the three examining captains, Pickard of *Aurora*, Crown of *Helicon*, and his own captain, Captain Lambert, to be examined in navigation, gunnery and seamanship. The latter was considered the *sine qua non* by most Old Navy officers. Marx got a second class in the first two but was disappointed to get only a third in seamanship. He had been so nervous under Lambert that on reflection he felt lucky even to get a third class:

> ...passed of the 18th in seamanship before Crown, Pickard and Lambert, the latter tried hard to pluck me and by so doing made me very nervous and I got a third and very lucky to get that with such an old beast.

Since Marx was one of Lambert's own midshipmen, did he lean over backwards not to show any favouritism before the other two captains? Had he taken a dislike to the sometimes difficult midshipman? Or did he simply think Marx not good enough? There is every evidence of Marx's nervousness in such a situation, but he certainly blamed Lambert to his mother:

> Johnny has passed his exam and is a sub lt. He seems to have a brute of a Captain who did all he could to make him miss stays. He took 2 2s and 1 3 and thinks he should have done better.

But at least he had passed. The highest dropout rate of midshipmen for the Navy was at this time probably about ten per cent.[11] But with two twos and one three, relieved that the exams were over and looking forward to his return to England, Marx's journal ceased temporarily at this point. He was still worried about George, who had now contracted fever, and he was sorry to hear that Captain Bythesea had been dismissed from his ship and 'severely reprimanded'. (Bythesea, then serving on *Lord Warden*, had gone to the aid of a stranded British steamer and in the rescue attempt had severely damaged his own ship. Despite his VC he was never employed again.) At the last moment Marx tried to change into the *Agincourt*, but he was pleased that it didn't work out since the Admiral decided to send all acting subs, of which he was now one, home to England.

Marx sailed for Plymouth, thankful that the frustrating days of being a senior midshipman were now over. There had been pleasures of friendship and travel in the last three years but there had also been uneasy days of anxiety and worry as he tried to come to terms with the Navy and his own personality. There would still be problems but he had met certain challenges and overcome some difficulties. He would do so again. He was proud to be going home as an acting sub lieutenant and now felt ready to become a successful lieutenant on one of Her Majesty's more exciting ships.

However, he would have been only too aware that getting a berth as a lieutenant was not going to be easy. It was hard to get ahead in the 'seventies, promotion was slow in a stagnant Navy and he still had more exams to do first.

---

1 I am indebted to Dr John Ashton FRCS and Mr Walford Gillison FRCS for medical information.

2 As related by a sailor from Gosport to Reverend Robert Craven of Southampton. *Anti-Vaccinator*, 2 December 1871.

3 Captain Thomas Brandreth of *Warden*, Rear Admiral and Controller of the Navy in 1881.

4 Captain Charles Pringle succumbed to 'coast fever' at the siege of Dahomey and died in 1877.

5 George Stanley Bosanquet, retired as an active Vice Admiral, 1892.

6 John Marx's Passing Certificate for Seamanship for the rank of Lieutenant.

7 Chambers, *Salt Junk*, p119.

8 Shadwell, 'Report on Higher Education of Naval Officers', p846.

9 Captain Crawford Conybeare was wounded and mentioned in despatches as a lieutenant in the action in Tamai in 1884.

10 Midshipmen Arthur Babington and Ernest Duncombe.

11 Jones, ibid, ch7.

Five

Sub Lieutenant to Lieutenant (1872–1875)

'I would as lief jump overboard...'

Marx did not resume his journal until the May of 1874. When he did so, he started by summarising the missing years:

> After a lapse of more than two years I intend to commence again as I find a journal is useful as it gives one ideas on subjects at different times and I find they change very much. For the last two years I have been in England having a jolly time on the whole but still there were some very dark spots, for instance Dorey's eye. My nearly being seduced by J.L. which would have been a great failure in hospitality and an abuse of one's opportunities, then of the Great loss on November the 15th. My time in the Brig [Martin][1] was pleasant considering everything but I hardly think I should like to sail with Gordon again. My habits have not improved and I must put a check on some of them at once or they will play the mischief later on. The Derby and Oxford and Cambridge boat race are two remarkable events in the time besides many others and I now deeply regret not having a journal of all my doings but intend to try and remedy it in future. I left the Brig in December having

joined her at the end of July... . I caught a most awfully bad clap in April while at Greenwich which lasted me some weeks and in future have intended not to get it any more. While at Plymouth I fled from flower to flower but was lucky on the whole. Mrs. Best a general purveyor of those sorts of goods who always had them to order and resided in Raleigh Street. Many the times I have been on the spree with young Mundy down there. He now poor fellow has gone to his last account and may he be able to answer all the questions favourably. He was a regular good honest and pleasant fellow and this is not one of those lying epitaphs which one so often sees. His bones are rotting on the sand to Coomassie where he died doing his duty from the effect of a shot in the head by some rascally Ashante and if we have another row with them I will go out if it is only to have the pleasure of avenging him. To us he always was a sort of brother and now he is deeply regretted by us all. George came back from India in the middle of January looking well but hating his profession which is the worse thing a man can do. There are few people I know worthy of being remembered but Miss R Shepherd, I forget her real name, is one. She had many good qualities and the thing which always surprised me was that she was what she was and after all I think it must have been by misfortune and a defective education... . Flory Conquer is married which puts an end to the day dreams of a good many young men... . The hunting was good and I enjoyed it very much... . When I got my appointment to the Warden I was on leave with two days more to run...had to hurry off to Portsmouth and get my kit together before we started. We left for Lisbon...and then on to Gib where I saw Creswell who had not recovered from his wound but seemed to be getting better.[2] We arrived at Malta on Feb. 11th and now I must bear a hand to get up to the present time...

It is interesting to see what Marx thought worth noting in his précis of the past. He was unwilling to dwell on the unpleasant memories.

In June of 1872, he had started at HMS *Excellent*, doing the gunnery training that he needed to qualify him as a lieutenant. By 1868, in the Old Navy, there were three examinations to be taken for qualification as Lieutenant: seamanship at sea, gunnery at *Excellent* and navigation at the Royal Naval College. By 1875, with the elimination of the navigating cadet, every executive officer had to show skill in that area and pass an examination in pilotage at Portsmouth.[3] By 1876 all sub lieutenants had to take the torpedo examination held at Vernon. All these examinations resulted in the award of first, second or third class certificates, important to the career prospects of young officers. Marx was fortunate in that he only had to take the first three to qualify as a lieutenant since these exams came at a very difficult period in his life, as we shall see.

It is unlikely that Marx enjoyed the gunnery training at *Excellent*. *Excellent* was the shore-based facility at Portsmouth, established under Captain Sir Thomas Hastings in 1834 to improve the gunnery of the Navy. It did little in this respect[4] but provided a great training in what was essentially the drill and military precision of soldiers. Drill was of the essence; military appearance and discipline everything. Admiral James had called it 'a place for playing soldiers'.[5] It appealed to some but it was probably anathema to the freedom-loving Marx who hated arbitrary restraint. The stringent conditions possibly exacerbated his subsequent illness.

When he had gone home at the beginning of June, taking his friend Creswell with him, Marx's mother thought he looked very unwell and said he had not recovered from his Malta fever. Marx had remarked on an attack of fever just before he left Malta for England but whether it was that, or malaria, or some sort of rheumatic fever or other infection, we do not know. Certainly Malta fever, or human brucellosis,[6] was prevalent on the island due to infected milk but whatever Marx's illness, at the end of June his mother received a 'painful letter from dear J who is ordered into hospital'. He was sent to Haslar, the Naval hospital at Portsmouth, for six weeks. With maternal devotion, his mother visited almost every day and sat with him as often as possible. She was distressed by his condition. 'Johnny unable to move in his bed and suffering terribly from rheumatism. He is so patient and good.' His legs were swollen and he was breathless – symptoms of rheumatic fever indeed, but rheumatic fever usually results in a damaged heart and ensuing problems; Marx apparently suffered from none of these and eventually, in July, after six long weeks, '...dear crippled Johnny came home at last! Thank God! Thank God!' But life at home continued to be difficult for him:

> We have brought Johnny's bed down into the painting room
> to save him the agony of getting up stairs.... . Johnny is still
> on his crutches...

It was a wretched year for Marx. He had to return after this weakening illness to *Excellent* to finish the rigorous training of the gunnery school and then in September he had to go home again, this time for the illness of his mother. He was with her when she died in November from 'a congested heart valve'. That was 'the great loss' referred to by Marx in his resumed journal. Interestingly, it is the only mention he makes of it in all his writings. Does that indicate too much emotion to speak of it, the stiff upper lip, or too little to think it worth expressing? Was he by now too distanced from his parents, or simply acclimatised to a naval culture that stoically marginalised grief? We can only guess the psychological impact of such a significant loss, as his mother had been the chief support of his life. Perhaps her early death contributed to Marx's recurring depression over the next few years.

By February of 1873, however, he had recovered his health and strength sufficiently to return to *Excellent* and obtain a second-class passing certificate, having served 'with sobriety and satisfactorily', and thereafter life improved. It only remained for him to obtain the navigation certificate at the new Royal Naval College, Greenwich, and his qualifications for the post of Lieutenant would be complete.

The naval college at Greenwich was an entirely different matter from the gunnery school. Greenwich was in London. Greenwich was exciting. Marx was one of the first sub lieutenants to go to this new college. Until 1873, all the courses in navigation had been taken at the Royal Naval College, Portsmouth, but by then it had come in for increasing criticism. The Shadwell committee of inquiry set up in 1870 had pointed out that foreign naval cadets entered their respective services at a later date and with a better preliminary education in the way of 'book learning and mental learning' than their British counterparts. The committee thought that although the traditional early entry of British naval cadets consorted well with 'insuring a supply of young officers…their minds being docile and plastic…their habits and modes of thought yet unformed…',[7] there was a need to make up for the narrowness of early, naval, sea-based education with provision for subsequent broader adult education and professional improvement, hence the need for a new and improved college. Asked to comment on the current facilities at the Royal Naval College, Portsmouth, the committee reported that despite a yearly average of forty-four officers who had taken advantage of the courses, 'the College has not succeeded in imparting to the public service all the benefits such an institution should be capable of conferring'. They picked out several reasons for this, including the material defects of the buildings, '…the College is wanting…in the accommodation expected in the present day for educational purposes, such as suitable class and lecture rooms, studies, etc…', the fact that officers attending voluntarily on half-pay were often incapable of coping with the advanced work and had no proper system of examination, and that the educational staffing was inadequate and there were not enough incentives to encourage officers to study. Also, the situation was exacerbated by the fact that the college was often crowded with sub lieutenants, some of whom lived on *Excellent*, and who only had the short-term interest of taking their gunnery and navigation exams for Lieutenant at the college. Their Lordships thought this was not what the college was designed for – it was meant for 'adult scientific education'.[8] Instructors should not have to bother with conducting final examinations for sub lieutenants or candidates for commissions to the Royal Marines. However, despite the Shadwell committee's recommendation, the new college did continue to cater for lieutenants' qualifying examinations and sub lieutenants like Marx found themselves, after January of 1873, at the new, imposing Royal Naval College in Greenwich.

Portsmouth had been dull and rather isolated, but Greenwich was exciting. It was near London, with all its possibilities of entertainment, theatrical and otherwise. Since most naval officers were from the South East,[9] relatives and friends were often nearby and there was all the promise of fun and relaxation at the weekends. We have no letters from Marx but he might well have written as William Ainger did to his sister, in 1874,

> *I have not yet got settled down properly. My chest has arrived. My servant has not thought fit to get the things up but I have warned him to have them up by 4 pm today or else look out for my stick (our servants are boys)... . [Have you] any warm chintz knocking around. I want some to put round my bed and washhand stand. You may send me some tea and sugar...I shall have a select few to my kettledrums... . We have had our first lecture on Physics today it seems very interesting.*[10]

It was a chance for more independence and for those that wanted to, to kick over the traces. In 1872 Sub Lieutenant Seymour Fortescue described himself as being part of the 'wildest and laziest class who ever went through Greenwich'.[11] Marx demonstrated in his usual manner: 'I caught a most awfully bad clap in April while at Greenwich which lasted me some weeks and in future have intended not to get it any more.' Despite distractions however, he managed to obtain a second-class certificate in navigation from the Royal Naval College, on 19 May 1873, with 849 marks out of 1,000.

Marx's overall performance in the sub lieutenant's examinations was average, despite having done badly in the arbitrary business of the seamanship exam. In fact his performance in the navigation exam was above average and argues a good level of intellectual mathematical competence. We don't have statistics for Marx's *Britannia* intake but statistics for the 1868 *Britannia* intake were as follows:

	1	2	3
Seamanship	35%	34%	30%
Navigation	6%	26%	50%
Gunnery	15%	32%	31%[12]

These and similar figures reflecting the poor quality of sub lieutenants' performance generally, and especially in navigation (Marx's second in navigation was a small feather in his academic cap) caused Admiralty concern. It led to the Luard inquiry in 1885.[13] There was a strong feeling among officers that if they had done poorly in their seamanship exam they had no hope for future promotion. At the inquiry, Lieutenant H. Evan Thomas said that nothing could remove the stigma of a third-class pass in seamanship. Nothing achieved at Greenwich would replace it. Lieutenant Carus Wilson declared,

> I think that the present system of awarding promotion is decidedly discouraging to sub-lieutenants. I mean the scale of promotion according to the certificates that they get, because if a sublieutenant gets a third class in seamanship, which is acknowledged to be due to the simple chance as to the officers he has on his examination, he thinks it is not worth his while to work for a higher class, having already lost his chance of promotion.[14]

Marx probably shared this view and thought his promotional prospects were poor. He was concerned to find a good berth as a lieutenant but was more concerned that it should be one that would be enjoyable and convenient to him, rather than looking for quick advancement in the promotion stakes. It was certainly a realistic attitude. It was difficult for any sub lieutenant to get ahead in the 'seventies. First Lord Milne had 'deplored the state of the Lieutenant's and Commanders lists and the impossibility of promoting anybody'[15] and 'On the subject of sub lieutenants and midshipmen…their case is absolutely hopeless…. . There is now on the Active list 1,000 of these officers,'[16] said Sperling in 1871. Marx didn't have the academic expertise or the 'interest' to be an exception. The average time for a sub lieutenant to wait for promotion was four years, it could take up to six or more.

Marx remained on the books of *Excellent* until April of 1874, when he was appointed to the *Lord Warden*, the ironclad flagship of Admiral Sir Hastings Yelverton, sailing to Malta. The *Lord Warden*, now commanded by Captain Codrington, was a good appointment, so Marx had presumably done himself some good in that quarter. A sub lieutenant's life was a considerable advance on that of a midshipman, he had a cabin of his own and as Marx's compatriot Tupper said, 'The treatment of an acting sub lieutenant was very different from that of a midshipman in the gunroom of a man of war.'[17] Nevertheless, it was only a stepping stone to the coveted post of Lieutenant and Marx's main concern was to find himself a good berth as soon as possible. He knew he had not sufficiently endeared himself to Admiralty to look for early preferment, but Captain Codrington took an interest in his future and offered him a chance to be one of the two lieutenants on the seaman's training sloop, *Cruiser*. This did not appeal to Marx. It hardly promised excitement and he had reservations about the Captain, Captain Dale. He was always wary of those in authority, so he decided to stay in the *Warden* instead and was made Flag Mate. It involved a lot of time interpreting signals and less time ashore. Marx found it arduous. 'The work is very hard. I have been copying signals on board the *Narcissus*…difficult to keep up.'

However, there was always the time out of the ship. An early highlight in May was a four-day canoe trip out from Valetta, which Marx made with Barr, a fellow-sub, despite being advised against it. He loved the freedom and autonomy of independent sailing, he enjoyed the challenge of wind and weather. Afterwards he wrote a long, careful account in his journal. It is worth repeating since it shows Marx at his happiest during this period of his life, enjoying one of the best aspects of a young officer's experience in the Victorian Navy:

An account of our Canoe Cruise of April 3rd 1874

After spending the previous week in collecting provisions…and preparing for our expedition…it was the first cruise of the sort and we were young hands at it, besides the consolation of everyone we knew trying to persuade us to abandon the idea as they said we should never succeed. But having pledged ourselves to go, we could not back out. We started at about 6 pm and had a fair wind and made a good show going out of harbour. At the mouth we met Thurburn, Wilkinson and two or three more who wished us God speed and then left us. We were congratulating ourselves on the beauty of the weather and the nice fair wind, but this did not last long for hardly had we reached [?] when the wind shifted dead ahead and blew really hard, the sea rising at the same time. So we were reluctantly obliged to shorten and furl sails, making the best stow we could as the moon was shut in by clouds. B had a great advantage over me in the coming pull being able to unship his mast and stow it away. We pulled steadily on in silence, thinking of the test our paddling would be put to before we reached our goal. The clouds cleared away and the full moon shed a flood of light over the island and made it look really beautiful but we had little time to waste looking at the scenery as the wind continued to freshen and our speed proportionately decreased. At last…I looked at my chronometer…it was 11 pm and still no sign of the statue which forms such a capital landmark on the little island where we intended to camp. After pulling on for some time with tired arms and very much disheartened, we at last sighted what we supposed to be the statue and immediately put on a spurt, B taking me in tow as my mast held much wind and I could not make much progress against the wind which was blowing a good 6.

They had great difficulty in finding their landmark in the dark, but eventually they ran in under the lee of the rocks on which St Paul's statue stands and putting their canoes side-by-side on the shore, they spread their sails on top and waterproofs underneath:

> and old B and myself crept in heartily tired and in spite of the hard stones and an occasional flap from a wet sail or a gust of wind from some corner not quite airtight, we soon fell asleep and did not wake till about 6 am when the cold wind…made us wish we had brought more raps. We soon turned out and made some cocoa over a candle and had breakfast (hard boiled egg and sardines) and then set off for a cruise to the top of the island to see if we could get a wash and anything extra to eat… . [They couldn't, but they found a well. The question was, how to get the water?] Luckily we had a toothmug and a ball of string, so we managed to have a lick and a promise and then went back to our boats…

The weather was bad and it was a long, hard pull. Marx was almost tempted to give up due to the fact that he could not get his mast down. It would keep holding the wind. Eventually they got to 'Commino' where, exhausted, tired and very wet, they had the bliss of a night in a local hotel. They sat on top of charcoal stoves to dry themselves and ate a wonderful dinner: 'I never enjoyed anything so much as our beefsteak… .' Next day the weather played its usual trick of starting well and then getting nasty. Marx had a row with Barr about stopping for lunch. He said they must get on. He feared being out on the sea in the freshening wind with nowhere to run for cover. There was always the fear of capsizing miles from anywhere. So after much discussion, they paddled on,

> …opening headland after headland…the wind completely died away…so taking old B in tow gliding along at about 2 mls an hour with spinnaker set and the heavy swell giving us a slight set in our favour…at last about 7 pm we arrived off Marso Surroes and heartily glad were we to land.

They rigged a 'tolerably comfortable shanty' on a level ledge on the cliffs with masts and paddles. They lit half a dozen candles to warm and dry the place, lighted a lantern to boil some cocoa, then 'Todled about in search of wood and adventures'. They couldn't find any wood, only an old fort with defunct guns. They returned to their shanty and,

> ...commenced our frugal meal of a tin of sardines and biscuit and cocoa which we found boiling over when we came back and although the fare was not very luxurious I enjoyed it much better than many a dinner consisting of multitudinous dishes. In fact I am sure one never knows what true bodily enjoyment is till one has worked hard and takes one's rest.

Marx waxed lyrical:

> I shall never forget the scene, the Marso surroes revolving light one moment beautifully bright and the next minute nearly obscured on the opposite point. The moon rising over the sea, with two or three fishing boats in the offing clearly seen in the wake of the moon. The old ruined battery at the extremity of the point on which we were which altogether made a scene not easily forgotten and which made one think of the old times when the French and Knights were in power. But one gets tired of all things, even eating Sardines with our fingers, drinking brandy grog and looking at the moon...

They spent an uncomfortable night: the rocks were hard, the wind was cold, the dew was heavy and dripped through the sails; and 'last but not least our legs were hanging over a precipice'. Next day they explored the ruined fort and found a corporal and private of the Maltese Fencibles living in a nearby tower and doing duty as policemen. Early suspicion gave way to friendliness, the officers were invited in – the only entrance being by a ladder to a door twenty feet from the ground – to look around. They found the room the men lived in 'smelt very strong of garlic and other abominations' and were thankful to leave it. They went up to the lookout roof and down to a well in the old magazine at the foot of the tower, where, delightedly, they stripped,

> …much to the astonishment of our friends and had a most refreshing bathe in the cool water. Our toothbrushes also puzzled them considerably. After our ablutions were finished our old friend carried a bucket of water down to the canoes, and after replenishing our water bottles and rigging the boats, we launched once more intending to complete our journey that day…

The last day was not without incident. They narrowly escaped shipwreck passing between a small island and the mainland, and nearly grounded on the reefs a good mile from the shore:

> The wind was as much as we could manage to stagger under with whole sails. The McKiver's pinnace passed us full of ladies and they could not make us out, two such ruffians in fisherman's jerseys and Southwesters as we were. At last as we opened a point, we saw a fleet of small skiffs and canoes and they turned out to be a lot of our fellows come round to meet us it being Saturday. So shortly after we ran on shore in a pretty little bay and had lunch and bathed. We got back to Valletta about 5 pm after a very pleasant cruise and were looked at and wondered at for a day or two.

It made a change for Marx to be admired! He enjoyed it.

It was the first of the many trips of exploration and sightseeing that he would make and record during the course of his career. This was, for him, one of the best aspects of a naval life. It was not the technique of sailing, nor the administration of a ship, nor the status and prestige of a naval officer that was the primary appeal of a naval life to Marx; it was the chance to see the world, respond to its challenges and meet different people. In this he shared the aspirations and pleasures of many naval officers who were amateur explorers, botanists and scientists.[18] He resolved to have an extra bonnet put on his canoe mainsail.

The work on *Lord Warden* continued to be demanding. Marx was kept 'very hard at it all day'. There were evolutions with other ships of the squadron, signals to be dealt with, watches to be kept. Marx was no malingerer, when the doctor insisted he had a touch of fever, he was annoyed to be put in the lists, no trips ashore. But at the end of June, when the ship was off Turkey and he was recovered, there was another chance of exploration. He and Midshipman George Wemyss walked the area around Troy, taking digging tools with them in the hope of finding hidden treasure, but only a few insignificant amphora materialised. Marx showed his ingenuity and disregard for convention when careless of appearance he went about in the strong, hot sunshine with an umbrella lashed to his waist. The more conservative Wemyss (commonly called Speckled Billy) got sunstroke.

There was also a diversion when Admiral and Lady Drummond and their three daughters as well as two maids and a governess came on board. 'What a nuisance they will be I think the Mohammedans are the only people who know how to treat their women,' declared Marx, but as so often his feelings changed: 'The ladies on the poop seeming to enjoy the fresh air, I wish Codrington would introduce me... .' He thought having his ladies on board did a lot to improve the Admiral's temper, who previously had had a tendency to 'blow up like blazes on the quarter deck' much to Marx's disapproval.

And then came some real excitement. For the first time, Marx was able to show something of his mettle as an officer and demonstrate his initiative and energy. On 2 July a bad fire broke out in the local city square. *Invincible* made a signal asking for landing parties to be sent and Marx volunteered and was given charge of a party. When they arrived, the square was 'in a tremendous blaze and all was confusion'. Commander Hilary Andoe of *Invincible* ordered them to start pulling down houses but Marx reckoned they were too near the fire and should have made a clearance further out. As it was, the fire overtook them and they had to retreat. He was dismayed and saddened to see that the people were 'all burnt out'. For several hours he organised the bluejackets in the pulling down and blowing up of the houses to contain and extinguish the fire. He noted ruefully that it was the Greek and Jewish quarters of the city that were most affected, 'while the Turks whose quarter was not touched looked on rather pleased than otherwise'. He helped the people to remove their furniture and household goods, 'which were not numerous' but they could not stop the progress of the fire. He helped 'a very handsome Jewess who would not clear out of her house until very late when the flames had nearly surrounded her house and was in a most painful state of Hysterical sobbing... '. He tried to get a Turkish man to help him but 'he threw down a large vase full of water which I had given him to carry and I tried to lick him but he ran'. He thought the *Swiftsure*'s men were 'very disorderly' but as a general rule the men worked hard. They found that a street full of wine was close to the fire so Marx sent all hands to try and remove the liquor: 'while we were rolling casks of wine a poor old woman was knocked down. I picked her up and set her down on her pins.' At the end of 'some of the hardest work I have ever had', Marx was pleased to hear that only two natives had lost their lives and noted tolerantly that 'two or three bluejackets were drunk which was not to be wondered at as the houses were full of wine'.

The incident did Marx some good. His confidence rose. He generally got on well with his fellows but now he was beginning to feel appreciated by senior officers aboard the ship. 'The Admiral has been pretty civil lately and the Captain is a brick... .' The ship sailed on to Smyrna and Athens. There was more sightseeing at Ephesus and Athens, and Marx felt that these were good days. Alas, the good days did not last. Marx had an increasingly volatile personality and was prone to periods of depression and anxiety when he felt that things were not going so well or that people disapproved of him. Perhaps he was over-sensitive, perhaps he too easily felt sorry for himself, whatever it was, in the middle of July, after arriving at Corfu, he started to complain for the first time of Captain Codrington:

…more bullyragging…the Captain is really a bully. He may put it down to principle but I hardly think it proceeds so much from that as from an innate pleasure in feeling that he has the power of making other and not inferior animals to himself miserable. He bullies everyone. Coffin [probably a petty officer] tried to imitate him but I ran him in.

There was a row with the Captain over the signal log and suddenly Codrington was no longer 'a brick' but 'a bully, I intend not to write up the signal log any more'.

Was it this setback that sent the young sub lieutenant back to his old ways? One sees here the beginning of another decline in Marx's spirits and sailing around the Mediterranean he did what he always tended to do in these circumstances, he looked for the comforts of the brothel; this time in a more than usually free way and suffered the consequences: 'In an unlucky moment I threw away my covering on one occasion and caught a severe attack of clap.' He and friend Barr had tried to explore the prostitutes' area around Caravan Bridge in Smyrna without success. They had nearly been taken up by a Turkish policeman. In Corfu, it was easier and on 19 July Marx wrote, '…my evil inclinations took charge and there is a good selection of tolerable game. I do not intend Chronickling each day but My usual routine was going on the shore each evening and going astray…'

Sometimes the local sexual activities took even Marx by surprise:

The Captain and Flag lieutenant being both on shore and the Adl. being on board, I had to do the duty. Some people came off, very nicely dressed indeed and wanted to see the Adl. but he told me he was indisposed so I took pity on them and shewed them round the ship and gave them sherry and got chummy in return, for which they gave me their card and asked me to come and visit them so I made up my mind to try seduction, as they were very nice. So not being able to get anyone from the ship I semaphored to Den Rodgers and we started off to the Caffe where they were stopping, expecting to find a very nice turn out, for although they were actresses they looked as if they lived on the fat of the land. So, after calling at the Hotel George to get some refreshment to buck us up, we started to try and find the address. Much to our surprise one of the gentlemen who had come on board and wanted to see the Adl. came up and asked if we were the officers from the flag ship and when we said yes, Old Barr, whom we wanted to get rid of, would keep talking with him, so we to create a diversion started off at last. We found the place and were ushered in. We thought it did not look up to much but then we did not know how they might live, so we went upstairs and sat down. They were civil and told us to make ourselves at home and take off our coats. The room was large with some beds in it but as they had told us to come and take pot luck, blind as we were, we thought nothing. They had changed their rigs for cool, drifting, gowns so we made ourselves at home. While we were talking, using the half dozen words of Italian we knew and they replying with a couple of English words eking out the conversation Mademoiselle Maria was called away and we sat talking with the other. At last we heard familiar sounds in the next room of a bed creaking and we began to smell a rat, so after walking round, looking through the keyholes much to the annoyance of the inhabitants we found that Barr (was on very familiar terms with) Maria which accounted for the bed creaking. So it turned out that the ladies were prostitutes and a dollar was the tariff.[19] The gentlemanly man who came off acted the part of pimp. A curious coincident: the Adl had gone with two or three youngsters to an operatic entertainment. Nobody went but him. He became very friendly with the ladies and made one of the youngsters ask them off to the ship next day. Another coincidence, he had packed wife, children and female servant off to a picnic that day. I daresay I wrong the Old man but I cannot help thinking he intended to have a little fun with them himself but his heart failed at the last moment... . Curious, I found out that I was attacked with the malignant disease on the morning after or within six and a half hours.

Marx spent most of his free time in Malta in his canoe, avoiding others and enjoying his own company and the activity of sailing in 'a freshening breeze on a rising sea'. He rejoiced in the fact that the Admiral now lived on shore, 'perfect bliss getting rid of him and Romilly'. (Francis Romilly was the flag lieutenant.)[20] The Lord Warden continued her Mediterranean cruise and there were fleet evolutions. Marx, in his disgruntled state, exacerbated no doubt by feeling ill, complained about everything:

the Admiral clearly shows that he is an Old fool, on deck he blows me up like blazes and I do not like him... . The mess has been going to blazes. Mr Soper, Messman, is the slipperiest blackguard on earth... . Brown was bowld out drunk much to my disgust as I knew I should get a wigging...

In fact he didn't, and Marx, always willing to give credit where credit was due and change his mind where necessary, acknowledged that 'the Captain let him off and behaved like a gentleman and I hope I shall always get on with him as I like him much'. He found his latest attack of the clap was not so bad. He took capsules that somewhat alleviated it. For a brief while he felt more cheerful. The Admiral had his ladies on board again and was 'less fidgety'. Marx took to gambling instead of sex when he went ashore, but this led to debt and he gave it up. Debt became the new problem. There were other problems: Soper the messman whom Marx despised, after many rows with the wardroom officers, gave notice: 'We shall have to take charge of the mess which is a damnable nuisance... .' Relations with other senior officers soured, '...it is an utter waste of life being humbugged about by the present set of men. I like Codrington but hate the others very much.' As his spirits fell, inevitably he tried to return to the old solace:

No women of known respectability to be seen at this crib though I went all over the town. The difficulties of my position are still apparent but I see no way of relieving them. No promotion. Nothing to be done except remain in a miserable position…

It is hard to see the young, sick, self-deprecating and utterly miserable Sub Lieutenant as a future Admiral and popular hero at this point. It was a time of great frustration for him and deepening depression. He longed for 'action of some sort', and promotion to Lieutenant. He wanted to get out of the *Lord Warden* into another ship. He despised his inability to avoid the brothel. Codrington's certificate in November seemed to confirm his failure, '…with sobriety and has complied with all regulations…' – hardly a glowing report. By 22 August he had reached rock bottom. Lying awake in his cabin that night, he heard voices down below:

And I became the unwilling listener to Romilly's opinion of me. I had not strength of mind to send down but could not help listening and the consequence was I heard no good of myself and have hated the man heartily ever since. My position is most uncomfortable and gladly would I exchange for any other position and what makes it worse I have written complaining of my hard luck and how I hate this life which will do me no good and I am afraid will make the Father unhappy…often and often I puzzle my brain to see what on earth can be done but at present I am chained to the present life though often I would as lief jump overboard and strike out for the nearest land… . I am becoming utterly broken in spirit and more, I hate and fear my kind and have lost all the natural buoyancy which I ought to have, I am in fact very unhappy, as much as any one can be with good health and natural animal spirits, though they are crushed out nearly. I do not know if my character is peculiar but people thinking badly has always had a strong effect on my mind. I nearly bolted from Hinds on that account.

The next few days continued in the same vein:

23 August – More rows and horizon looking black.
24th – same.
25th – Determined to go at any price to get out of the ship. Very miserable indeed.
26th – Very miserable.

He tried to lift himself out of depression:

27th, 28th – After much consideration I have come to the conclusion…these melancholy fits are caused by feeling seedy combined with a succession of bad luck but the darkest cloud has a bright side.

He cheered up with news from home and determined 'to try and fight against bad luck and not become a coward…a man is a slave of his feelings'. He resolved to

…have a yarn with the Skipper and see how the land lies. He was alright and I am at present of opinion that he is in favour of my staying so I will, but I must admit his manner on deck is not always as gracious as it might be…. [Still it was a struggle to stay cheerful.] I find my work most disgusting. The Admiral is an old fool. I daresay a good man in his day but past his work and is particularly jealous of his authority while the Captain takes almost entire charge and the Admiral has to lean upon him but occasionally he takes it into his head to act on his own judgement which is usually wrong, and makes a mess of what he undertakes, which enrages the Captain. The Flag Lieutenant is jealous of the Captain and thinks he ought to have all to do with the concern and the Secretary thinks much the same, so between the lot there is anything but harmony....most of their follies and mistakes are visited on my luckless pate...

Depression deepened. Now he not only longed to quit the ship, he wanted to quit the service as well:

...the sooner I quit the billet the better and then again, these cursed accounts of mine are not settled and altogether I am in the tub and am almost of the opinion it would be better to quit the whole concern while yet there is time to turn my hand to something else. Getting sick and tired of the whole concern I went in the list after the Adl. dinner and to speak honestly, am in no hurry to come out again to be bullyragged at pleasure by three such b-grs as these people are.

But again, when he came out of the list and felt better, he decided he did not 'lead so much of a pig's life as I did previously' and things began to improve again. On 10 October 1874, Marx had a chance to demonstrate his courage and earn the sort of commendation that could result in early promotion. The *Lord Warden*, which had been edging along the African shore in an effort to keep out of a strong wind before slanting across towards Gibraltar, was just coming abreast the Rock, steaming against the wind, when,

...about half way across a cry of man overboard and I had a slight view of a blue frock floating aft, apparently the back of a man. Lobb [another bluejacket] jumped overboard all standing [e.g. fully clothed as he was]. The lifebuoy not going and the Kirbie (another lifebuoy) not being thrown well it occurred to me I ought to go. So taking off my frock coat and cap I went in a header after them. I am afraid I thought more of a medal than anything else but when once overboard I found I had my work cut out and gave way hard for Lobb and we succeeded in supporting him by the collar for some time. At last he made an effort and caught me by the brace which I not liking, set to clear away as quickly as possible but could not for some minutes, but at last succeeded in freeing his hand which I took in my own and held him at arm's length, Lobb doing the same as we were both much tired. The man opened his mouth and could not shut it about this time, although we told him constantly to do so.

The Kirbie lifebuoy was floating some distance to leeward and I proposed to Lobb to get it but he would not. I quitted my hold of the man for a minute but made an effort and regained it. At this time I could not help thinking as I swallowed buckets of salt water of care and comfort and comparative safety on the lifebuoy to leeward if we only left our charge, but we could not and held on spitting and splashing as well as we could. At last I turned around and saw the life boat coming and told Lobb we had to keep our backs to the ship as the seas broke over us. At last the cutter came and with so much weigh that the stroke oars man who caught hold of me nearly came overboard too and dragged me away from Lobb and the wretched man to whom they gave an oar. I thought they were sunk and rang out for someone to dive after them. After a bit they dragged the other two into the boat and then I would have given anything for the Instructions for restoring the drowned. The man frothed all round his mouth, a yellow nasty looking stuff. Lobb was sick and I felt very bad but could bring nothing up. When we came alongside Kellet brought the boat straight bows on which rather discomposed me. The man was taken up on a bowline and some stuff came from his stomach but he never spake or breathed his name, Fred Bryant, he was working on the port lower boom when the lead struck him and knocked him overboard. I felt all right and went on the poop again though rather shaky. After a brandy and soda with Piggot I went to bed at 9.30…at about 2 woke up seedy. Went forward and at 2.30 thought my last night had come, having cramp in the chest which nearly stopped my breath.

It took him two or three days before he recovered. Bryant, sadly, did not. Marx received a bronze medal from the Royal Humane Society in recognition of his valour in this brave and difficult rescue. He was not pleased: 'A bloody penny to wear on my breast… '. He determined to get a silver medal.

It seemed, after this, that things might really be improving when after falling through the ship to the lowest deck and becoming severely bruised, though incredibly without anything broken, he found the Captain evinced much more feeling than Marx had thought him capable of. 'I like him more and more,' he declared, and then enigmatically, 'I wonder if he divines the reason why I am never familiar or never speak to him… .' To add to his growing confidence, on 10 November Admiral Drummond at last gave Marx an acting lieutenant's vacancy aboard the recently commissioned Mediterranean battleship *Invincible*. The court martial of *Invincible*'s Lieutenant Arthur Baker had made the fortuitous vacancy. Marx was cautiously pleased:

I rather like the new ship, have got cabin and new messmates.

But he also found it quite the 'rummiest ship I have ever been in. Old Tomms[21] and Buckle,[22] the doctor, do not speak and fight on every occasion. Glasspole, Chief Engineer, and Hembridge,[23] are atheist…and try to ram it down our throats… . Commander Polly[24] is a good sort, a tea totaller but smokes a good deal and is a gentleman… . Old Turner[25] has a swollen testacle and secondaries and has gone to hospital. Williams[26] has a bad throat and will not speak and thinks he is dying…Barker[27] presents a drunken sort of person a very good fellow and gentleman when not in liquor which he generally is…'

The French Squadron were in. Times got better. There was dining and dancing, they gave and received entertainment, they 'talked French with amazing fluency after Dinner' and exchanged yarns. Marx told of the French lieutenant who when choking on a piece of bird at dinner, declared, 'Well, at least not everybody dies of syphilis!' Marx met Madame Powlowski, and her husband. They were Russian and she was a prima donna singer. Marx enjoyed her company and admired her greatly, though he did not think he 'would get much change' out of her. It was a pleasant enough time spoilt only by disquieting news from home:

> Why on earth must George go and get spoony on Constance. I was going to say God d-m him but won't. The only girl worth two damms in the world that I know of. Good God, one would think the world was large enough and that he might choose my ewe lamb, the only chance I shall ever have and do feel angry especially as he has made a confidante of me and therefore renders me powerless to act on my own behalf. His name has been coupled with half a dozen, that girl in Ireland, Kerry and more, but what a nuisance the man must come all the way from India to interfere with me. I shall remain neuter and see how the land lies. He has not a sous, nor has she. There may be a chance in the waiting game. I will try, but honestly swear that if I find she prefers him, to help him to even the same difficulties that lie in my path as in his; Cousinship, No money, no hopes or prospects.

Marx was still brooding resentfully about not getting a silver medal. He vowed he would

> ...get it yet or give up the ghost, [which] would not be a bad thing to do as it would enable two people to be happy and live comfortably, but I much doubt if they would be happy. He has a temper and she, though as sweet as an angel talks rough to the younger sisters and so, I suppose would to her husband after a time. It is not worth breaking one's heart but may be an

incentive to do something that others do not care about (nil desperandum) shall be my motto for the future. I wonder if they will give me my promotion though I do hope they may, but much fear there is no chance, too many men get medals and do braver actions than I can and do not get it. I have no interest to back it.

But perhaps the act of early heroism, in the attempted rescue of Bryant, and the leadership he showed in the fire in Turkey, did make up for the lack of interest because finally, on 3 January 1875, 'the Admiral came on board at 2 pm, my afternoon watch and called me to him and gave me my commission...'. Great was the rejoicing thereof: 'my joy was great...little did I expect it, had dim visions of waiting two years more, stood the required champagne and felt a great swell... '. Admiral Drummond had telegraphed Admiralty for the appointment of Marx as a lieutenant on *Invincible* but they would not, so Marx was to take his passage home in *Crocodile*, to have some leave in England before getting his first post as Lieutenant elsewhere. Perhaps Marx had more 'interest' than he thought. Admiral Drummond seems to have liked him and Admiral Phipps Hornby had always been 'interested' in the young man. But even so, it was a surprisingly early commission after only two years. Nevertheless, a commission was not an appointment. Marx now had to go home and wait for a ship.

It was typical of the new young lieutenant that before he left, he had one last adventure. When he found his gear had been put in the forehold of *Crocodile* ready to leave, and he wanted to go to a final ball at the Maltese Casino with his friend Pengelli to say goodbye to Madame Powlowski, finding that he had nothing to wear and no one else's gear would fit him, especially their boots, he took himself off to the club and asked the head waiter to rig him out. When the waiter said no, Marx offered him a sovereign to borrow his new suit:

I got into his things by holding my breath and buttoning one button of the waistcoat. The coat sleeves coming a little beyond my elbows, the trousers a little below my knees but again boots was the rock on which I split, none were large enough so I sallied forth with a club waiter in search of a shop and having at length knocked up the sleepy owner of one who at first was rather annoyed and wished to fight in which wish I promised to gratify him if he would sell me a pair of boots first. In all his shop he had but half a dozen pair. 5 to small and one pair much to big but I decided on them as more comfortable and at last fixed up all round at 11.30 pm, made my debut in the ballroom the centre of the admiring gaze of the Multitude. I immediately secured a dance or two with the Powlowski and having drunk bad sherry with the husband spent the remainder of a very pleasant evening in her society. In spite of having a very slight cast in her eye and one shoulder a little higher than the other as the women who are jealous of her say.... Though I could never see these blemishes she is by far the pleasantest woman I have ever met and the recollection of her will always be a green spot in my memory...

These last ingenious and forceful stratagems that Marx used to get himself fitted up to attend a ball he wanted to go to, showed a resourcefulness and determination when he had made up his mind to do something, a disregard of convention and propriety, an instinct for independent action, that presaged a successful career in the Old Navy. The worst had passed. Despite his lacklustre reports, the future looked good. But how long would it take to turn his lieutenant's commission into an actual posting?

---

1 HMS *Martin*, sailing brig borne on *St Vincent*. Commander Hand reported that Marx served 'very much to my satisfaction'.

2 Creswell was wounded fighting pirates in China in 1873. He was invalided home and later left the Royal Navy for the South Australian naval service

3 For discussion of this, see Vice Admiral B Schofield, *The Story of HMS Dryad*, Havant (Hampshire, 1977) and Lieutenant R Dickinson, *History of HM Navigation School 1729–1966*.

4 *Reminiscences*, p41. In 1878, '…there was not a lot to be learned by the gunnery specialist in that day as compared with all the scientific gadgets under his charge today…'

5 Admiral Sir William James, *The Sky Was Always Blue*, p26.

6 The actual bacterium for Malta fever, then called *Micrococcus militensis*, was not discovered by Sir David Bruce until 1887. It took another ten years for the association of that same organism to be related to spontaneous abortion in cattle.

7 Shadwell committee report, ibid, p844.

8 Idem, p847.

9 Jones, ibid, vol 1.

10 RNM PAL 136/81, William Ainger, to sister Caroline, 15 October 1874.

11 They assumed they had all failed and rioted mildly. They were all under arrest in the guardship for a month. Sir Seymour Fortescue, *Looking Back*, p73.

12 Jones, ibid, ch8.

13 1885 Committee to Inquire into and Report on the Education of Naval Executive Officers (the Luard Report).

14 'Evidence to Luard Committee', p395.

15 Admiral Sir E Bradford, *Admiral of the Fleet, Sir A K Wilson*, p40.

16 Sperling to the *Army and Navy Gazette*, 29 July 1871.

17 Tupper, *Reminiscences*, p39.

18 '…went over to the Admiral [Fairfax] and talked over my orders but he was much more interested in a wonderful croton [fern] he wanted me to get for him than in the French Commission or anything else… '. Clayton to his wife, 15 April 1888.

19 A sub lieutenant's pay was £66 per annum. A dollar was a crown, e.g. five shillings. It would appear to have been an expensive entertainment!

20 Lieutenant Francis Romilly was made Commander in April 1877 and subsequently lost his life at Majuba in the Boer War in 1881.

21 Staff Surgeon Francis Y Toms.

22 Surgeon, Fleetwood Buckle MD.

23 William Glasspole, Chief Engineer and Henry Stembridge (probably) Assistant Paymaster.

24 Commander Lewis B Solley.

25 Lieutenant Charles Turner.

26 Lieutenant Arthur Williams.

27 Chaplain, Reverend Frederick Barker.

Six

Second Lieutenant (1875–1880)

'...loafing about holds and orlops...'

John Marx took his passage home in *Crocodile* full of enthusiasm for his new life as a lieutenant, but on arrival at Arlebury he found that poor George had been burnt in a bedroom-fire accident while staying with friends. A coal had rolled out and caught some clothes alight, which then, unbeknown to him, had set fire to the bedding. George had put the flames out with his own hands. Concern for George took a little of the shine off the news of Marx's promotion. George recovered and Marx enjoyed a few days of leisure, visiting friends and hunting with his father before he set about putting his affairs in order. He went to London and found that his account with Coutts bank had been badly managed and he could not rely on any decent funds to help him. A lieutenant's pay was only about £200 a year, Marx certainly did not want to spend any time on half pay. His chief concern was to find a suitable posting as Lieutenant as soon as possible, so he went to Admiralty to plead his cause with Admiral Phipps Hornby. He particularly wanted the chance to go on the forthcoming Admiralty Arctic expedition. Not only did it offer the prospect of exciting action, it carried the chance of early promotion as well. (After the Arctic expedition in 1875, Lieutenant William May, who acquitted himself well, was promoted to Commander over the heads of 260 other lieutenants.) But Hornby said there was no chance of the Arctic for Marx. He had not yet distinguished himself sufficiently in Admiralty eyes. So Marx decided he might improve his career chances by returning for a further course of study and training at the new naval college at Greenwich. (The attractions of London life?) These courses were designed to promote the 'scientific' officer; the new officer required for the coming New Navy, an officer versed in the new technologies of steam and armament. They do not seem to have been popular at first. There was much prejudice against 'the scientific officer':

> No officer who is worth anything will go to Greenwich after his practical course unless he is obliged to do so. He is then longing to get to sea or on the staff of the gunnery school to let off all the knowledge he has gained. The only men who would wish to go to Greenwich would be the confirmed bookworms, who will never make practical officers, and those who want to marry and elope...[1]

Perhaps it was talking to Admiral Shadwell that had prompted Marx to take the new courses. He was staying at Arlebury at the time and Marx notes the fact that they took the sacrament together. Admiral Shadwell, as we have seen, was a significant figure in the Royal Navy, having led the Admiralty inquiry of 1870. Shadwell's chief concern was for the advanced training of lieutenants. Possibly he persuaded Marx that in advanced training lay the new lieutenant's best career opportunities. Perhaps it was the thought of London life again that attracted Marx. Maybe he simply decided, like some other officers, that it was a way to stay on the 'active list'. Whatever prompted him, Marx attended the Royal Naval College in Greenwich for the session 1874–75 and the session 1875–76, from April 1874 to June 1876. Here, he passed a satisfactory examination in marine surveying and meteorology, and gained an honorary certificate for proficiency in physics, chemistry, steam, marine surveying, meteorology, military surveying and drawing, combustion, practical shipbuilding, naval history, international law, structural arrangement of ships and military tactics.

The extra study at Greenwich seemed to pay off. In May of 1877 Marx received an appointment as Second Lieutenant to the battleship *Achilles* in the Channel squadron, under the redoubtable Captain Hewett VC.[2] *Achilles* was an impressive ship. When built, in 1863, she was the largest broadside-armed ship any navy had ever had. She was iron hulled and built along the lines of *Warrior*, the first iron ship, but she had greater armoured protection. In 1874 she had been rearmed with twelve nine-inch muzzle-loading rifles (MLRs) in battery and two seven-inch and two nine-inch MLRs on the upper deck. The only warship to have originally had four masts, giving her the largest sail area ever provided in a British warship, in 1877 she was reduced to a more manageable barque rig. Although difficult to handle because of her great length, she steamed and sailed well under most conditions. She carried a complement of 709 men.[3] It was a good appointment, such as any aspiring young lieutenant would have been pleased to have, and when a few months later *Achilles* moved with the Channel squadron to the Mediterranean, it was even better.

Marx's account of life in the Mediterranean prefigures that later time in the fleet, in the New Navy, when Captain Michael Culme Seymour, currently of *Temeraire*, would become Admiral Culme Seymour of *Ramillies* and operate the Mediterranean squadron with his handpicked 'band of brothers' – the Mediterranean clique.[4] It was a life of socialising with fellow-officers, visiting the homes of senior officers, calling on naval wives; dining, dancing, picnicking. A life, it seems, only punctuated by sea-borne activities. A life that some thought was simply a euphemism for 'a yachting holiday'.[5]

We return to Marx's journal in December of 1878. There may have been other journals which he kept and which have been lost. This journal is different from the earlier ones. Marx is older now and the pleasures and exigencies of naval life leave less time and inclination for long accounts of his activities. This journal is noticeable for the brevity and enigmatic quality of many of its entries. Perhaps Marx feared that his pages, each always marked at the top 'Private' might come to unwelcome attention. This journal was not used for the cathartic expression of emotion and reflection as earlier but rather simply recorded events and persons. Much of the handwriting is particularly bad and rushed. This argues a life of social activity where there was little time for reflection and psychological angst. Added to which, Marx was now a man of twenty-five and his adolescent anguish had passed. He had come up in the world. On 15 July, he had even fulfilled his avowed intent to obtain a silver medal from the Royal Humane Society. The citation read,

> That the noble courage and humanity displayed by Lieut. John L. Marx RN HMS *Achilles* in having on the 15th July, 1877 jumped overboard in a heavy sea, at 36.45 N Long 0.46 E 1 500 Fthms to the rescue of John L. Burke, Boy 1st class, who fell overboard, and whose life he with assistance, saved, calls forth the admiration of this General Court and justly entitles him to the Honorary Silver Medal of this Society.

This time, a lot more than 'a bloody penny' to wear on his chest !'

1877–80 marked the admirable Phipps Hornby's 'epic reign'[6] in the Mediterranean. The support of Admiral Phipps Hornby, the man who had applied for Marx's nomination to the Navy and brought him up through the Flying Squadron, meant that Marx now had some overt 'interest', both psychologically and in career terms. In *Achilles* Marx was accorded much family hospitality by the great man. In March of 1878, Captain Hewett became a rear admiral and was superseded in April by Captain Algernon Heneague.[7] Hewett gave Marx the best report he had had since his early days with Bythesea on *Phoebe:* 'With sobriety and in every way to my entire satisfaction. A most trustworthy officer of the watch. 17 May 1877–17 April 1878.' It had been a good relationship between the Captain and his young Lieutenant and Hewett remained supportive of Marx's interest in future years.

The new captain, 'Pompo Heneage', was renowned for his dandyism and affected speech: 'Gunnery Officer, vot larvely hair you haf. Vot do you put on it? Myself, I break two eggs ofer my hair efery morning... .' Dress was his obsession. Before he emerged on deck in the forenoon, his valet inspected the tall, thin figure from all sides to remove the tiniest speck of dust or fluff.[8] Marx makes no comment as to Pompo's eccentricities in his diaries, perhaps they were exaggerated. He seems to treat the Captain with respect and always refers to him simply as Heneage.

When we return to Marx's journal in December of 1878, *Achilles* was in the Gulf of Ismid. On 2 January 1879, he witnessed the shocking day of the *Thunderer*'s 'vast catastrophe...[when] the gun burst, the shot having slipped a distance of 8 feet four inches, killing Lieut. Cocker and Lieut. Daniel RMA (such a nice fellow).... 10 others died and 37 were wounded.' The actual cause of this tragedy was never proved beyond doubt but it seems probable that one of the *Thunderer*'s twelve-inch, thirty-eight ton Woolwich muzzle-loader guns had been double-loaded by mistake. On 3 January Marx attended the large funeral with the Admiral and all the captains. There was a firing party of 100 marines from the *Achilles*.

Throughout January and February of 1879, the fleet under Admiral Phipps Hornby was watching the progress of the Russo-Turkish War from Besika Bay, near the entrance to the Dardanelles. The British government feared a Russian occupation of the Dardanelles, but anxious to avoid trouble and vacillating, they ordered Hornby, in the flagship *Alexandra*, to take no part in hostilities but to keep the Dardanelles open. The Admiral was ordered 'in the event of tumult at Constantinople, [to] protect life and property of British subjects'. This put him in an invidious position. He transferred his flag to the *Sultan* and made preparations for action, but as inconspicuously as possible. Although poised to attack Russia if necessary, he sent a message to the Turkish commander at the mouth of the Dardanelles:

> If you fired at me, I should be bound to fire at you; and then we should be playing the Russian game, which would be very disagreeable...[9]

The Turks backed down and the crisis subsided. Marx recorded laconically, on 11 February, 'We were going to fire but the *Sultan* was nervous and refused, so we did not and went back to Ismid.' In fact, it was Hornby's tact and restraint that helped to keep the peace. The Russians promised to evacuate the area and events came to a peaceful, if anxious, conclusion. In August, the Admiral was rewarded with a Knight Commander of the Order of the Bath (KCB) for his diplomatic moderation during the crisis. 'For many months Europe had been on the verge of a general war. No individual perhaps did more to avert that catastrophe than the Vice Admiral.'[10]

The pleasurable activity of naval life in the Mediterranean returned: Marx went riding, shooting with officers from the other ships in harbour, seeing the sights of Constantinople and availing himself of its other amenities. On 8 February at Malta, he was dismayed to find he 'had a fearful suspicion that all was not right from Constantinople...'. The detailed accounts of his disease are interesting in that they cast light on the medical treatment, or lack of it, at the time. He recorded them, meticulously but briefly:

9th – Hard lump. Shewed Preston, no amaguidal [inguinal?] glands to speak of. He speaks favourably. Am in a stew, went for short ride.

19th – my lump no better.

21st – rather seedy, an opening had come in top of lump, very small with but little discharge. Went for a walk with Barcroft, determined to begin baths, slight discharge, small hole – determined to begin baths.

23 – had a slight swelling of the lower gland on the opposite side, the hole still open took baths.

24th – Drill. A good day. Swelling in right groin a little increased, no decrease in hardness of lump.

25th – lump biggish in right groin, went for a small ride with Barcroft who walked.

Wednesday – lump big, dressed it with blue mercury [poisonous, but would control infection].

Saturday – Went out where the beagles met...had a capital day.

Sunday – Sore, still bad, no glands

Monday, 17 March – called and went in at the Hornbys and passed a pleasant half hour, am convinced that I shall have the secondary business to get over.

A week's attack of ague and fever [presumably related to Marx's general debility].

Wednesday 30th, no further sign, gave up vapour baths on Sunday, after [lots? 66?] of them.

Recovered from his debilities, Marx returned to the life of a watch-keeping lieutenant on a large ship. There were evolutions and exercises to oversee and he had a particular responsibility for the instruction of seamen and boys. In his final certificate, Heneage congratulated him on this: '…this officer has undertaken the instruction of Seamen and Boys to my entire satisfaction'. There were the small interests and altercations of life at sea: when Captain Heneage came out of French Creek without the assistance of a tug and did it well, Admiral Luard did not approve and referred it to Admiral Hornby. Horny said Heneage might do as he liked. Marx enjoyed the diversion of a good day out with 'a whole lot of snotties'[11] in Athens. He was gratified when *Achilles* 'wapped *Research* and *Monarch*' at cricket. But even pleasure palled when boredom set in. He began to find life tedious, 'still doing 2cnd Lieut. duty and loafing round holds and orlops,' when he wanted something more exciting and demanding. However, not all the duties of a watch-keeping lieutenant were uneventful. On Sunday 15 May, Marx was in charge of a funeral party to bury the remains of William Regan, a stoker who had died. He described what happened:

Putting the corps in a carriage we moved to Vourlah, where the English Consul met us. He could not talk much English and told me everything was ready. So we moved on through the town until we came to a church where a procession of Greek priests met us. We moved on again and the road got so bad the carriage could not get on, so we carried it and at last, after a mile arrived at the burial ground which was densely crowded with people. Blake[12] had gone on ahead and I saw him at the gate, beckoning him to me, so I pushed my way to him and he told me that the grave was much too small. We got the party inside the gate formed round the grave and tried to enlarge it but in doing so opened up another one, which stunk like blazes and the concrete was as hard as possible. Then I went in search of another spot where I was told I might dig a grave and having selected a spot, we got men and commenced to dig. I posted the firing party with fixed swords as sentries and made my way back to Blake who was in great tribulation being nearly pushed into the grave with all the mourners. We got them inside the space...the people crushed in a good deal, but by dint of stamping on their bare feet they were kept back. After the first foot of grave had been dug, we came on skulls and the ground appeared freshly moved a little below. It was one festering mass of human remains the like I never wish to see again. The stench was overpowering.... . I reported the business to the Consul.

Then it was back to the social round. In July Marx went to Smyrna in Heneage's despatch ship, the *Helican*, 'with the Hornbys who went to put up at the Augusta... . Down[13] and his brother, Hext,[14] Heslop,[15] Blake formed our party, a lot from the Flagship and some from *Temeraire* [Captain M Culme Seymour's ship], *Raleigh* and *Monarch*'. There was sightseeing at Ephesus, shopping and gift buying in the bazaars, fun at the pulling races in the Regatta, although *Achilles'* officers won nothing and 'there was a lot of dissatisfaction from the way Lake started the races'. There was a diverting paper chase with the Hornbys and a delightful tea party at the Admiral's, although while dancing with Mary Hornby, he 'got more home truths put into me by Miss Mary Hornby than I had by any other person in so short a time'. Perhaps Mary Hornby felt she could speak freely since she was to marry Lieutenant Francis Egerton in November. There were also the inevitable reminders of mortality. '2cnd Lieut. Rowe killed himself by falling from the topyard...Captain Seymour fell overboard at the Admiral's races and had to be rescued…Hockin nearly drowned when he fell in and his monkey jacket stuck half off.' But there was rejoicing when news came through that Admiral Hornby's son, who had been reported dead, was all right.

Achilles was due to go to back to Besika in July, the Russian affair was still smouldering. Bluejackets from the squadron were distinguishing themselves in bar brawls with the local Russian sailors.[16] Marx expected action but,

> Last night a Turkish gunboat came with a telegram for the Admiral from the Ambassador at Constantinople, saying we were not to go as the Russians refused to continue their evacuation if we did.

Again, Hornby held back and peace prevailed.

There were more diversions: shooting, riding and sailing races continued with the other officers at Lemnos. Ship work took a back seat: 'Got a damn wigging from Heneage, the – he is – for the work not going on properly on the Forecastle.… .' Shooting trips and camping out with May, Down, Hext and any available friends took up all free time and was 'great sport…'. Was it this attention to life outside the ship that meant 'the Commander [William Molyneux] and I had a row, he threatening to suspend me from duty'. Marx was in trouble again on 30 September when *Achilles* was involved in a collision with *Alexandra*:

> …about 4.15 we collided with the Alexandra. Gregory had just relieved Hockin,[17] and the fleet in groups, the two signals alter course 4 pts to Port and reform groups were hoisted together. The first was hauled down and Gregory Starboarded and kept the helm over two long. We had been leading but the second signal always orders the proper lead to lead and the Alexandra steamed on and we fell off 8 instead of 4 pots and came close to the Flagship who starboarded to, but too late as we were

into her starboard side rather brushing along, and whipped the Admiral's galley and another boat to pieces. Her stern struck us first before the main mast and her starboard screw which was heaving round made a slit in a plate 14 in long by 4 broad at the broadest part. We closed watertight doors and the compartment of the double side quickly filled, no other damage was done beside smashing our pinnace's davit.

As a result Marx 'got two signals whipped into me for being on the Starboard quarter of Admiral. They are getting smart... .' But he was able to redeem himself to some extent, by showing his resourcefulness. He stopped the hole with a plate 'with two things like post bars' which greatly reduced the amount of water, and filled it up inside with wood and caulked it: 'it is now tight'.

The ship moved on to Cyprus but here Marx thought his old symptoms were returning, he had spots on hands, arms and feet. Again, he took to vapour baths and the trouble seemed to disappear. Now, for the first time it seems, the work on the ship really interested him. He was given responsibility – something he wanted to do. He had to take over from Gregory, the flagship's Lieutenant who was on a court martial as a result of the recent collision. Marx was now called upon to manage the ship's steam tactics. Phipps Hornby had initiated steam tactics in the Royal Navy and his fleet had to be expert in them. After the first exercise the Admiral signalled Marx that his movements were 'well executed and satisfactory'. According to Admiral George Ballard, a sub lieutenant in *Achilles* at the time, such a signal 'was enough to elate a ship for days'.[18] It improved Marx's standing on the ship in everyone's eyes. In November there were more steam trials and although *Alexander* was by far the best, *Achilles* and *Monarch* were equal. *Raleigh* 'could not steam a bit' and *Temeraire* broke down. 'The Admiral drills a good deal,' reported Marx.

After the drilling there was relaxation again in Malta in December. Marx as usual enjoyed the dining and dancing, the opera and the races, though at the races he declared, 'the Hornbys are b-dy rude'. We may wonder what he had done to prompt that? There was a succession of visits to the wives of the squadron, and an enigmatic account of a letter he had written to a Mrs Talbot which caused problems: 'It is of no use handing down the story of the letter and the mistake I made and how I suffered for it and in fact it aint finished…' but Mrs Talbot must have forgiven him because at the final dinner with her, 'everything went off satisfactory'. At the end of December, the squadron left Malta for Gibraltar:

All the ships cheered as we left. Molyneux tried repressive measures on the men but they broke the bonds and cheered lustily.

1880 started on 1 January with lots of good resolutions: 'By Malory's advice I left off baths having had them for over eleven weeks and Malory now vows I am cured "Thank God," may he prove correct.' It seems incredible to think that after writing this, on the very next day, 2 January, Marx was prepared to go back to the old risk. He records, 'I went over the rock with Gunn in the afternoon and <u>fell</u> in the evening,' and two days later on 4 January, '…my guard got away in the evening for an hour and again <u>tripped</u>'. Did temporary physical pleasure really outweigh the danger and discomfort when things went wrong? What about the all-pervading fear of syphilis at this time; evidenced in social life, in art and literature, in Marx's own diary? He saw his colleagues fall foul of the disease, and although it could only be caught from a syphilitic prostitute, did he know this and if he did, could he tell? One can only say, ''twas ever thus'! But whatever the present pleasure, he was as vulnerable as any Victorian moralist to the long-term promptings of a nagging conscience. He certainly did not approve of his own behaviour. How many of his naval colleagues experienced the same problems? Statistics relating to this are hard to find.

From Gibraltar *Achilles* went to Lisbon. It was time for her to return to the Atlantic fleet. Lisbon provided sightseeing, dining and opera again. There was the grand event of the King's ball though Marx thought the ball was 'not up to much no end of orders and medals but they must have got them for fighting with their wives'. At sea, all through February, 'there was no end of drill'. The Admiral was working his fleet up and Marx had to keep a regular four watches. He found the drills tedious and complained that there were drills 'even on Saturday night'. A sailor fell from the yards and was killed; competitive evolutions took their toll of life. Admiral Ballard thought that the perpetual competition added zest to life, but at a cost, a single commission generally took six or more deaths from evolutions.[19]

There were still all the little aggravations of life at sea: Hood made a mess of bringing the squadron in; Heneage was out and while he was away, the ship shifted her billet; the ship's dog Rover was stolen and later found; Lord Brassey's[20] yacht came out and they had to make sail in the dinner hour for his convenience; in March, Marx was witness to the inquiry about the loss of men and a pinnace. Personal worries also intervened. Gunn was in the list with secondary syphilis and this time Marx did feel nervous for himself. Then a particularly unfortunate incident occurred, while Marx was coming back from a shooting trip with May and Hubbard:

...we were just going home. We were standing on a road talking about which way we were to go, when a man we had with us I think touched the gun on my shoulder, or it slipped off my shoulder. I tried to save it but failed. The muzzle went into the ground some 2 in and then fell, exploding left barrel and breaking the lock. The shot went all over the place, some 25 into Hubbard's leg, some 10 into a miller's boy, most of them into his leg, in his neck and into his face. 3 or 4 went into a small boy. Some dust and stones struck Hubbard in the face injuring his eye. A little crowd soon collected. We extracted as many shot as we could, gave one boy £1 and walked in...

How much did Marx care? He took the trouble to record the incident carefully in his best handwriting, and said how glad he was that

Hubbard's eye was 'all right' but he expressed no sadness for the other unfortunate victims. This should probably not be construed as lack of sympathy but rather part of the unflinching gaze upon adversity for which naval officers were successfully trained. In the same entry Marx wrote, 'Jolley, A.B. fell from foreyard and was killed.' Old Navy officers were 'inured to hardship' for others as well as themselves.

Touching at Gibraltar on the way home, there was a chance of sightseeing in Spain. Marx went on a trip to Ronda and Gaucin with Commander Molyneux and Lieutenant Hammond. This was the exploration and travel he delighted in; the makeshift camps and local inns to stay in, the local inhabitants to meet. This was a final outing before the ship went to Berehaven for more steam trials and returned to the Channel squadron. But Marx had a volatile temperament and was always prone to fall out with his seniors, so it is not too surprising that by the time he returned to Ireland in May, there had been trouble with the Commander. 'My guard and I do not sail with Molyneux again if I knows it.' However, on leave in Plymouth, he was happily dining with Molyneux; a willingness to forgive and forget was also part of Marx's temperament.

On 11 June 1880, it was home to Arlebury and a spot of leave. All Marx's energies were now directed to improving his position, trying to find a good berth as First Lieutenant on a ship of his choice. Now Hewett said he would do what he could to assist Marx to a good posting. He tried to get him First Lieutenant on the gunboat *Miranda* but failed and Marx was disappointed. Captain FitzGeorge asked him to go as First Lieutenant on *Salamis*. Marx said he would think about it. He knew that Millett had not succeeded there, as Admiral Hood had found much fault with the ship. So he refused *Salamis*, but the old indecisive Marx doubted his decision, '…think I am an ass to do so'. The field of possible social influence increased. On 3 August, 'dined with the Duke of Edinburgh on board the Hercules, met Kemble Winslow (Spy…writes for Vanity Fair), the English Consul Townsend, Delmege Dr, the young princes' tutor Dalton and others.' On 25 August, he was asked to go to *Royal Adelaide* as a lieutenant but again refused. He called on Captain Grant to thank him. But the *Royal Adelaide* was the flag and depot ship at Devonport and not likely to go anywhere. He wanted something more exciting. Meanwhile, he was hard at work preparing *Achilles* to relinquish her present commission for a new one. There was always much to do at the end of a commission. Molyneux was 'pushing on everybody', something Marx always hated.

September came and another short visit home. Sister-in-law Con and niece Daisy were flourishing (though perhaps in relation to the 'cousinhood' Marx thought young Daisy 'a fine child but still there is a want which one feels'). Again there was a lively local, social life to be had, with a great deal of hunting. He hired 'a tubb' for a month. However, he was disappointed to learn that a newspaper report that he had been appointed to *Vernon* had proved false. He was also disappointed to find he was passing blood, but this time thought it must be due to bladder or kidney disease. He was given 'nasty stuff to drink for three months'. The doctor said there was no disease but he would probably never be entirely well. He continued his search for a good new posting. He found the Sclater-Booths 'most kind and cordial', but neither Sclater-Booth[21] with his political influence nor Admiral Lord John Hay,[22] nor Lord Northbrook,[23] nor Phipps Hornby could assist him with getting a First Lieutenancy when he went to see them at Admiralty, although he declared them all 'kind and civil'. At last an offer came his way that did please him. On 29 November 1880, Marx came home from hunting to find a telegram waiting from Captain Aldrich[24] inviting him to become First Lieutenant of *Fawn*. *Fawn* was a surveying vessel working on the East African coast. It was a promising and interesting assignment to a man of Marx's temperament. It was not on the face of it a great advance in his career, but it offered him the adventure and autonomy he longed for. No more humdrum watchkeeping on a battleship that never went into battle, now the chance of individual action and responsibility in the necessary and significant surveying work of the Old Navy.

Local congratulations were forthcoming and the neighbourhood socialising and hunting before taking up his appointment seemed more enjoyable than ever. His troublesome medical symptoms returned but this time the doctor declared it was disease of the 'prostrate' [sic] gland and it was curable. He left home in good spirits. Just before leaving, he made a cryptic remark in his diary: 'I gave Edith the ring and explained matters as well as I could.' There are several Ediths referred to in Marx's journal – it was a common name – and it is difficult to know who this Edith was, but it seems likely she was the 'dear Edith Jervoise' whom he had earlier referred to as being ill, a cousin on his mother's side. Why he gave her a ring is uncertain, or what were the matters he explained as well as he could – the difficulties of relationships conducted at three-year intervals? Was it the same ring that 'the festive aunt', Fanny Duberly, had given him earlier? We do not know but we shall hear more of Edith. Now Marx was happy simply to be leaving home and going to his new life as First Lieutenant on HMS *Fawn*.

---

1 Admiral of the Fleet, Lord Chatfield GCB, OM, *The Navy and Defence* (London, 1942).

2 Vice Admiral Sir W N Wrighte Hewett KCB, KCSI, VC. Hewett became a Rear Admiral the following year and a Vice Admiral in 1884. He gained his VC in 1874, leading a naval brigade in the Ashantee War.

3 Conways, *All the World's Fighting Ships* (1860–1905), ibid, p9.

4 Andrew Gordon, *Rules of the Game*, p300.

5 Comment in House of Commons debate.

6 Gordon, *Rules*, p186.

7 Admiral Sir Algernon Charles Fieschi Heneage.

8 See G L Lowis, *Fabulous Admirals* (London, 1927), p28.

9 W Clowes, *The Royal Navy* (1903), p294.

10 Clowes, idem, p299.

11 Junior midshipmen.

12 Reverend George Blake, Chaplain.

13 Lieutenant William Down.

14 Henry Hext, Marine Lieutenant.

15 Colpoys P Heaslop, Captain, Marine Artillery.

16 *Daily Telegraph*, 24 June 1879.

17 Lieutenants Joseph Gregory and Percy Hockin.

18 Admiral G Ballard, *The Black Battlefleet*, p46.

19 Ballard, *Battlefleet*, p46.

20 Lord Sir Thomas Brassey, KCB, wealthy MP and Permanent Secretary, 1884.

21 Mr Sclater-Booth, Conservative MP for Hampshire.

22 Admiral of the Fleet, Lord John Hay CB, KCB, GCB.

23 Thomas Baring, Earl of Northbrook, who was First Lord of the Admiralty in May of 1880 until July of 1885.

24 Pelham Aldrich had served in the Arctic, 1875–76, and been promoted to Captain, accordingly.

Seven

First Lieutenant (1880–1883)

'I am uncommonly sorry to part with them...'

On 28 December 1880, First Lieutenant Marx, now aged twenty-eight, arrived in Malta to take up his three-year commission on HMS *Fawn*. She was a screw sloop of 750 tons displacement, commissioned for surveying service in the Red Sea, with an executive of twelve officers. Since Marx was to spend three years with these officers it is useful to see who they were. The Navy list of January 1881 records the following:

Commander:	Pelham Aldrich
Lieutenant	John L Marx
	Thomas F Pullen
	(N) Edward C H Helby
	Francis W Keary
	Herbert E P Cust
	Edmond J W Slade
	Andrew C Williamson
Staff Surgeon	James L Sweetnam MD
Paymaster	John Hynes [Marx refers to him as Hynds or sometimes Hinds]
Ch Engineer	James Legate
Sub-Lieut	Gerald C A Marescaux

Marx was keen and enthusiastic. When he went to look at 'the craft' he found her 'cleared out but rigged and clean in his part of the ship'. He took a small working party on board and started the preparations for recommissioning the ship. It did not take long. On 31 January 1881, having been successfully commissioned, she set off for Suez.

There was a brief stop at Port Said where Marx availed himself of the local amenities in the usual way and then it was into the Canal. Marx admired the engineering feat of the Canal and found it 'a wonderful place', where he nearly caught 'a fine fellow of a tiger shark...'. The mail came in at Suez and there were letters from cousins Edith and Ethel. There was also a letter from George. Apparently the cousins were finding times hard financially and George and Con had determined to offer them £500 a year if they were hard up. It seems a generous offer from the newly marrieds. Marx heard later that the offer was refused.

Relations between Marx and Captain Aldrich seem to have been good from the outset. They had dined together and played tennis before leaving Plymouth, but the First Lieutenant suffered an early embarrassment when on 4 February there was 'a regular black squall one of the most remarkable I have ever seen and as we had been coaling and all the boats were anchored off I was caught with my trousers down...'

The first destination was Jeddah. The entrance to Jeddah was difficult, 'a wonderful place for reefs...and one is advised to enter with the afternoon sun as then they are more visible...' but they managed it safely, relying on the lookout in the foretop who could see them more clearly. The officers were pleased to find there was an opportunity for sport on a nearby island but when Marx and Lieutenant Hynes went out for a day's shooting, they met a party of 'Upper Nile blacks' who tried to get rid of the two lieutenants by saying they were suffering from smallpox, 'which I believe was a yarn and that they were slavers as the Dhow was close at hand'. They saw more dhows down the river. It put an end to their shooting expedition, but there was no attempt to investigate the slavers further though naval officers were generally assiduous in this task, and Marx was no exception as he showed later.

Naval officers could do nothing without evidence of slaving equipment in empty dhows and indisputable evidence linking individual traders to specific ships. Nor could they act unless the slaving ships were in international waters.

As First Lieutenant of a surveying ship Marx had plenty of opportunities for sport as well as work. There was always the chance of hunting ashore and he was particularly keen on bagging antelope and gazelle, as well as shooting the various birds and pigeons to augment their diet, a sporting necessity when ships ran out of their last live meat. There were also various social and sightseeing activities to set against the more mundane work of navigation: triangulation, sounding and surveying. But the weather was a constant problem. In the Red Sea it was always blowing hard and causing damage to the ship and her boats, a ship that was not that sound to start with: '…weighed and found our rudder rotten in the head, badly so, confound Malta dockyard'. The southerly wind raised much surf, which could upset an experienced sailor and lead to tragedy:

> Bennet, 2cnd class PO who knew the passage through the reef…left the ship about 9.30 with the Whaler, missed the center of the channel and getting too much on the Port hand going in, was swamped. I went in the life boat and picked Cundy and Hunt from the Whaler. Bennet and Cadogan swam on shore. William Cox was drowned.

Going out in the steam pinnace to reach the coaling dhows one afternoon, the screw shaft broke in two at the coupling and the pinnace started drifting out to sea in bad weather. It got dark. Marx had to use the light from the furnace to make enough light on the foresail to attract the attention of the ship's lifeboat to rescue them. By the time it arrived, the water was 'up to the thwart and the fires put out'. On another occasion, 'when it came on to blow, one of the big coaling dhows got tangled with the ship and had to be cut free, much to my relief'.

On 2 May *Fawn* anchored in Aden. The men were relieved to be ashore and the freedom led to some horseplay. There was a row. Some bluejackets knocked over Mr Walsh, the political resident. There was a trial and it was decided to send some of 'our troublesome people to prison', a useful way for captains to get rid of black sheep. The weather presented further problems. One evening was the hottest and closest Marx had ever known and two men died the following day from 'heat apoplexy', while two more were taken ill. The cutter was upset in a heavy sea necessitating another rescue. The ship was busy taking soundings, and there was an admiral's inspection to be prepared for. 'A high old state we are in but must do our best had a thorough good clean inside and tried to paint outside but could not finish.' But all in all the inspection, when it came, was a success. The Admiral complimented Lieutenant Marx on the cleanliness of the ship but he found fault with Lieutenant Keary for gunnery drill and blackguarded him in front of the men. Marx was shocked that the Admiral should do so; he thought it in 'bad taste…'

In August the ship called at Mauritius. Marx went ashore up to the Champ De Mars and saw 'all the beauty and fashion'. In the evening he went to the theatre and met Mr Lawford, a man in the 'Oriental Bank', whereupon he 'fell into badish company'. We may conjecture as to what that meant. He decided to opt for more healthy exercise and determined to climb the notorious rock, Pieter Both. He failed to reach it on the first attempt with Jones, Able Seaman (AB) and met Lieutenants Cust and Keary on the way back, who had tried to do the same but failed to get any higher than the shoulder. Marx typically determined that he would try again and 'fetch the top…'. It is interesting to note that he took no guide, but went with one Philp, a chief petty officer. It argues an easy relationship between officer and rating, perhaps more typical of the Old Navy than the New. Before they could leave however, there was a sprung mainmast to be repaired and a ship to be caulked, then intricate preparations of equipment to be made if he was to succeed a second time: 'one rocket, 10 tent pegs, 40 fathoms of lead line, 11 fathoms of white line and 1 and a half of brown, water and food, to be found…'

The climb started well enough as the two men 'commenced trudging':

...the first difficulty was the 30 feet sheer flat rock at an angle of 80 degrees with a slight crack in it. Here we put five tent pegs and soon reached the top, secured our rope and a piece of bamboo. It was by this time nearly dark so we wended our way down and went to La Laura where the Manager Monsiur Apatie offered us a bed and we sat and watched him pay the coolies until 8 pm when we were getting hungry. He showed us our room and had mattresses put there and then ceremoniously closed the door.... I went round to Mr Apatie's room where he was just commencing dinner and said we were hungry....after some show of reluctance shared his grub with me and gave Philp some...went to bed and slept...no breakfast in the morning...he having gone out and left word that if we wanted anything we could buy it in the village. So we bought 10 eggs and some bread intending to have a square meal when we reached the shoulder and left La Laura at 7.45 am, reached the shoulder at 8.45 and went straight up the 30 feet we had prepared the previous night, we then got up some distance further without much difficulty until we came to another difficult place but Philp who worked like a man got 2 tent pegs in and we surmounted this, the last difficulty. We were soon underneath the button (10 am) but it came on to rain and blew hard and do what we could, we could not get a rope over the top in spite of our bow and a sling so at last, at noon, we determined to try our rocket and fired him to leeward over the rock but the wind caught it and the end of the line not being secured, rocket line and all went down a thousand feet into the valley below. I sat down ready to cry for being such an ass but it was our salvation we still had the 1 and a half in line left, so cutting off a fathom we knotted the yarns, tied them to a stone and so at last Philp threw it over and we soon had the 1 and a half in [?] and made fast on the Port Louisa side to a big rock on the opposite side to 2 tent pegs. I went up first and when I was nearly up I found that the rope was slipping but luckily got my arm in the crack and wriggled up but I was rather in a funk I must acknowledge but when I got to the top I put the rope in the crack and Philp came up like a shot. There was a piece of lead on the top on which were scratched a lot of names. Haig's amongst the number.[1] We put ours down and then came down…

Marx enjoyed more climbing at Mauritius with Lieutenants Keary and Cust (Cust turned out to be a good and ingenious cook), and the redoubtable Philp. It was a season of relaxation, outings and local dances. Marx enjoyed returning the favours by preparing for a dance on *Fawn*, the officers rigged double awnings over the quarterdeck and single ones from the funnel aft. There were two stages alongside and another awning made from the studsail, over them. The inside was lined with flags and 'lots of green stuff'. A threat of rain passed and the dance was a great success, the deck looked very pretty and they had a lot of people. Marx enjoyed the company of 'Miss Reilly a nice girl… . Thus ends one of the pleasantest six weeks of my time.'

Fawn was a surveying vessel and October was devoted to the ship's task of surveying in the Red Sea. Marx found Delagoa, off Port Melville, 'a most difficult place to find one's way about owing to the badness of the chart and the scarcity of leading marks and the number and character of the shoals…a beastly place for anchoring, blows hard, strong tides and a good deal of sea'. He described the method of surveying: '…running the lines out by boats in the direction of the reef, the boats maintaining their lines of bearing on the ship and getting their distance from her, the ship then shifting her billet a mile or two and the boats doing the same thing'. There were also soundings taken at suitable intervals. It was a skilled job for which the Navy had trained a specialised branch of navigating officers but other executive officers like Marx had to be able to supervise the work.

On 22 October, the ship anchored at Mozambique and Marx went for a walk in the evening to see the place. Apparently he saw it to some purpose since the event is marked with a large asterisk! A couple of days later he dined with Captain Mather Byles, 'Byles is a beast by all accounts...' but he does not say why. Marx reckoned that in the event of war, there would be an increase in naval recruiting. Byles said the Russian crisis had seen a drop in naval applications. Byles had just been promoted from Commander to Captain for his action on the gunboat *Mosquito* in the seizure of the Suez Canal, so perhaps there was some jealousy there. Then it was sailing from Mozambique to Zanzibar, where on 4 November the officers went to visit the Sultan who gave them a grand reception. Marx was impressed with his army, 'Sultans army seems in good condition well armed and well dressed,' but less so with the cakes, sherbet, and otto of rose, which was put on each man's handkerchief as he held it out. He remarked that the Portuguese were not taken much notice of by anyone.

This reception was followed by the 'hardest working week'. The feed pump broke down and when the ship wanted to go into Aden, she failed to get pratique. She had to join *Dragon* in quarantine at Kamaran. Pratique was a certificate of health, which allowed a ship to enter a port. There had been some illness aboard *Fawn* and local fear was exacerbated by a cholera scare locally. Marx had spoken of the men suffering from sunstroke but does not mention fever. Various diversions relieved the tedium of the quarantine: a boat full of pilgrims going to the Hadji broke down and the travellers had to be rescued, 'they were a turbulent lot'; *Fawn* kept an armed boat handy and the *Arab* sent one in case of emergencies. A runaway slave came alongside, 'but we did not take him in as he was well fed, fairly clothed, had not been beaten for a month and said that he and his chums were as strong as camels'. Meanwhile the officers of *Fawn* entertained themselves and the men with boat races. The Captain sailed the galley against the cutter. 'I beat him by three minutes,' said Marx. Keeping the men entertained in a quarantine station was a common problem for captains. It was also commonplace for governors to baulk at having the men on shore after the quarantine period had expired.' The local governor here was no different. Marx declared him an obstructionist, putting every difficulty in the way of the men leaving the ship in case they still carried any infection. The Governor declared, 'The taxes being collected, the people were in a disturbed state,' and yet he would not 'put his pen to paper to that effect' Marx complained. But eventually they were cleared and could go into Aden.

The beginning of 1882 was spoiled by the fact that Marx shut his hand in a cabin door and could not hold a gun. To be deprived of shooting animals and birds (and even the possibility of men should trouble erupt) was a trauma indeed. Triangulating the group of islands off Zabayek was hardly compensation and then, to cap it all, as he started out for Zebassar at eight a.m. on 16 February, Marx 'smashed the whaler'. Afterwards, he said 'I think I did not take care enough,' but there was a furious row and Captain Aldrich took charge out of Marx's hands. Marx was furious, and, despite his growing maturity, his old resentful, stormy temperament showed itself again. Too angry to say a word, he sulked on the poop. Next day he sent in his resignation. Perhaps tempers had calmed by then. The Captain refused to accept it and no more was heard about resigning.

April and May were taken up with more surveying in the Red Sea and recording ship's soundings, but the wind was often blowing so hard they had to abandon it. At Mocha

> …the side of the condenser air pump casing carried away and we were about one hour before we could share the Engines and then anchored under Table Island coming back working only one air pump…next day went out Sounding, the marks were heliostats and answered beautifully.

A heliostat was an apparatus with a mirror driven by clockwork to reflect sunlight in a fixed direction. But many of the days were marked by 'blowing so hard we did not make much way…'. They went to Mocha 'to run meridian distance'. On a walk ashore, Marx found 'a b-y house' but there was no asterisk.

Then it was back to Aden in May for docking. It was just in time. They were running out of coal and had to burn tar and pitch mixed with coal dust and some broken spars to make the fuel last. In dock they had to remove all the powder and shell from the ship and make it ready for cleaning. They also had to clean the dock. By this time naval officers realised that docks were notorious centres of disease and this dock was no exception, 'a filthy place and we had it pumped out first and then cleaned…and lots of lime sprinkled about it…'. While this was being done, the men had to be accommodated in the local barrack. This proved to be not an easy thing to do, since hammocks and bags got lost and mixed. Marx decided that 'In future every man shall carry his own bag and hammk and shall not lose sight of it.' In dock they replaced the copper on the bottom of the ship, which was bad in places, but the screw shaft had only dropped slightly, so on the whole Marx thought there was not much the matter with the ship.

With *Fawn* now in dock, there was again opportunity for relaxation: 'jolly picnics', dining, dancing with the local society, especially the ladies, made a pleasant interlude before returning to sea, en route for South Africa. Hounslow took the ship out of dock and did it very well according to Marx. He remarked on the fact that the Captain likes 'carrying on and does it. I do not like it'. He liked to deal with the technicalities of sailing the ship and was at his best in emergencies, as when unfortunately a copper seam was opened shortly after leaving the dock by an accident with the jib boom:

15 June – Directly after midnight, the Jib boom carried away and we spent two hours getting in the wreck the whole of which we saved. I had hardly turned in when a man came down that the Captain wanted me and that the ship had made 16 inches of water in the last 15 minutes. I doubled up and got the watch on the downtons [Downtons – a make of pump] next minute. I went down between the tanks and there the water was washing about furiously. By this time we had 2ft 7 inches in the bilge. We opened the sluice and turned on the main engines, the stoke

hole plates were well covered and matters looked bad. The men worked the pump and all the engines were got under way. We found that the water did not gain and at 4 am we knocked off the hand pumps but kept the main engines going…the thing was that the water over the stokehold plates washed the ashes down into the bilge and choked the suction. The Jib boom had knocked off the head shoot [a pipe from the heads down to the waterline] and the water was coming in at 2 and a half inches an hour afterwards.

16th – The water now comes in at the rate of 1 and a half inches an hour. The weather being comparatively fine and sea smooth.

17th – I discovered the leak. It lies under the head at the juncture of the lower head beams. When the Jib boom carried away it knocked off the head shoot and in doing so we suppose we must have disturbed some copper and opened out one of the seams.

With typical naval invention the jib boom was put to good use. With some added canvas, it was used as a triangulation marker for Delagoa Bay. No sooner had this nerve-racking incident taken place than it was followed by the incident of the sinking pinnace.

24th – Delagoa Bay – Put 10 bags of coal and five breakers of water in the Pinnaces which we got the boilers into all ready for landing tomorrow…. . 12.30 am Simpson Q Master called me and I turned out in time to see the first Pinnace was nearly flush with the water. I turned out the crew but as Collins was on the boom, down she went and he was washed off…I saw him clear of the boom and doubled down, called the Whalers away at forehatch…jumped on the poop and there saw a serge jumper floating astern which I hailed for Collins. It not answering, I slung a life buoy at it and let go the stern one and then had the satisfaction of hearing that Collins was safe on board. I turned the hands up and tried to weigh the

Pinnace…after hauling at her for 1 and a half hours, I gave up until morning.

Next day:

> I had nearly finished securing her when the Captain came on board after having had a bad night star taking, the galley swamped and the crew wet through. The ship was dragging so I let go Port anchor. The Captain was anxious about the ship and weighed the Port anchor and stood out and I had to leave the Pinnace. Clancy and Norman who had been active at first in securing her, neglected to do anything and away she went to the bottom again…as it was blowing hard the captain determined to buoy her and leave it till a fine day, the buoy was the broken heel of the Jib boom.

There followed a long and detailed account with a beautifully elegant diagram explaining how Marx managed to rig a derrick to lift the ill-fated pinnace. Nor was this the end of their troubles. The bad weather continued to take its toll. On Friday 30 June, the Captain and Morescaux left the ship with 'a galley leaking like a sieve' and returned with nine timbers smashed. On 10 July the spanker and main trysail split. Marx detailed all the many endeavours to combat the effects of unpredictable wind and sudden storm on the suffering sloop: 'The middle watch took in all sail but made it again… . A flash of lightening is quite sufficient reason for making all snug at once.' The whales although impressive with their many spouts could also be dangerous: '…saw a thrasher attacking a whale'.

Marx seems to have enjoyed the challenge of keeping the ship afloat. It is not surprising perhaps that he found anchorage in Simon's Bay, even with its 'Grand Hotel which is kept by a swindler', its socialising, and the presence of Miss Salmon 'who dances <u>well</u>', tedious in comparison. Captain Aldrich and Hynes had their wives out. Perhaps he missed their single company and wished he had a wife of his own.

All his life, he never failed to comment on a pretty woman and at this time he always detailed in his diary a list of all the respectable ladies in town he visited, commenting on their charms or otherwise, but in August he declared himself 'sick to death of Cape Town'. He did not, like some others, fear the smallpox in Simonstown. He said robustly that there was only one case of it and went to see the marionettes, declaring '…fine chance of getting the smallpox'. The Salmons were at Cape Town and he got to know them better. This cheered him. He still thought 'Mrs Salmon nicest woman out'.

October was an interesting month. *Fawn* had to settle astronomers on Nos Vey, an island off Natal in St Augustine Bay, as part of the Navy's preparations to monitor the 1882 transit of Venus. Captain Aldrich explained what was happening to the local residents and landed a party from the ship with tents to set up the establishment of what he called 'Venus Town' on the south end of the island. Ingeniously, the sailors made 'a large raft of the huts and placing an iron base on the top, successfully floated the whole lot ashore'. The astronomers took up their residence and seemed to like it but the work on the island was hampered by the sand, which covered everything.

As we have seen, Marx was always interested in the world around him and the people who inhabited it. He seems to have had little of the prejudice often exhibited by imperial Victorians. He said of a local native chieftain's son, 'Prince George has been on board he wears a red tamo shanter cap and a red lamba and is acknowledged by all the natives as the best dressed man in these parts quite eclipsing the King in the splendour of his person. He is a very intelligent man fond of vermouth and takes quite a leading part in the politics of this part of the world. The King is old and feeble but much respected and looked up to…not so, his three sons who levy blackmail on the local traders.' Although much of Marx's journal is brief, sometimes to the point of obscurity, he took a lot of time and trouble in writing up local customs and scenes. Here, he gave a description of the local slavery system and the despotic power of the King:

The system of slavery is very curious a slave can hold slaves and if a slave is hungry he goes to his master and asks for something to eat and his Master is bound to give it to him. If a slave goes away to find work he makes a small present of a fathom or so of cloth to his master and that is all, on his return if a slave is iltreated by his master he can complain to the king who generally takes him as his own slave and finishes his master. The principal seems to be that everyone is the kings slave and that his power is unlimited…

He noted that 'our surveying parties are treated civilly on the mainland so far there seems no chance of a row'.

Officers were always at risk of any number of diseases in these waters and in this climate. On 18 October, Marx had what he thought was a 'bad fit of the gravel', and declared that really he had better look out or he would not 'fetch England'. He managed to keep going. It was a relatively peaceful time. Astronomers' instruments were set up and surveying started. There was time to make and mend clothes. The men established a firing range. Marx dined with the missionary Fathers Parry and Sidgram. The astronomy of the occasion interested him. He saw Saturn and his ring, Venus and her crescent, Jupiter and his bands; 'the wonderful Nebula in Tukan…'. But the gravel continued to trouble him. It hurt him when he moved. This discomfort was probably due to stones in his bladder. In a tropical country, if the body is perspiring a lot and there is not enough water, it will become dehydrated, the urine concentrated, and stones will easily form. In addition, if Marx was harbouring any element of genoccochal infection it would exacerbate the situation and make him pass more urine without replacing it. Alcohol would also add to any dehydration, though that never seems to have been a problem for Marx. In any event, he must have suffered considerable pain.

He was diverted by meeting the intriguing Captain Thomson, who 'gave me 4 snakes all alive OK. He has a guinea worm in his left eye which cruises round underneath the hard covering of the eye sometimes he does not see it for 3 months at other times it come to the front and gives him much trouble.' On Friday 10 November, he noted 'nothing of importance' but again the asterisk appeared. Apparently his debility did not succeed in promoting abstinence. Twelve days later he had another slight attack, 'some pain, put turpentine on bandage'. A tar bandage was a common remedy.

On 6 December, to everybody's delight and relief, there was a 'fine day for the transit of Venus, the transit came off about 4.50 in the afternoon and was very successful. I fixed a sextant eyepiece in my glass and saw everything very well. After the ingress I looked through the six inch telescope and saw the whole thing well, it was same with the naked eye at sunset.' Then it was time to pack up the instruments and return the successful astronomers to shore. The ship had her new sailing orders for Natal and Simonstown.

On 4 December the ship arrived in Natal. But now the 'poor old *Fawn*' was suffering. As she sailed on to Simonstown, the water came in through the quarterdeck ports and she was rolling heavily. They were also running out of supplies and had it not been for the men of *Boadicea* who brought *Fawn* 'all the duff and stuff they had left "good for them"', their Christmas Day would have 'been a very poor thing, our Christmas decorations and dinners being very small'.

January of 1883 started with toothache. Marx went to Cape Town to have it removed. Cape Town obviously provided other amenities. The asterisk appears again, '...had tooth out and other things'. He went calling with Hynes and visited Mrs Veal, Mrs Rowe and Mrs White. He went for a ride and met the Admiral and his wife, '...what nice people they are. Rode home with them.' Mrs Salmon came on board later and they went horse riding together, 'a pleasant ride'. In a seemingly unlikely remark the doctor said his disease might be gravel but was probably neuralgia. The discomfort did not stop him from organising the painting of *Fawn* and having it completed in a day. He had 'twenty eight brushes going'. They cleaned the brass with tobacco soaked in hot water, which 'answers well'.

Then, after nearly three years away, it was time to return to England, the commission almost over, officers and men happy to be homeward-bound. But to their frustration the winds on the return sailing remained very light, both before and after St Helena. 'The South East trade is a snare and a delusion... .' Marx anxiously recorded the winds each day as they sailed from Ascension to Plymouth. It meant they had to burn their scarce coal and only had a meagre two tons left as they approached the Scillies. There, briefly, the wind turned foul and the main yard was damaged. It was followed by a calm and the ship only drifted until the yard could be got up. The situation was worrying – to be so near and yet so far! 'We were placed on an allowance of water yesterday but as weather seems favourable we got up steam for distilling... .' Thankfully, the wind finally became favourable and on 15 April, just in time, before fuel and water ran out, they arrived and made fast to a buoy in Plymouth Sound – 'Hurrah,' cried Marx.

Sheerness was the place appointed for the concluding inspection, carried out by Captain 'Darcy', as Marx called him.[3] Aldrich said the Captain was much pleased, but Marx had his reservations – he thought the ship was clean enough, but the men were 'rubley'. Inspection was followed by dismantling. The ship went up to Chatham, where she was 'put in the basins miles from any where' and the crew had to work hard to prepare for paying-off day, clearing out the ship and leaving everything in good order. Getting the tanks out was a difficult job. Sails had to be stripped and returned. After that came three days' leave, a trip to town ('I fell') and the return home, to find George, Con and Daisy flourishing. There was the usual hunting, driving about in George's dog cart to Alton, calling on the cousins at Chester Street where Ethel was 'very nice as usual', but Marx declared 'the situation desperate' with Edith. It is difficult not to come to the conclusion that Marx was suffering from some degree of unrequited love here.

He dined with Captain Aldrich and Mrs Aldrich, noting that Mrs Aldrich was very delicate but pleasant. The letter came from Admiralty to confirm that the inspection had gone well and Marx was pleased. It would be useful in finding him another good berth. At the end of the month there was the final ship's cleaning and finishing of all the ship's stores, '...now there is nothing to do but return the sails after they have been stripped. Everyone has worked uncommonly well, especially Mr Mallard and Hockin, carpenters.' Like so many officers and especially captains, Marx experienced an emotional reaction to leaving his command of three years. He had given three years to the maintenance of 'poor old *Fawn*' and bonded with the men who had risked life and limb together. As Victorian muscular Christianity made itself felt, and the 'stiff upper lip' took over, such sentiment must be repressed. Admiral Fisher declared,

> I had the most trying parting from that ship's company of the 'Northampton': and not being able to stand the goodbye, I crept unseen into a shore boat...[4]

> Captain Clayton confessed, I said goodbye to them and very nearly broke down in doing so, I did not think I was so foolish but most of the men had been with me the whole commission and I felt very sorry at parting with them.[5]

In 1883, Marx contented himself with 'I am uncommonly sorry to part with the ship's company.' Strong sentiment. The actual paying-off day was 4 April. There was a sense of anti-climax as they waited for the final closing of the commission. Marx could hardly find any work for the few men that were left. But they gave 'poor old *Fawn*' a clean-up for the last time. At nine a.m. Commander John Musters of the steam reserve came for inspection and expressed himself pleased with the ship. It could be finally paid off, the men given their wages and all accounts settled. Marx and Aldrich walked down to the train 'to see the last of the men'. Then Marx said goodbye to Aldrich who 'gave me a rattling good certificate'. He went to town to square up his business with his agent. He found him 'damned slack...had ommitted to pay a half years interest to Coutts'. But the 'rattling good certificate' made up for it:

> John Locke Marx has served as Senior Lieutenant on board Her Majesty's ship Fawn, under my command from 1 December 1880 to 6 April 1883 during which period he has conducted

himself with sobriety and in every way very much to my satisfaction. The ship having been chiefly engaged in surveying work – a great many extra calls have been made on his patience and zeal, which have however always been very great from beginning to end.

Captain Aldrich informed Admiralty that not only was Marx 'trustworthy and reliable' – he 'spoke French'.

This testimonial marks the beginning of Marx's career as a naval officer on his way up. Aldrich had seen at first hand Marx's virtues – his ingenuity, his enthusiasms, his organising capacity and the new cheerfulness and confidence in his temperament. His next commission would confirm that temperament and competence. But before then, there was some additional torpedo and gunnery training to be done.

---

1 Article and illustration in *The Graphic*.

2 See year 1886, in 'Captain Clayton and the Australia Station, 1885–1886', Mary Cross, MA Thesis, University of Exeter (1994).

3 Probably Admiral St George Caulfield D'Arcy Irvine.

4 Fisher, *Memories*, p144.

5 Clayton's letter dated 25 August 1888.

Eight

Voluntary Courses – Torpedo Training and Gunnery (1883)

'*I do not think much of them...*'

After his successful appointment in *Fawn*, Marx went to Admiralty to ask for leave and look around for further desirable promotion. At the Admiralty he saw Admiral Key,[1] who was civil but refused him leave and could promise nothing. It was not customary to give leave at this time when a foreign commission was to be followed by a home appointment,[2] and Marx was posted immediately in April of 1883 for the recently revised (1882) additional lieutenants' training courses in torpedo and gunnery at *Vernon* and *Excellent*. In fact he ended his time on *Fawn* on 6 April 1883, and his service record puts him at *Vernon* on 7 April 1883. Before going there, he called on the MP Sclater Booth who was at home and had lunch at 13 Chester Street and saw the cousins. Again, we have a cryptic reference: '...saw the cousins...am much afraid it is hopeless...'. In the evening he went to Portsmouth as his request for leave had been refused and he had to join *Vernon* early next morning. On 10 April 1882 he went on board *Vernon* and began the lectures.

Vernon was the relatively new torpedo training school established by Jacky Fisher in 1876. It taught the use of the new electricity, and the innovative, secret, Whitehead torpedo. Compared with later developments in the torpedo, the Whitehead was a very primitive weapon. It was an underwater shell, launched through a torpedo tube and designed to explode upon a designated target. It had a range of about 300 yards at a speed of seven knots and carried an explosive charge of 100 pounds of gunpowder. Much was made of the 'Whitehead secret' – only lieutenants and above were allowed knowledge of it in the early days – the 'secret' was the hydrostatic depth-keeping valve which controlled the 'horizontal rudders' and hence the depth.[3] The use of these autonomous weapons was still something of a hit-and-miss affair.

Marx found the lectures at *Vernon* tedious after life in the Red Sea and although he does not say so, it is likely that he resented having to work again so soon after returning from a sea-going commission. Although life at *Vernon* was more relaxed than life at *Excellent*,[4] it was the same routine each day, and after only a couple of weeks he declared that his life was becoming 'all work, which won't do'. He started socialising again, calling with friends, a pleasant dinner at the Hornbys', a visit to Aunt Fanny who was looking younger than ever. He decided to raise his sights and approach Admiral Hornby about the possibility of a Royal Yacht appointment. Every year, three lieutenants' names were sent to the Commanding Officer (CO) of *Victoria and Albert* and these were forwarded to the monarch who chose one. Traditionally, such posts were supposed to be for good service but the chief requirement of a Royal Yacht lieutenant was that he should come from an impeccable social background. Of sixty-six lieutenants serving on the *Victoria and Albert* between 1860 and 1914, ten were 'honourables', one was a prince (Louis Battenberg) and one a lord (Lord C Scott). Marx was not an obvious Royal Yacht man, by temperament, class or career success. Nor did he like having to submit himself to the indignity and submission of asking for such an appointment. He remarked, '…it was not a highly satisfactory interview. Lady Hornby came in the middle, I was hungry wanting my lunch, hating the job, damned nervous and made a balls of the whole thing.'

The love affair with Edith, if indeed that is what it was, was not prospering: '…had it out with Edith, same old result. Obstinate as usual, think I will conquer, came down quite seedy with thinking and went to bed, wrote her a letter.' Next day he sent Edith £10 for 'the girls of some place', presumably to please her by supporting one of her charitable activities. He was impatient. Two days later: 'No answer from Edith, why does she not write…?' He went to Arlebury and told Conny 'something of my trouble…'. But since *Vernon* was at Portsmouth there was still the prospect of diversion from the troubles of Edith. Marx called on Mary Egerton, who was as nice as ever, he met Miss Cowper Coles and visited a bevy of other society ladies. On Friday 11 May, he went to town and 'nearly fell foul at lodgings…'. Only nearly? Was he thinking of Edith? If so, his feelings were shortly to be alleviated by meeting another delightful cousin – 'Binney, very nice, fresh….she paints prettily and is altogether a cousin worth knowing.' Binney took him on some local sightseeing and he was very sorry to come to the end of such a delightful visit.

The work with the Whitehead torpedoes became more pressing. There were exams to be passed and exercises to be undertaken. Marx already had a poor opinion of the primitive torpedo weapons – he had worked with them on *Lord Warden* and been unimpressed. He was even less so now. 'I do not think much of them.' They could also be dangerous:

> Peter Gallwey had his hands cut by the fans of a Whitehead. He was uncommonly plucky about it but what pained him most was that he had been nearly 3 years at the work and never met with an accident…

The exercises involved shooting with a Whitehead from a second-class torpedo boat up the creek. They were difficult to control and often went off their course. Marx never had the career-oriented enthusiasm for torpedoes or gunnery that Fisher advocated in a successful officer:

> If you are a gunnery man, you must believe and teach that the world must be saved by gunnery, and will only be saved by gunnery. If you are a torpedo man, you must

lecture and teach the same thing about torpedoes...

However, he had to prepare to pass the exam, 'One has to work to pass this exam...really doing something for exam.' On the morning of 31 May, he took volume one of the Whitehead paper and on the morning of 1 June the volume-two paper. Both afternoons involved practical exams. Marx really does not seem to have been concerned about these, compared with his earlier angst about qualifying examinations. It bears out the idea that *Vernon* was indeed more 'laid back' in its approach. In the evening he went to town and went to the aquarium with friends. Next day he visited the very wonderful fisheries exhibit and 'called on Lord Alcester[5] who said he knew all about me...' and called on Lady Drummond. Marx was beginning to search out interest for his next appointment.

After *Vernon*, Marx joined *Excellent* for the additional lieutenants' course on hydraulics and gunnery training, but his diary was still more concerned with his social life. He showed 'Ella', 'Rose' and 'Kitty' around *Vernon*. Mary Purefoy and friends came aboard for tea. The delights of tennis with the ladies figured highly. The Bonham Carters were 'very amusing'. He tried to see more of Binney but to no avail. One evening when he was coming off he had a narrow squeak: 'I fell overboard coming off and was drenched really in smooth water a great coat does not make as much difference as one would think.'

Marx went back to Arlebury to pass time till he could find a new appointment. George was at home ill and Marx was worried about him but he decided that it was time to look for a house of his own and take steps to ensure his own future – more searching for *interest*. He visited Sir Michael Seymour,[6] who

> ...was 82 and well, he drinks a bottle of port per day eats mutton and bacon no butter or beef. He told me about the Capture of two French frigates by his father in 1813. Also of his convoying 300 ships, one line batteship two frigates four brigs and that they did not lose one.[7]

Marx was impressed. He saw Lord Northbrooke again, who 'was kind' but could apparently offer no help. He tried a new doctor, Lee, who said he was getting well and free from gravel, and he saw Mrs Poore,[8] whom he had known as a sub lieutenant, '…as nice and pretty as ever, but getting older, her children all have whooping cough'.

For his new abode, Marx fixed on 109 St Thomas's Street (its whereabouts is unknown, whether he ever lived there or simply rented it out is uncertain) and went to Coutts in London to arrange the mortgage. The first payment necessitated an overdraft of £31 on his account. It was a dubious step on the small salary of a lieutenant only earning about £200 a year and his life was still mainly in ships and naval establishments, both working and social. Social life at *Vernon* (close to *Excellent*) was very popular with naval personnel and locals alike. The balls given on board were in great demand and local ladies were not beyond inventing invitations as Commander Poore's wife remembered. In July there was trouble at a *Vernon* ball involving Stanhope, a naval officer and a certain Mrs Robinson:

> Farmer, a doctor and a pimp, says he saw Mrs. R. come out of the lavatory twice in company with Stanhope. Moberly RH was the ball committee man he went to. He placed it in the hands of the committee, they weakly wrote to Stanhope asking for denial. He gets a written one from Farmer and shows it [to] Moberly who simply states that Farmer told him and asked him to place matters in the hands of the Committee. Farmer is a low beast. Stanhope by my advice saw Hornby who is a gentleman and gave him good advice.

Social life centred on Arlebury was still Marx's main source of pleasure. Whatever his current feelings for Edith, he was always able to appreciate other attractive women and at Arlebury he was taken by further acquaintance with the lively cousin Binney, '…got letter from Binney which I answered hastily and I regret it rather as I always do when one speaks in a hurry….' However, George's illness had become worse and Marx was worried. He visited his brother at home and was sad to see him in such a state. In August of 1883, a telegram arrived from Conny. Marx must come home again, George was now seriously ill. This time, when he returned, Marx found his brother in great pain. The situation was critical. Dr Wilson Fox made no bones about it and pronounced the case hopeless. Marx's diary simply records:

Saturday 4th – much pain, got a nurse.
Sunday 5th – More pain, terrible.
Monday 6th – Still terrible pain.
Tuesday 7th – almost insensible, poor fellow, Oh God help him!
Wednesday 8th – at about twenty minutes to six all was over, quite peaceful. Edith came in afterwards and did not know what had happened. Oh, God help him!
Thursday 9th – a sad day preparing for the funeral, answering many letters. Poor Con, Edith and Ethel so good.

The funeral was held two days later on the Saturday, and many people attended. After he had retired from the Army by sale of his commission in August of 1877, George had been notable in the local militia as a captain in the 1st Hampshire Rifle Volunteers and as a local JP. His funeral was a sad local event: the fire brigade marched alongside to the burial in the family grave at Tichbourne. As with the emotional loss of his mother, Marx makes no further reference in his diary to what must have been the second most tragic episode in his life, this loss of a dearly loved brother. Emotional inhibition, or admirable emotional strength? On the following Sunday, Marx went to church with Con and Edith and Ethel. Again, he took the opportunity to tackle Edith, but '…she will not alter'. He returned to Portsmouth saddened by the loss of George, and disappointed by his lack of success with Edith. A few days later there was a half-holiday from *Excellent* and again Marx went home and tried to persuade Edith, but 'Edith like steel'. It is hard to imagine what this is, if it is not an affair of the heart. Marx allowed emotive frustration, but no details of Edith, to reach the pages of his journal. Edith alone never has any comments made as to her appearance. It is puzzling and open to several interpretations. Was she not attractive? Was Marx drawn to her personality alone? Seems unlikely. Did the virtues of a 'lady' produce a different response and require a different approach? Constance, perhaps Marx's first love, later married a second time to Mr Arthur Wood and took Arlebury to her new marriage.

Marx's year at *Vernon* and *Excellent* had finished and he was becoming anxious about finding a new billet. He went to Admiralty where he saw Clayton and Beaumont,[9] but he got nothing to advance his career. At the end of the month he heard that he had passed with a second, 'though a bad one'. In fact he had got 307 marks out of 350 for his torpedo examination, and 410 out of 600 for his gunnery. When he went home he 'found Edith flown'. He felt depressed and unwell again. He consulted Wilson Fox, who said he could not tell but thought Marx had a stone in his kidney. He advised no violent exercise, no hunting, 'no nothing'. Marx became even more depressed. He went to Admiralty again to see First Naval Lord Sir Cooper Key,[10] who 'had of course forgotten all about me, although he said he would do what he could'. Then it was back to Arlebury to find 'E' (a decorated letter on the page, this time) 'like a stone'. Things looked black. 'What with "E", No Ship and WF I am pretty well knocked out of time.' He took refuge in hunting, shooting and going on a trip to the Lake District with friends. In the natural beauty and freedom of the lakes, in the company of happy companions, his spirits revived and at length he was rewarded by the moment he had been waiting for. At the hotel he was staying in, a telegram from York arrived, asking if he had received a letter from Admiralty. He had not. Next day a telegram from Admiralty did arrive. It offered him command of a gunboat, the '*Swinger*…which I accepted', declared Marx with masterly understatement.

Then it was all hustle and bustle. He and Con immediately went down to London but they missed their train at Crewe and had to sleep at Euston Hotel. This was too good an opportunity to miss. In high spirits Marx found it all 'rather sport', and marked it with three big asterisks. Next day he went to Admiralty and began to buy things for his trip. Con lived at Chester Street, Marx stayed at Norris Street. After seeing Lord Northbrook, he took the opportunity of another asterisk, and next day a further asterisk as he bought more gear and saw more people at Admiralty before he returned to Arlebury. There was a final flourish at home as he recorded one last asterisk before he had to leave. The prospect of prospective celibacy had to be addressed. This is probably not the last time Marx addressed it but it is the last time we see an asterisk in his journals and it is the last written record of his sexual life. Now that he was to have command of his own ship he would have other things to think about and a different image to uphold.

1 Admiral Sir Astley Cooper Key was First Naval Lord of the Admiralty Board.

2 Admiral Sir Reginald Bacon, *A Naval Scrapook*, 1877–1900.

3 I am indebted to Professor Nicholas Rodger for this concise description.

4 *Vernon* men cared nothing for appearance and usually dressed in old sweaters and seaboots. The *Vernon* men never paraded for drill. See James, *The Sky Was Always Blue*, p48.

5 The former Admiral Sir Beauchamp Seymour.

6 Admiral Sir Michael Seymour GCB. He himself was involved in early actions, notably in the Second China War, 1857–1860. He was first and principle ADC to Queen Victoria in 1899 and retired, after a career of fifty years, in 1900.

7 Admiral Sir L Beaumont, at this time Private Secretary to Lord Northbrooke.

8 Admiral Sir Richard Poore's wife, who wrote two books about her own 'naval life': *Recollections of an Admiral's Wife, 1903–1916*, and *An Admiral's Wife in the Making, 1860–1903*.

9 Rear Admiral Lewis Anthony Beaumont KCMG.

10 Admiral Sir Astley Cooper Key CBKCB, GCB, First Naval Lord, September 1879 to July 1885.

Nine

Lieutenant and Commanding Officer (1883–1887)

'Hoisted my pendant – what a rum thing to do!'

In the autumn of 1883, Lieutenant John Locke Marx presented himself at Plymouth, to take command of HMS *Swinger*. She was a single-funnel, three-masted composite screw gunboat of the Ariel class, of about 430 tons displacement, measuring something in the region of 125 feet by 22 feet 6 inches, with an armament of two sixty-four pounder MLR and two twenty-pounder breech-loading (BL).[1] Her speed was between nine and a half and ten and a half knots and she carried a complement of about sixty men with an executive of seven officers. Marx was pleased. *Swinger* was destined for the Australia station and that spelt not only the interest of a foreign, imperial posting, but the prospect of autonomy. He might still only be a lieutenant but now he would be a lieutenant and the Commanding Officer of his own ship. He wrote eagerly, 'Hoisted <u>my</u> [underlined twice] pendant. What a rum thing to do!'

His officers arrived and joined him at Plymouth. He was pleased to see he looked to have a 'fine ships company all ABs, over five years service and special leave men'.[2] It would make his first experience of command easier. It was a small executive:

Lieut. & Commander	John L Marx
Lieutenant	(N) Henry H Torlesse [navigating] (in lieu of a Sub Lt [N])
Sub Lieut	Henry H Bruce
Surgeon	Archibald McKinlay
Asst. Paymaster in Charge	James W Dixon
Engineer	Ferdinand J Fairclough
Gunner	Frederick Garland

Marx adds to this the important ship's mascot – 'Dog Swinger came aboard today.'

The new Commander's first task was to pay the official calls on both admirals at Plymouth, Vice Admiral Charles Curme[3] and Admiral Sir Houston Stewart.[4] He also called on Edward Kelley, Captain of Steam Reserve. There were other social calls to pay and various preparations to make for the commissioning inspection before leaving. The lighting of the ship concerned him:

> Orders have come…to have her fitted with Colomb lamps; if this is done it will interfere with the sleeping accommodation of the crew and at present we have only the exact number of berths for them. I also wish to point out that this ship has no lamptrimmer to look after, or lamp room to accommodate these lights, and beg to request that this ship may be lighted with the ordinary service lanterns.

Admiralty asked for a spare jib boom, topmast and topsail yard to be returned, Marx asked to keep them, 'considering the length of the voyage which this ship is likely to undergo'. He also asked for a twelve-month supply of lead pellets for shackles and a mould for making them, instead of the six-month supply he had been given, and he told Admiralty that he thought one of the carpenters' crew at age fifty-two, 'by his appearance', was not up to the job. He requested a new bugler boy since the old one had had to go to hospital. Constance and Ethel travelled down to be with him for the last few days and he enjoyed their company when he could.

Swinger's first steam trial turned out badly. In a heavy squall, 'our square sterned gig swamped, shackling on to the buoy and such a pandemonium I have not heard for a long time. I was sorry about it as Admiral Curme heard it.' The men were saved but the gig was lost and drifted up the harbour. He went and saw the Commander in Chief who was sympathetic: 'he did not blackguard me as he had himself been out with the brigs and knew how hard it blew'. But he found Admiral Curme inclined to blame him and was pleased when Captain Kelley exonerated him. However, the later full three-hour steam trial went well, and on 18 October they 'swung ship'. This was a matter of adjusting the ship's compass to best effect. He was gratified that Edith came to say goodbye 'by the last train, very good of her taking all things into consideration'. Next day, on 22 October, he attended a levee at Admiral Sir Houston Stewart's. Members of Admiralty also came down to attend it and Marx was sorry that he had not taken the opportunity to speak to Lord Northbrooke. He might have missed a chance to do himself some good and he regretted that he would have been thought lacking in courtesy.

The commissioning inspection took place at Devonport on 24 October and went well. Captain Bosanquet of the *Cambridge* inspected the ship and expressed himself 'much pleased. A good beginning, God grant it may all go straight'. The inspection was followed by the full speed trial. There was some swell, but the little ship did well. In six hours she covered sixty and a quarter miles. After the steam trial, Marx had his last two days of relaxation; a trip in a hired steam launch with Con and Edith, 'I have seldom enjoyed myself so much, and a walk around Devil's Point, it was good of them to come down.' Then came the sailing orders and the men got a last special leave. At nine a.m. sharp on 29 October, with everything ready, *Swinger* was ready to leave. But before Marx could get his signal, asking permission to part company, affirmed, he had to return some lamps. Admiralty's administration may have been penny-pinching but it was well administrated and effective.

1 Left: Francis J Marx, John's father.

2 Right: John Marx with older brother, George.

3 Top Left: The young Midshipman Marx.
4 Bottom left: HMS Swinger, Marx's first ship as Lieutenant and Commanding Officer.
5 Top right: The young Lily Heath.
6 Bottom right: Lily as John's Marx's wife.

7 Above: Breech Farm, the Marxes' first house.

8 Left:
Commander John
Locke Marx.

9 Admiral John Locke Marx.

10 Above: Clatford Lodge, Marx's house from 1906–1939.
11 Below: HMS Dominion, Marx's last battleship.

12 Above: Marx with his beloved horse, Stilton.
13 Below: Almost the last outing with the Tedworth Hunt, picture from the Tatler.

*14 Top right: Marx by
the bunker he built at the
beginning of WWII to
resist German
occupation. It is still
there!
15 Top left: Kapitan
Leutnant Ziemer, the
German Commander of
UB 23.
16 Right: The 'Grand
Old Man'.*

Marx saw the last of Con and Edith waving goodbye on Devil's Point, and then it was 'away into space with a fair wind...'

Their first stop was Madeira, which Marx thought '*not a bad place*'. He found the '*sleighing great fun*' (being pulled downhill in a basket toboggan which continues to this day). Then it was bowling along at seven knots to the next destination until the wind became slight and he had to get up steam. He did not want to use too much coal at this stage. He asked the Captain of a passing steamer when she had lost the trades. The answer was that they had never had any, and sailing in these seas was 'a hard job'. Having to steam in the light winds, Marx took the opportunity of target practice. Admiralty required ships to discharge a certain amount of ammunition in quarterly target practice. A period of quiet at sea could be useful. Nevertheless, Marx was relieved when the ship picked up a wind and they arrived at St Vincent. He enjoyed photographing the place. He visited the Consul and Governor of Cape Verde islands. He went quail shooting but '*never saw a feather*'. Setting off on 18 November, *Swinger* was again becalmed: '...if we had had no steam should have been in a hole as we were fast going in shore'. He described his sailing technique. In a fair wind, he was

> lying our course with Port studsail. I have now got an inner Jib as Mizzen Topmast staysail an [?] Achilles launches Jib as Mizzen Topmast staysail. I also use it as Lee Topmast studsail, Fore staysail as triangular lower studsail, QDK awning as lower studsail...going between 5 and 6 knots with trade, close hauled topmast studsail.

On 23 November, with the light going and night coming, Marx got into the disturbed region at the edge of the trade and 'it rained, thundered lightened etc all night'. It was a heavy squall. It wasn't until midnight on the 27th that he passed from the unsettled Guinea to the more favourable equatorial current. On the 29th, he 'bore up under fore and aft sails for Ascension which improved our speed...', the equatorial current set them to the South West, and they anchored in the southwest corner of Clarence Bay.

Ascension in those days was a military post famous for its turtles and little else except its rollers, which were huge Atlantic waves rolling straight into the open anchorage, giving sailors a spectacular exhibition of their power. Here, Marx met Captain Arthur Brooke of *Opal*. Brooke had been on an expedition up the Niger to Iga in the paddle vessel *Alecto*, with *Flirt* and *Starling*. He told Marx all about it. Marx was impressed and recorded it in his journal:

> Captain Brooke called a palava of chiefs, they came when he made mention of Queen Victoria and said she was very angry with them for stopping the traffic. They set up a yell and some 17 out of 25 bolted. A few minutes afterwards the beating of Tom Toms was heard and in a few minutes the store was surrounded by armed men. Mackintosh who was with Captain Brooke recommended a retreat to the boats and they walked out through these blackguards who were armed with poisoned arrows to their boats. Captain Brooke had put a guard in the West African Company steamer which was moored close to the shore but they could not have fired without hitting Capt. Brooke's party. When Capt. Brooke got on board, he gave the order to load and then tried to send his own interpreter, who was a very good one, to the chiefs to tell them that they must apologise or he should burn the town in an hour. The messenger came back in one and a half hours and said that the chiefs would not apologise, he then ordered the West African Steamer to get out of the way and when she began to move, the natives sent a flight of poisoned arrows at her. All this time they had noticed the women and children clearing out of the town. So then Capt. Brooke opened fire which was returned by some carronades, one of which I saw on board Starling and another one burst when the town was cleared. The boats were sent in and burned the town and destroyed the crops as much as

possible. Tommy Saunders said that there were several creeks up which the boats had to go and not being able to see one another made it more difficult to fire for fear of shooting their own party. They burnt the town during which proceeding Hayes, a Midshipman, and 3 men were hit. The men died and Hayes is supposed to be dying. They could only get two pilots and went down the river flying. Men all right but shortly afterwards the symptoms showed themselves and they found that they had been congratulating themselves too soon.

There was little time for socialising with Brooke and others (Moore, Healy, Elias and Saunders), Marx was given despatches to take to Cape Town. He took in forty-one tons of coal for the voyage but even so, only reached the Cape after an anxious time, fearing that '*the coal would not hold out*'. It took twenty-one days less five and a half hours. Reflecting on his recent visit Marx discovered he had 'Behaved uncivilly to Moore A.P. by a mistake', and typically decided, 'I will write and tell him.'

Swinger arrived at Cape Town on Christmas Eve, and apart from the fact that the sailmaker and Roberts AB got drunk, Christmas Day passed off quietly. The men of *Swinger* celebrated by dining on board *Boadicea* and the officers dined with the Admiral on Christmas Eve and Christmas Day. There was holiday socialising in Simon's Bay, but in January *Boadicea* sailed, '…very sorry am I that I shall see them no more as they are a good lot,' said Marx.

January 1884 started well. Marx was making a good impression: 'The Ad. said to me that which made me proud. Good luck to him.' He had tea with Mrs Salmon and found her again, the nicest woman. Presumably she also was attracted to the young lieutenant. He enjoyed much of her company. He visited all the leading families of Simon's Bay and gave a critical account of one of the social events of the season, Emily Van der Riet's wedding.

The ceremony was in the Dutch Reformed Church. No names of the people who were married were mentioned and altogether it was a loose sort of ceremonial, Mrs Johnson saying what larks they would have. The Rev. Bob Wilshire and Father Rooney made good speeches. Old Van der Riet lost his head. The bride groom's name was Brink. He wore tight shoes and looked a fool. The liquor was nasty. Mrs. De Ridder pretty woman. Young. Some gray hair. Women say she paints.

When Marx left Simon's Bay on 10 January, after having had a good time, especially with Mrs Salmon, '...how much I like these people...', it was blowing a northeaster. The lighthouse keeper, having said that the winds were light and southerly, '...how we cussed him. I was much tempted to turn back as I much wanted a ride with Mrs. Salmon the nicest woman of her sort I know. I photographed Mrs. Salmon's horses and have made a mess of it but am now trying to rectify it...'

All the time, Marx was learning more about sailing and the behaviour of his 'little ship'. On 12 January he wrote:

About 10 am going on the bridge I noticed a heavy breaking sea ahead and the officer of the watch went to the masthead. On coming down he reported that there appeared to be much wind as the sea was breaking heavy. We soon steamed into it and found that it was a perfect calm overhead but a heavy tumbling breaking sea, the temperature of the water was very high 75 and 76 and when it went down about 1 pm the sea disappeared. This was followed next day by a fine south westerly gale. The little ship became difficult to steer with the slightest thing showing abaft. At about 1 pm she broached too. Reefed foresail and single reefed foretopsail. At first was afraid for the mast but clearing lower deck, I trimmed a little forward and sent all the men on the stern gratings but she would not pay off and our weather boat by main rigging got a bump and some heavy seas lopped in. After half an hour, I slewed the

150

head off the Fore Topmast staysail and she paid off. Another time I intend trying putting the men on the weather side of the QDK aft. The barometer fell to 29.60, at least I believe that was the correct height. One aneroid showed 29.43 and two others 29.60.

The wind fell and they arrived at Fremantle after a long, tedious passage with no decent winds. He anchored inside the reefs 'in about 22ft of water half a mile WSW of the lighthouse'. He found *Undine* and *Harrier*[5] there. They were schooners and had taken forty-five and forty-two days from Zanzibar, 'they are pretty dirty and the men <u>regular pirates</u>'.

Visiting and socialising, calling at harbours on the way, Marx enjoyed the trip along the coast from Fremantle to Sydney. In February it was Albany, with dances, shooting parties, picnics. Marx 'left the place with regret'. In March, it was Adelaide — 'the best laid out town I know,' though he found the port very dirty. Adelaide liked Marx:

> HMS *Swinger* came up the gulf on Sunday.... The craft is a jaunty looking gunboat of composite build and suitable for carrying and working 2x64lb and two 20lb pieces, with two machine guns. In her rigging aloft the *Swinger* is remarkably neat, and is built on a pretty barquette design with a long bowsprit and jibboom. She has a finely moulded hull, although it is extremely narrow, and in all her equipment is essentially a natty gunboat. By the courtesy of the Officer-in-Command, she will be open for inspection for a week...and so afford an opportunity for the people to admire one of the Queen's ships, which although small is in point of discipline equal to any one of the Imperial Fleet.

> *Adelaide Advertiser*, 10 March 1884

Then it was a visit to Melbourne, less desirable, 'a [Mr] Stuart tobacconist wore a wig and was in other ways peculiar. Gave me a description of what went on in Melbourne that did not improve the morality of that place.' There were various other diversions on the way. Dog Swinger got a fit at Torrens Island. The ladies who came on board to view the target practice had hot water accidentally pumped all over them! Then on 31 March 1884, Marx arrived at his destination – Sydney, the centre of naval operations in the Australia station.

From 1884 onwards, the threat of Russian invasion, and other predatory foreign interests in the area, had forced Admiralty to take a greater interest in the Australia station. It was becoming more important politically as the new colony grew in importance and this meant the Navy was now required to perform manifold new functions on behalf of the government: imperial power and status must be represented, the Pax Britannica implemented, missionaries delivered and cared for, natives supervised, diplomacy preserved, and occasions of distress, where appropriate, alleviated by the all-encompassing Royal Navy. With the coming of the telegraph in 1884, the station could be centrally run from Admiralty and in 1885, with the coming of the impressive Rear Admiral George Tryon, the station was upgraded to Admiral status.

The station already had its own governmental strategy for the rule of law. The High Commission of the Western Pacific, set up in 1877 and operating out of Fiji, had made the Australia station 'a centre from which law and order might be diffused throughout the unannexed islands of the Pacific'. It meant that offences committed in British islands could be dealt with in the same manner as if they were committed on the high seas. This allowed naval captains to use their own judgement in the application of imperial law where there was no access to a civil court. But it led to confusion over the exact legal status of the various parties concerned and in 1881 it was decided to give naval captains the legal status of Deputy Commissioner. This lessened the autonomy and powers of the Royal Naval captain. Until then he had been virtual judge and jury in the islands where the natives were concerned. Where there had been 'outrages' (murders and killings by natives) it was up to him, abiding by law and Admiralty orders, to find the miscreants, apportion guilt and exact suitable retribution. An 'act of war' on natives was regarded as legitimate punishment. After he became a Deputy Commissioner however, his quarterdeck was no longer the legal courtroom, malefactors were now subject to civil jurisdiction, fines and imprisonment instead of the appropriate naval exaction. It was to this work that Marx was now called in his capacity as representative of the official Deputy Commissioner, Hugh Romilly.

When he arrived in Farm Cove at Sydney, Marx found the flagship *Nelson* (Captain Atwell Lake), the sloops *Miranda* (Captain Thomas Acland) and *Espiegle* (Captain Cyprian Bridge) the gunboat *Raven* (Lieutenant and Commander C Cross). *Undine* and *Harrier* had already arrived. The first thing Marx did was to dine with Commodore Erskine and enjoy the usual initial visiting befitting a new lieutenant and commander, before preparing for his first inspection. It was set for 9 May. It was an anxious occasion for Marx. His reputation among his peers was at stake and senior officers were on hand to note the results. Captain Lake of the flagship took the inspection – a man described by Admiral Bacon as one of the strictest officers serving in the Navy. But it was a good report:

> The *Swinger* has a fine looking Ship's Company. The men were very clean and well dressed and drilled with much spirit. The Ship is clean below, the mess deck being especially so – considering the time she has been in Commission and the recent considerable change in her armament, the Gunnery drills were fairly well carried out. The present plan of passing up powder is not efficient, and alterations have been suggested. The steadiness and silence of the guns' crews, when clearing for action were not quite perfect.

On 10 May Marx sailed to Brisbane to start work: 'the dreaded island work', patrolling the islands of Micronesia, Polynesia and Melanesia. 'Dreaded' because of the climate and the threat of fever, the tedium, the hazards of uncharted reefs, the danger from hostile natives, and the difficulty of keeping the ship provisioned on long voyages in remote areas. However, even here, there was always the pleasurable opportunity for good sailing. It was a challenge to see who could sail fastest: '...taking the ship in through the Howe Channel we beat the *Raven* and the *Diamond*'. *Raven* was another composite screw gunboat of the same type as *Swinger* but *Diamond* was the most important ship on the station after the flagship. She was a wooden screw corvette, with fifteen sixty-four-pounder guns and 225 men, as opposed to *Swinger*'s two sixty-five-pounder guns and 60 men. Marx was delighted to have sailed faster. He noted another sailing detail in his journal: 'The *Diamond* had been on shore, her chronometers were also 5 minutes out and she nearly went on the Investigator reef in consequence...'. It was only a three-day visit to Brisbane but Marx managed to visit and comment on a number of ladies he met. He significantly 'made the acquaintance of one, Miss Lily Heath'. There was no further comment.

Marx's first task in the islands was to investigate an outrage. Outrages were the murders and attacks that were made among the peoples of the islands, involving local natives, traders and settlers. He also had to police the local labour trade and make sure there was no blackbirding (illegal employment, often with abduction, of natives). Marx described this trade in his memoirs:

> At that time, the whole sugar trade of Queensland depended on the Kanaka labour. Labour ships used to go round the islands recruiting natives and, of course, their earnings depended largely on the time taken to get back with a full cargo of labourers, so that the temptation to collect them by fair means or foul was very great. These labour ships were usually manned by one or two whites with a crew of islanders who had learned a little English – mostly bad language. The Queensland Govt. had gone so far as to put a government official on each labour ship to see that the natives had fair play.

On 15 June, Marx reported that he had communicated with the natives off Cape Hunter. He commented on the difference in the natives' attitudes: 'The people were very timid at the anchorage but not a bit afraid further to the Westward.' Sailing to Rossel Island, he had 'some of the nastiest navigation it was ever my luck to have'. Captain Clayton of the *Diamond* had also declared the area 'a villainous place full of reefs, a few days more like yesterday and today will turn my hair grey'. Marx left Rossel to sail for Teste and Blanchard. On the way, he and his men boarded *Hopeful*, a labour vessel they thought was carrying contraband black labour or other items. She seemed to be all correct but they could not question the occupants as they had no interpreter, essential for effective police work. They passed the Bell Rock and anchored at Blanchard, this time encountering a group of 'niggers who came down to the beach with spears. Fairclough was in a terrible funk and so I sent for Bruce and the Chief Engineer [and] went on board.'

On 3 July at Dinner Island, Marx again showed his resourcefulness. He decided he needed to supplement his diminishing coal. He made the acquaintance of Epinouso the Lefoo teacher and told him that he needed wood. The native teacher said he would cut some. This was the first time Marx had used wood to fuel the engine. He was anxious as to how well it would perform. On 4 July the *Elangowan*, the London Missionary Society ship, came in carrying the missionary, the Reverend McFarlane, and Hugh Millman, a police magistrate from Cooktown. *Swinger* had sprung a leak but Duggan repaired it for them. Meanwhile Sub Lieutenant Bruce was 'wooding' on board while Marx organised a big meeting of natives ashore and 'told them a lot of rot'. He described some of the rot in an official letter to the Commodore: *'I explained by means of the interpreters that the man-of-war had come not to prevent their going willingly but to prevent their being taken by force...'*. After that, Marx weighed anchor with the *Elangowan* in tow. He was relieved to find that the wood burnt fairly and gave them about three knots.

Constantly on the lookout for illegal traders, it did not take long for Marx to be involved in a major incident. He touched on it briefly in his diary, but perhaps the incident is best told from his memoirs. It was 9 July 1884 on a hot and lazy afternoon:

The monotony of our cruise in the Engineer group, to the Eastward of New Guinea, was broken by seeing a sail on the horizon one afternoon as we were sailing along with the sun on our backs, sitting aloft in the masthead looking out for reefs which were very common...the next thing was to overhaul her and see what she was.

As soon as she saw us she altered her course and turned away from us, so we raised steam to give chase. We threaded our way through various reefs, constantly having to turn back and find another passage in the hopes of getting alongside her before sundown...we just managed to do so and told her to anchor, so as to allow the Magistrate whom I had on board to examine the recruits. It was my good fortune to take Mr. Hugh Millman on board my ship before I went for the cruise...

Having anchored the ship on the lee side of one of the reefs which was not above water, Millman went on board to examine her. He found that they had about sixty boys, for forty of whom they had no interpreter, it was quite impossible for them to understand the nature of their engagement. ...having satisfied myself that the men had been illegally obtained, I had the Captain and Mate on board. I said to Bruce, one of my officers, 'We have caught this fellow red handed and he must not get away now. I'm going to send you on board tomorrow to keep an eye on him.'

'Yes Sir, I see,' he said, looking a bit glum.

'First of all, we will hear what he has to say for himself,' I went on.

'Shall I send for him now, Sir?'

'Yes,' I replied, 'we will get it over.'

When we had asked all the necessary questions and obtained all the information from him that we could, I said, 'You are a pair of rascals and a disgrace to any country. I am going to send you into port with one of my officers on board.'

The Captain of the disgraced ship, with a face like thunder slouched off muttering oaths and threats under his breath – something about: 'Waiting until he could get hold of me, and cursing me, my ancestors, home, possessions and anything else.'

Then started the job of making out the numerous certificates that were necessary. This occupied everybody who could write on board the *Swinger*, until midnight when I sent the Captain back to his ship on his giving me his word of Honour that he would 'play no monkey tricks' and would loyally support the officer I was going to send him into port with.

About midnight that night we went to bed thoroughly well tired out after a day at the masthead conning the ship and half a night spent in making out the necessary forms. Previously to this I first told the Captain of the *Forest King* that if he tried to get away during the night I should sink him.

I had hardly been in bed for what I thought was five minutes when the Quarter-Master came running down and reported that they were throwing coca-nuts overboard from the *Forest King*. I came up with my binoculars and saw that it was men they were throwing overboard. There was no land for them to swim to. They would simply be drowned or eaten by sharks, so I called away the boats and the men went away in their jumpers, not having time to put their trousers on and proceeded to rescue these men. We picked up seventeen or eighteen but more than half the forty men were missing in the morning.

This is how the Captain kept his word of Honour.

The next morning I sent Sub Lt. Bruce and four men to take charge of her...who I provided with pistols, handcuffs and irons in case of necessity.

Sub Lieutenant Bruce took the *Forest King* safely to Brisbane. He had some trouble with the Master but when he commandeered all the liquor on board, and threw it into the sea, there was no more trouble.

Marx had to return to Brisbane to be available for the Vice Admiralty Court of Inquiry into his actions about the *Forest King*. He was gratified when '*Diamond* came in and Dale [Captain before Clayton] said I had done a plucky thing taking *Forest King*. I like him...'. Not everyone was pleased with what he had done. The vested interests of the traders were threatened and feeling ran high against him in Brisbane. Douglas, Chief of Police, warned him not to go into the main streets in his uniform. He had to take a back street to get to the court. It was a great *cause célèbre* in Brisbane – three barristers were told off for the naval side, including the Chief Justice's son. The famed Virgil Power stood for the prosecution:

Sydney Morning Herald, 9 October 1884:

> The case of Regina v. the owners of *Forest King*…
>
> In this case the owners of the *FK*, which was recently seized by HMS *Swinger*, are charged under the Polynesian Kidnapping Act with decoying South Sea Islanders for employment to Queensland, and the action is for the condemnation of the ship, her goods and effects, as forfeited to her majesty. The Defendants, on the other hand, claim the restoration of the ship and £5000 damages for her restoration. The case is likely to occupy the court for some days.

Marx was anxious. '*The trial is started the Governor and Griffiths premier approve. So hurrah I hope to win…*'. The trial took three days. It opened before the Chief Justice, Sir C Lilley. Marx thought the cross-examination by Power '*very distasteful. The trial was a troublesome affair. I thought at one time it was going against me but nil desperandum we pulled through in the end.*' He recalled later in his memoirs that the morning when the verdict was to be given, he had met a man who had been at the Queensland Club the night before where the Chief Justice, half-drunk, and lying on a sofa, had expressed his views and was heard to say, 'I suppose I must give a verdict for that – Marx.' In the event, he exonerated Marx and declared there were reasonable grounds for seizure…. Marx was relieved. Had the case gone against him, he could have been in trouble. He had the satisfaction of receiving a letter from Commodore Erskine on 5 November 1884, which summed up the incident and vindicated him in Admiralty eyes:

> Having perused the evidence given on the Trial, I am of the opinion that, having received Mr. Millman's report, and having satisfied yourself, after further investigation, that 5 natives had been recruited from New Guinea without a possibility of the terms of their agreement being explained to them, that you were

not only justified in the course you pursued, but that it would have been a failure of duty had you not sent that Vessel before the Vice Admiralty Court for adjudication.

Under the circumstances, while regretting that the '*Forest King*' has not been condemned, I entirely approve of your proceedings in the matter, which I trust will have good effect.

At Brisbane, Marx took the opportunity to renew supplies of beef and tea and ships' biscuit. He suggested to Admiralty that since the ship could only hold biscuit in the tin-lined bread rooms, otherwise it went bad (sixteen cases held on deck had gone bad since leaving Sydney), and could not hold more than fifty days' supply, the biscuit should be supplied in bags instead of boxes. It could then hold 120 days' supply. He asked for extra oars since the ship had so much work to do, and a new assistant paymaster, since his old one had suffered from a 'friendly fire' accident: he had been shot in the foot during a landing party, 'poor Dixon was shot by C. Scott AB I was awfully cut up about it poor chap MacKinlay got the bullet out that night... .' When Marx left Brisbane, it was with some relief: 'I was not sorry. I liked it for some reasons and for some people but had too many worries to make it altogether a pleasant recollection. Miss L. Heath paid me a pretty complement [sic] such a one I doubt if I ever have again in my life.' In view of future events, let us hope that he did.

In November Marx returned one of the native labourers who had escaped from Port Mackie to Murray Island, 'this labour traffic is villainous...'. A few days later he returned three other native boys rescued from the labour trade –

the New Guinea boys I returned at Vaga Vaga were received with Great Joy, the speech I made was that I was very glad to see these people again and that I had brought back 3 boys they said they were glad to get back the three but why had I not brought back the remainder that their engagement was long up and the friends believed that they were dead and had cooked food for them and thrown it away...

This entry ends with,

> …got into Killerton at 9 pm…. . One of the Chiefs from Rabo
> had had a rare good cannibal feast that day as they had killed
> three men and eaten two of them he was very sick on board
> the Nelson that night.

There is much controversy over the nature of cannibalism in the South
Sea Islands but there is no doubt that naval officers of the time believed
it to be a common practice. Even if they had not observed it themselves,
they felt that there was plenty of evidence to indicate it. Marx had
conversations via an interpreter, with a native chief on Skelton Island
in the engineer group and was told about cannibal feasts. Here, he saw,

> The only cannibal pot that we came across. It consisted of a
> stout pot some 18 in in diameter and 6 or 7 ft high. The top
> was carved into the shape of a man's head and below this carving
> about 5½ feet from the ground was fixed a large round board
> about 4 ½ feet in diameter and an inch and a half thick. The
> lower part of the pot had two figures carved in its sides. The
> platform when I saw it had sprouting coconuts on it but the
> Chief said that its original purpose was for distributing the
> bodies of the victims from, the Chief cutting up the body and
> giving it to others reserving the head for his own share. Mr.
> MacFarlane the New Guinea missionary was with me on this
> occasion his object was to place a native teacher there The chief
> having given up Cannibalism after the Brooker feast.

At the end of the year, it was time for Commodore Erskine's reign
on the Australian station to come to an end. Marx went aboard *Nelson*
to say goodbye. So far, Marx's commission had redounded to his credit.
He was making a name for himself, albeit a small one, and when he
left, the Commodore said that he had 'never told the *Swinger* to do
anything which had not been done to his entire satisfaction'. He also

wrote to Marx '*to take the opportunity of expressing my appreciation of the zealous and efficient manner in which the duties you have been called upon to perform in the Swinger have been at all times carried out*'.

The work of the Australia station now continued under Admiral Tryon.[6] Captain Clayton, who was to continue as Second in Command on the station went to greet the new admiral. 'Tryon is such a big fellow, over six feet and big in proportion. I hope he may be as nice a fellow as the departing Commodore is.' Although still only a lieutenant, Marx's work as a captain and de facto Deputy Commissioner continued. It involved further trouble with natives and difficult white men. He was gratified that the new Admiral Tryon was pleased with his work and wrote him several letters approving of his actions. When, in May of 1885, it was back to Sydney for another ship's inspection by Captain Lake, the result was even better: 'The Ship is efficient and very clean. The men are well trained in Gunnery, small arm and cutlass drill, and fairly smart aloft,' Admiral Tryon complimented him on it.

Marx's next sailing orders were for the New Hebrides group, to 'call at various Islands and superintend the labor traffic...'

> *You are to render such assistance as is in your power to British subjects carrying on legitimate trade, or located among the Islands.*
>
> *You are not to use force against, or inflict punishment on the natives, nor are you to land men to enforce a decision, or for any other reason, against them; and you are only to do so should it be absolutely necessary to save life. Your action with them is practically limited to enquiry and report.*

Tryon's letters to his captains always showed a keen understanding of the diplomatic niceties involved in their work, and a surprisingly progressive and sympathetic (considering the tenor of much Victorian imperialism) attitude to the natives. He sent a private note to Marx asking him for a description of Noumea and signs of any French activity in the area. The struggle for new colonies was mounting – Americans, Germans and French officials were in the area. Marx's report when received prompted the grateful thanks of Tryon and Admiralty.

> *I am directed by their Lordships to convey to you, and to Lieut. H.H. Torlesse, their appreciation of the zeal and care shown in making this sketch survey which will be of use to the Hydrographic Department.*

Tryon referred to Marx's admirable report on the defences of *Noumea* and *New Caledonia*.

On 8 June, Marx received another set of sailing orders. This time there was a little more room for autonomous activity, perhaps reflecting Tryon's increasing confidence in his abilities.

> *2 You will act in harmony with His Excellency the Special Commissioner, still you must in each case decide for yourself as to the course you will adopt, for the responsibility rests with the Naval Officer for every action taken by him.*

> *3 Special attention is drawn to the Station Orders, as to your dealings with the natives and to the Pacific Act. While protection to legitimate traders is to be given, wrong doers are not to be supported, and natives should be protected from the lawless acts of white men…*

> *4 The main object of your service in the North is to supervise vessels and trade where civilization and barbarism are in contact and to promote good understanding and good order. It is hardly possible to overestimate the value of successful efforts to establish friendly relations with natives.*

> *5 You are not to remain at anchor at any one port for more than a few days.*

7 You are at liberty to call at Townsville or Cooktown to refresh your crew, taking care that demands to keep up your supplies are sent to the Depot Sydney in ample time with a statement showing when and where they should be sent, and how long the stock on board will last.

8 You are to visit especially those ports frequented by traders and also mission stations, and you are to acquaint me of your actual and proposed movements by every opportunity and always leaving word at the last port of call where you have gone.

In the pursuance of these orders, Marx's commission on the Australia station was full of incident. His accounts cover a lively experience: natives and white people were murdered – he had to investigate the murder of Mr and Mrs Webb who had been killed and had their heads cut off by natives who then tried to attack him with spears as he returned to the ship. He fired shots into them and they dispersed. He had the job of burying the remains of Mr and Mrs Webb. Accidents occurred – a large canoe he was towing, full of men and pigs, overturned with great loss of life. There was much 'benighted beastly navigation' that had to be managed, especially around Aroma. New land had to be annexed for the Queen. Clayton described how it was done:

This small, unidentified island is an old volcano, the inhabitants thought it was going to begin again and prudently retired. We saw some sheep and some goats. I hurried back to the flag staff which was soon erected, my proclamation in the name of the Queen, in a strong glass case screwed on to the staff. Another one put in a bottle and buried. Then the Union Jack was hoisted and we off caps while I read the document and another bit of Great Britain was taken formal possession of. If there had been any inhabitants we should have fired a royal salute but there were none.[7]

The constant request by missionaries and local government officials for the presence of British warships meant that ships were always in demand. Missionaries were vital as unofficial government / naval helpers. Chalmers, the great London Missionary Society missionary, was particularly useful – and kind. He gave Marx his rug on one cold occasion, and presented the men of *Swinger* with a Christmas pig. 'He was a wonderful interpreter and generally went abroad first to make the preliminary attempt on the various villages, in fact a first rate fellow altogether. He disregarded safety first...'

Dog Swinger died. An event significant enough to be recorded.

A major incident in 1886 was the occasion on which Marx was attacked by natives. New South Wales newspapers were full of reports and rumours: Captain Marx had been killed, Captain Marx had lost an arm... . Here is a description of what actually happened as Marx gave it to Admiralty:

6 July 1886 – I anchored on the East side of the large bay on the North of St. Agnau. The natives came off the following morning but were at first shy however after having been given some tobacco they became more assured and brought off yams etc.

2 Wishing to obtain information about the murder of Gerrett...and also to find out the movement of any white traders that might have been there I landed at 4 pm, taking the usual precautions of a covering boat & on shore I met one of the natives who had been on board during the morning to whom I made a present, the other natives were very shy but I distributed some tobacco amongst them through the medium of the same man.

3 After about 10 minutes when I was within 10 yards of the boat and there being three of our party on shore close to me I handed him some more tobacco for things he had brought down. As he took it with one hand, he struck me over the head and right hand with a large trade knife he had in the other and jumped into the bush. Dr. McKinlay who was close to me fired at once at him but without result.

4 For this outrage on his part I can give no reason whatever except that he had told the interpreters that some men had been taken away a long time ago by white men (who they were I could not find out) and it may have resulted from a desire to revenge them.

5 A large number of men with arms were seen hiding behind a rock at the same time I think his premature action spoiled a plan for an attack on a larger scale.

6 Seeing that making any more enquiries was hopeless I returned on board and on the following day took the ship to the bay in hopes of learning something about the cause of the attack but the natives would not come near us. After waiting an hour I left for Dinner Island.

7 St. Agnau is seldom visited is very mountainous and covered with bush and the natives bear a very bad name.

Captain Clayton, who had also had his troubles dealing with recalcitrant natives, sympathised with Marx but thought he should have been firmer in his reaction. As senior officer, he followed up the incident:

Got into communication with the natives where they attacked Marx. They were very defiant and insolent and refused to give up the man and said they would fight us. This all comes because he did not promptly punish them. I fired a few shells to clear the bush of any lurking gentlemen and then sent Shakespear [First Lieutenant] in to burn the small village. He had a terrible job

landing as the surf was very heavy. However, after much trouble
he got on shore, of course very wet and did all that was required,
destroyed a few canoes and burnt a few houses, rather an
inadequate punishment for trying to kill Marx but there was
nothing else be done...[8]

Marx regarded the native's attack as revenge for the labour traders who had kidnapped some of his people: '...their immutable law is a head for a head, what is worse they don't care much whose head it is as long as they succeed in getting one, fortunately they were unsuccessful in getting mine'. Marx thought the native had wounded him rather severely, but he did not try to obtain compensation for the injury until many years later when he was told it was too late. It is worth noting that both Marx and Clayton were able to appreciate the good qualities of the natives. Both admired the dignified Chief Koapina. Marx noted, 'Caopina came in. He holds himself aloof from the other natives, is a fine man.'

The most important incident of Marx's commission on the Australia station had nothing to do with his naval life, heroic or otherwise. It was his marriage to Lily Heath in 1866. It comes as a great surprise because Marx's diary for 1886 is missing, and although Lily is mentioned in 1885, as with his first love Edith, we have no information as to her appearance or character. Indeed, at this point it seems his wife might have been any one of three sisters. In his first visit to Brisbane in 1883, Lily appears as one name among many of the colonial girls he meets. In the fortnight's visit to Brisbane in September 1885, for the trial of *Forest King*, Marx meets her family, the Heaths, and for the first time has tea with the mother! 'Sunday, 13 September, Tead with the Heaths. Mrs. H. anxious to know if I am engaged... .' This certainly sounds like the fishing fleet in operation. Colonial girls and their mothers were generally regarded as fishing for desirable British naval officer husbands. No doubt Mrs Heath was no exception. Her husband was Captain (RN) G.P. Heath, Queen's Harbour Master at Brisbane. '...walked back from church with Miss L.H.'. There appear to have been three Heath daughters, Isabelle, Ethel and Lily. Marx socialised with all three but at the end of that first fortnight he tried to send a letter to one of them: 'Tried to send a letter to Miss Heath by chucking it on board *Pilot* schooner and then by throwing it on board *Ariel* labour schooner whom we passed under sail. I wonder whether for good or ill, they both went to the bottom of Moreton Bay.'

At this stage in Marx's enigmatic account it is difficult to know which Miss Heath it was. The plot thickens. When Marx returned to Brisbane at the end of November, his first two days were spent calling at Government House, seeing among others Isabelle and Lily Heath. Then almost every day was spent with the Heaths:

5 December – bought D'Acourt's horse for Miss Isabelle Heath, £30, badly ribbed up.

8 December – spent evening with the Heaths, asked I [Isabelle] an important Q, reply indefinite.

9 December – rode early in the morning with Isabelle and one or two others, repeated my question.

It seems that Isabelle had now taken his fancy. Then Marx had to leave for Sydney. A naval life did not lend itself to courting; managing things by letter was not easy. When an answering letter came, 'Got answer from Isabelle Heath, very nice letter, unsatisfactory, well, I feel a load like a millstone off my neck bad for Heath burns his cheque £30 and said nothing about it.' Marx's brevity now turns to total obscurity. It is difficult to know exactly what happened here. The likely explanation is that Isabelle's father did not want his prospective son-in-law to be out of pocket over the gift of a horse to his daughter, especially in a deal that turned out to be bad, so he endeavoured to give him a cheque to defray the cost. Marx refused to accept the offer and burnt the cheque. In a memorandum of 'Things Lent' etc., at the front of the diary for 1885, he notes again, 'Burnt Capt. Heath's cheque £30, Dec. 15th.'

However, it would seem his devotion to Isabelle was short-lived and Marx was glad to find himself free again in Sydney among 'some pretty girls'. Miss Ethel Heath was in Sydney and he enjoyed her company with others. Marx concluded his diary for 1885 with, 'The last day of the old year not an unpleasant one and one in which I have learnt much.'

It comes as a surprise to learn that on 13 April 1886, in Brisbane, Lieutenant and Commander John Locke Marx married Celia Georgina Heath known as Lily. They married in St Mary's Church, Kangaroo Point, Brisbane. Unfortunately and frustratingly, we have no personal diary for 1886, only naval papers, so we can never be sure what made Marx decide to marry Lily Heath. Did he just think it was time he took a wife and she was available? Naval officers generally married at the rank of Commander. Early marriage was frowned upon. Did Lily just want a meal ticket to England? According to family understanding, she said she would marry Marx but told him she did not love him. So far as Marx was concerned, he had a naval life, which suited him, and domesticity never weighed heavily on him. Perhaps he just wanted legitimate sex, perhaps offspring. He was thirty-four years old. Lily was twenty-five, 'getting on', in old-maid terms! It seems not to have been a particularly happy marriage. Marx retained his particularity for a pretty woman and the separation of naval life made marriage difficult. We have to go to his diary for 1887 to learn more of the relationship. It seems to have been ordinary enough to start with, 'an explosion, I to blame…'. They went to events together and by January of 1887, Lily was pregnant and feeling unwell. Marx was at Sydney with her and they set about looking for somewhere to live together.

But other changes were now afoot. Tryon was leaving the Australia station and was replaced by Admiral Fairfax:[9] '*the Officers received him in sword and frock coats on board Nelson*'. Marx went down to say goodbye to him. It had been a good relationship. Marx had been able to send Tryon private letters and Tryon had had confidence in Marx's judgement. It was time for Marx too, to return home. His commission had come to an end and he received his paying-off orders for 3 May. But the last days were not good days. There was malaria and suspected typhoid in *Swinger*, Roberts was very ill and one man, Baker, died. Lily's pregnancy was going badly. She was *seedy* and not very well. As the baby became imminent, she was the main concern of Marx's diary but there were still other matters to be dealt with. On 4 May, when 'Lake paid us off and said the ship was dirty', Marx had to see the Admiral and expected 'a bad prospect'. But next day the baby arrived:

> Lil's pains awful, confined at 7.45 am. Girl. Cox attended, Nurse Druse, Mrs. Silvester lent a hand. All well. Saw Admiral and explained matters to him. Court of enquiry aboard Lark. Pullen (Captain) says he is to be tried for loss of £32 from Cash Box. Lake again. What a brute. Saw Admiral and told him about Lake.

Life improved again as Lily recovered – 'Lil doing well, and infant' – sister Isabelle and the family came, last social visits were made, and final arrangements were put in hand for the paying off of *Swinger*. Marx did not record his feelings on this occasion, but we may imagine what he felt. Officers and men had been together for three years, in close proximity, sharing all experiences, good or bad, depending on each other for professional competence, bravery and good company. It was a wrench to leave them, but he had other things to think about now – a wife to settle in England, a child to care for. Having said farewell to his men, he was ready to take passage home on HMS *Tyne*. On 9 May 1887, with Lily, the baby, and a nursemaid who 'nearly dropped the infant in the sea', safely on board, goodbyes having been said, he was seen off by a flotilla of ships and well-wishers as he took his leave of Australia. It had been a particularly successful commission. He was well placed now in the promotion stakes, at a transition time when the Old Navy was about to expand into the New Navy and make different demands on its officers. What would come next?

1 Conway, ibid, p111.

2 Special leave – a reward for long and good service.

3 Rear Admiral Charles Thomas Curme.

4 Admiral Sir William Houston Stewart KCB, GCB.

5 C Cross and F Pike, respective Lieutenant and Commanders.

6 Vice Admiral Sir George Tryon had been educated at Eton and joined the Navy when he was sixteen years old. His successful and promising career came to an end when he was commanding HMS *Victoria* and gave a wrong order to *Victoria* and *Camperdown* to turn six cables towards each other. Captain Albert Markham of *Camperdown* obeyed in the face of obvious danger and the two ships collided with great loss of life. Tryon himself was killed.

7 Description of annexation by Captain Clayton. Letter to wife, 1 August 1886.

8 Clayton in letter to his wife, 16 November 1886.

9 Admiral Sir Henry Fairfax CB, KCB.

Ten

Commander (1888–1895)

*'Come as soon as you can and help us, we are
in a mighty tight place...'*

In July of 1889, after another short period of top-up torpedo training
at *Vernon*, and work on the central battery ironclad, *Hercules*, Marx's
competence and zeal on the Australia station was rewarded by his official
promotion to the rank of Commander. In June of 1888, Tryon had
recommended to Admiralty that he should be promoted: 'Sir G. Tryon
specially recommends for promotion.'[1] For the time being, Marx's
detailed daily journal ceased. Perhaps marriage inhibited accurate reports
of his activities, perhaps life was so busy and satisfying that he no longer
needed the catharsis and interest of a daily journal. He was now living
with Lily at Breech Farm, Bighton, the other side of Alresford from
Arlebury; a house he had fallen in love with on his return to England
in 1877. Perhaps he felt it was dangerous or unbecoming in a senior
naval officer to acknowledge such vulnerability in a daily journal, as
he had done earlier. Perhaps he thought it dangerous to leave a diary
accidentally accessible even if every page was marked 'private'. For
the moment we have to rely on other sources: Admiralty
communications, letter books, personal papers and the brief entries he
now made in his intermittent diaries.

The Victorian Navy was now in transition. It was changing from the predominantly 'ad hoc' sailing Navy manning the imperial Pax Britannica in a scattered fleet of corvettes, sloops, schooners and gunboats, to the 'efficient'[2] steam / turbine Navy of battleships, cruisers and destroyers that would be amalgamated into the central, home battle fleets and characterise the New Edwardian Navy. The increase in naval finance after the Naval Defence Acts of 1889, which had pleased an anxious populace, marked the beginning of this growing, powerful New Navy that was eventually ready to take on any nation that threatened its hegemony. Indeed, its power and prestige became increasingly supremacist and mythical:

> The Navy is very old and very wise…her wisdom is on record…it works in the unconscious blood of those who serve her. [3]

Her admirals became men with 'keen and level gaze', not only exercising the 'vigilance and toil'[4] demanded of them but also making an impression 'by the magnificence of bullion, epaulettes, medals and white-clutched sword'.[5] Every little boy proudly wore his sailor's uniform. In view of this change, a rule-of-thumb terminology may be used to chart the development: the Old Navy ran from roughly 1860 to 1885, the Transitional from roughly 1885 to 1895 and the New Navy from 1895 to 1914. Officers themselves perceived this change. Looking back over a long career, Lord Chatfield declared, 'It was a transformation, not only of material development of the service, but of the mentality of the whole personnel.'[6] In this perhaps he was not entirely accurate, Marx never quite developed a New Navy attitude.

Marx's first commission as a commander came in *Belleisle* towards the end of the transitional period. *Belleisle* was one of the older ships, a second-class, armoured, twin-screw battleship launched in 1876; a ship of the First Reserve Coast Guard Service at Kingstown. Marx had some valuable experience here, as the ship was involved in the steam tactics and gridiron manoeuvres of 1891 and 1892, which would stand him in good stead in the mechanised New Navy. Captain Frederick Boardman declared his Commander a 'very good zealous and valuable officer', but Marx's next commission was probably more to his liking. It came in one of the newer ships that marked the transitional period, the third-class, protected cruiser, *Blanche*. She had been launched in 1889 and was now stationed off the east coast of Africa, at Zanzibar. There was still much of the Old Navy work of the Pax Britannica to be undertaken by these transitional cruisers, since the increasing numbers meant a need for more commanders and captains. These were good years for promotions.

Blanche was a Barracouta-class cruiser. The Barracouta class was four small cruisers designed for service on distant stations where docking facilities were limited. They were sheathed in wood and copper and among the first to be fitted with a true protective deck, triple expansion engines and a main armament of six four-foot seven-inch quick-firing (QF) guns, four three-pounder QFs, two machine guns and two torpedo tubes. *Blanche* carried 120 men. The posting promised action. These cruisers often performed the function of a gunboat. Ships on the east and west coast of Africa were likely to be involved in all sorts of clashes with recalcitrant natives and aggressive tribal chiefs. Punitive expeditions by naval brigades were often mounted against them and this involved the supportive action of the gunboat. The prospect of individual action in one of the new armoured cruisers was more to Marx's taste than any tedious peace-time posting in a large battleship.

In the course of 1893 there had been numerous difficulties with the natives of East Africa, particularly in relation to the confines of the Imperial British East Africa Company, and inland in the neighbourhood of Lake Nyassa and the River Shire. The difficulties arose from the continuation of trouble that had occurred on the Witu coast (about 230 miles north of Zanzibar) when nine German traders had been murdered, by orders, it was said, of the Sultan, Fumo Bakari. A punitive expedition, successfully led by Vice Admiral Sir Edmund Fremantle in 1890, succeeded in avenging the crime with little resistance and no loss of life. However, by 1893, Fumo Omari, successor of the Sultan of Witu, had grown restless and dangerous. He began to commit outrages and it was decided that a further punitive expedition by officers and men of the naval brigades was necessary to restore the required order. In August of 1893, just prior to Marx's posting, a brigade led by Captain George Lindley of the cruiser *Blanche*, Commander Lewis Sampson of the sloop *Swallow*, and Lieutenant Francis Cole of the gunboat *Sparrow*, had set out on such an expedition. This time there was resistance and brisk fighting. Pumwani, Omari's stronghold, was taken and a stoker and two officers were killed: Lieutenant Maurice Fitzmaurice of *Blanche* and Sub Lieutenant William Gervis of *Sparrow*; several men were mentioned in despatches and Captain Lindley gained the Companion of the Order of the Bath (CB). Marx must have looked forward to the prospect of continued action in the region and a chance to distinguish himself in a similar way.

The chance came in what was known as the Lamu Forest expedition, Lamu being close to where the brigade started inland. This expedition arose from the fact that Fumo Omari was not prepared to knuckle down under British control. He reinforced Pumwani despite agreement not to. This was not to be tolerated. So in October of 1893 another naval brigade was launched against him and this time Marx was involved, as he was senior officer in the area. On 2 October, stationed at Kismayu, Marx received handwritten orders from Commander Frank Henderson in the third-class cruiser *Racoon*, at Lamu. They show the detailed preparations that were made for this sort of naval operation. As Second in Command, Marx was left at sea with *Blanche* to co-ordinate the operation:

Orders:
Communication can be made by runner to Mkwumbi in six hours.
The Launch on requisition to Superintendant of J.B.E.A. Co.
can be at your disposal, the lighter only being required in case of
re-embarking.

For sending anything down, or up, one of the Steam Cutters of
the Ships with small boat in tow should be able to do all our
work. Until the creeks are well known Mr. McLallan will kindly
supply a pilot.

Telegrams Important telegrams in cypher. Those to Consul General must be by (*mode of sending*) by Army and Navy Signal book.

Telegraph Wire If broken down, the Swallow must keep up necessary communication to Malinde – only 60 to 90 feet [?] distant.

Medical Until return of Blanche Surgeon of Swallow must not disembark for good though his services might be necessary, temporarily at Mmkumbi.

Sick or wounded. If there should be unfortunately any large number, I am sure a portion of the Residency might be turned into a Hospital, until the opportunity occurs for sending them to Zanzibar. I gather at Mombasa there are no nurses.

Coal Ships must not be run out of coal – it can always be sent from Zanzibar, if necessary to incur the expense. I have ordered 60 tons for this Ship by the Kilwa, a little might be spared if required.

HMS Swallow Use every effort that there may be no delay in sending the Swallow's landing party to the front.

Seeing that the launch is ready on Wednesday morning to go straight alongside on arrival – the lighter would not be required. Use our Ship's boats it is quicker.

If arriving Tuesday use steam boats.

Inform me, by carrier, of Swallow's arrival, and when her party can be at Mkumbi.

The Senior Officer will consider the Ship's presence under his orders and in my absence carry out the ordinary duties of the Division, referring to me, what only can be answered by myself.

<u>Order</u> No ship to be detached from Lamu, except for communicative purposes to Melinde, returning at latest following day.

Any required deviation from the above order (except caused by direction of Commander in Chief) <u>must be referred direct to me for approval</u>.

Detailed instructions were also given to the men before leaving: From Henderson on *Racoon*, 1 October 1893:

The landing party as told off will be alongside and ready to proceed sharp at 4.30 am on Tuesday next. The Cutters of the different ships being used as required for conveyance of their own men – One officer in each boat, the remainder in the steam launch, store will be placed in the lighter.

<u>Kits</u> Officers to carry one suit of white, one suit of blue, cap, cover and helmet.

<u>Officers</u> Khaki suits may be worn on the march and unless otherwise directed.

<u>Men</u> To have complete kit (worn or carried) as follows:
  1 blue suit
  1 white working dress
  2 Pairs of socks
  1 Check shirt
  (for sleeping in but optional)
  1 white hat

1 blanket
2 flannels
1 cap and cover
1 Knife lanyard
1 Towel (To be carried and mustered with men as
sunshade, placed in three folds over right shoulder
if under fire)

(All this to be rolled in blanket lengthways and tied with 5 stops)

Ammunition   Each man to carry 40 rounds
Each ship to carry 60 rounds

Each ship to provide requisite spare pistol ammunition.

The remainder of spare ammunition will be provided by Racoon (6000 rounds)

Sufficient ammunition to be carried by our own carriers attached to companies to complete 70 rounds.

The ammunition bag may be left behind (in case of necessity the haversack may be used)

Racoon and Blanche provide magazine with rockets etc. etc. – the list is forwarded herewith – also 2 cases of dry gun cotton, 2 of wet each, Bickford's fuze and one Battery to be provided with wire.

Victualling By the Racoon. Cooking and Mess utensils, soap and tobacco to be provided by our own ships.

Spirit Ration Spirits will be issued in the evening

Underline On Tuesday Morning The men will be given optional Cocoa at
3.30 am

Optional Cocoa Parade at 4 am

Dress Hats, Blue Suit, leggings, haversacks and water bottles.
(haversacks to be worn on the back)

Surgeon's Party Surgeons of Racoon, Swallow, with their Sick
Bay men.

Blanche taking medical charge at Lamu
Surgeon of Swallow attends at field base
Field boxes provided by Racoon.
Camp Routine and Orders
Senior Lieutenant of Blanche responsible, assisted by senior
Lieutenant of Racoon
These two officers will carry out the ordinary duties of Field
Officers

There were other communications before the expedition was ready to
set out. Marx was given a rough plan of the country around Lamu,
and Henderson wrote anxiously,

> …since I have given my orders the Consul General has
> apparently woke up…and requires a ship at Zanzibar…demands
> on the present squadron are heavy…. It is a pity that twin screw
> ships have not a complete logitudinal bulkhead, then we might
> make six=three…in great haste…it won't be much of a show
> unless I am there.

Although Marx must have enjoyed the buzz of preparing for the
expedition, he was not part of the main fighting party and was probably
disappointed not to be so. He oversaw the operation from *Blanche,*

receiving and sending messages, despatching various boats as required, receiving on-the-spot reports from Henderson. It was a short-lived affair. By 5 October Henderson was reporting to Marx that all had gone well, the party was returning to the ships, the weather had been good and the men were doing well, with 'very hard work'. He also bemoaned the fact that he was 'extremely dirty'! Marx received a final letter from Henderson to be sent on to headquarters at Simonstown:

To Navy, Simonstown

Have completed expedition…Tamwani defended and fire opened upon us – formed, advancing quickly, the gate smartly charged. Gate very strong and loopholed – otherwise fire and defence very weak – one seaman of Racoon slightly wounded…advancing to the westward at Pandengras…shelled the village, then rapidly advancing, the gates were secured without resistance, natives burning village as they left…decided to advance no further, returned Tamwani in the morning and completed destruction of gates. Moved to Tongeni through forest – one village was fired by natives on our approach – gates destroyed. Near Tongeni a strong stockade and [?] were shelled – only distant firing met with. Stockade and gates destroyed. Consider from prisoners, district has been quite surprised. Regret that permanent occupation is not following. Further operations useless without it…Men all well. Racoon.

Henderson was always very conscious of the health of his men; not only a humanitarian gesture but also expedient to the efficiency of the brigade. At the end of October, he wrote to Marx, 'The Swallows have had a little fever on board – but all relapses I think. I hope your people are getting stronger. I am very thankful that we have no sickness or a single one of fever.' He had insisted on the surgeon remaining in *Swallow*, there would be other medical assistance in Zanzibar. The Consul General was down with fever and had to be hospitalised.

In December of 1893, Their Lordships were pleased to express their approval of the Lamu expedition and 'the manner in which the service has been performed'. Names of officers and men would be noted. A number of Zanzibari troops had been involved and the Sultan was thanked for his co-operation. Marx had taken a backseat in the action but at least his name would be noted in the endeavour.

After the Lamu expedition things quietened down, though there was still anxiety that the dissident Somalis in the area remained worryingly well provided with ammunition. However, the Consul was satisfied that if steamers appeared regularly to protect the few Europeans working in the area, it would avoid the necessity of sending a man of war and save future punitive expeditions.

In July 1894 there came welcome sailing orders for England via Sierra Leone, St Vincent, Cape de Verde islands and Las Palmas. It was to be a short holiday for Marx after so long away, not much time for him to make a good relationship with Lily and his now seven-year-old daughter, Constance, and his little four-year-old son, George. Family memory remarks that there seemed to be little overt love shown to the children as they grew up, but Marx was away from home most of his early married life and as his contemporary Captain Clayton noted, 'A Captain of a man of war is too much of an autocrat and it is not a good school for managing children or people not accustomed to discipline.'

Orders soon came to return to Africa to take command of another protected cruiser, this time the *Barrosa* on the west coast of Africa at Sierra Leone. Commander Marx was ordered to join her at Zanzibar.

After 'a long and dusty journey' to Brindisi, travelling in a British India steamer that was full of cockroaches and had a captain 'with the best vocabulary of all I had ever met', he arrived at Zanzibar and was pleased to find the ship 'in capital order'. He looked forward to his new command. Since *Barrosa* was like *Blanche*, another Barracouta third-class, twin-screw, protected cruiser, launched in 1889, she was reassuringly familiar. She carried 160 men. His executive consisted of three officers: Lieutenant Marcus R Hill, Edward L Booty (navigating officer) and Walter H Cowan; the paymaster was Stanley Elliott; the staff engineer, William Smith; the surgeon, Joseph McDonnell MD. The boatswain, Harry Clarke, was provided 'in lieu of a Sub-Lieutenant' – does this indicate shortage of junior officers, now there was a greater demand for officers in the expanded New Navy?

No sooner had Marx arrived than he was involved in an incident with a slaving dhow. It was flying a German flag and he captured it. It is an interesting story and again, best told in the detail of his own words, as he remembered the incident some years later. Contemporary letters bear out the truth of this undated account:

> We arrived at Zanzibar at 9 am one morning…I found the ship in capital order went on board the Barossa and my old friend Lindy much delighted at going home. When I finished taking over the confidential books a German dow [sic] came sailing in the harbour with a dirty rag as a German flag. Lindy said it was a slaver, so asking Lindy what the procedure was, he said, 'Send a boat and see what she is like and if she is reported as a slaver, take her.' At that I called away a boat and sent her to deal with her. On his return, the Lieutenant reported that her hold was covered in sand which was foul and that she carried a great deal of extra water. By this time L— had gone and my next procedure was to see Sir Reynold Rod who was charge d'affare at Zanzibar at the time. He was down with fever and in bed but he very kindly received me. He was looking very ill and not wanting to trouble him more than possible, I told him I had taken a German dow. He said, 'You must let her go.' I told him that knowing the international law, I could not do that as it would lay me open to an action for damage for detaining the ship. He then said, 'You'd better go and see judge Harding who deals with all English cases of slaves.' So I wished him a speedy recovery and set off on my travels to the judge. I set off to find the judge as soon as possible. The port authorities came off at once, telling me that I should probably find the governor at home. So, I put on my official dress, took the corporal marine in his. On my interviewing him and telling him of the arrest of the German dow he said to let her go at

once, 'I won't have her in my court.' So I said I was very sorry for that as she was undoubtedly a slaver and I don't intend to let her go. I have arrested her, she's a slaver and by international law she ought to be arrested. So I said goodbye and thanked him on his receiving me so well and returned to my ship.

The German dow was then becoming a nightmare. On considering the matter and having read up the International Law on the subject, I decided to try my luck at Dar Zalaam, so being a senior officer I raised steam 12 knots and having got the dow in tow so that she could not break off straight away, I decided to take her to Dar Salaam. She was a beautiful dow, quite new of 90 tons and the weather was simply glorious and the following day I arrived at Dar Zalaam. Everything in Dar Zalaam was perfect, the buoys freshly painted and all the houses in good order and the whole town showed the Germans tried to make themselves comfortable and the town as magnificent as possible. So I put on my best suit and folded the German flag in the best piece of tissue paper I could find, and proceeded to Government House where I found the governor, who was a Prince, a very charming person. I told him I had taken a German dow, which was undoubtedly a slaver, and had brought over for him to adjudicate on and had brought over the flag which had been disgraced and presented it to him. He was most courteous and most charming. I asked him if I might hand over to him the dow, she was bran new and 90 tons and I wanted no prize money and so the matter seemed settled.

He very kindly asked me to dine that night and I went to dinner. That night I dined with the Governor and the princess, his wife – a very charming lady…the Captain of the Condor was also dining there, a very nice fellow.

I told the Governor I had to sail in the morning and on arrival on board I found a large number of weapons on the quarter deck which had been sent on board from the dow by the German authorities. I had them put in a bread bag and sent them to the governor with a letter to say that it was quite impossible for me as a British officer to take anything out of a prize.

I then gave orders for steam to be raised by 4 am…having quite decided that the sooner I left and let the matter of the slaver to settle itself the better. So we sailed at 4 am. When I got to Zanzibar I saw Matthews, the Sultan's Prime Minister who apparently thought I had done the right thing, so I felt satisfied.

While in port I made it my business to see slaves who had been liberated and to get from them, through an interpreter, an account of their capture and journey to the coast. In almost all cases their capture was accompanied by wholesale slaughter, ravaging and destruction of the villages. On their way to the coast their treatment was exceedingly bad and when they fell out they were either speared or left to die of hunger and thirst. Of course, the women had had the worse time and when they could no longer carry their babies they had to be thrown away. When they reached the coast they were crowded into the holds of dhows. The holds were covered with sand. There was no sanitary accommodation and they were in this pestilential hole the whole time. Fortunately for those I had interviewed in Zanzibar they had only a day or two's sail; but for those taken to Arabia, their trials were very much longer. I asked several of them if they would like to be sent back to the places where they came from. They said they did not know where they had come from. The best answer I got was from one who said that Africa was like a big sea where there were great fishes and little fishes and he was a little fish and did not want to go back...

Slavery was still in existence in Zanzibar at the time I was there; but the slaves were really well treated and when they got old and useless they were given a piece of land and they built themselves a hut and lived in one of those parts called Shamba or smallholder. The entry of slaves was forbidden but there's no doubt that slavery did go on in the adjoining island where spices grow.

After a month, having heard no more of my slaver, I made a short visit to Dar es Salaam. The officials were most cordial and told me that the dhow had been condemned. They took us to see the crew who were expiating their crimes in neck irons, a remnant of the old regime for bringing in slaves. I shortly afterwards received a notification that the Germans had taken the dhow into their public service and had paid a small sum for her. My crew got £5 a ton prize money for having taken her. I also received a letter from the Admiralty to say that I was not to take any more dows as the Emperor did not wish any more dows to be taken, and the Captain of the French man o' war who escorted his dows every evening asked me if I should examine them. I said certainly not when under his escort. And I considered I was very well out of a delicate job.

The capture of slaving ships was a constant headache for British naval officers. They were committed to the task of freeing slaves. It was disillusioning to find that governments were not always of the same mind. Slaving ships could only be seized in international waters and these waters were clearly Turkish territorial waters.

Marx now had orders to sail from Zanzibar to Sierra Leone, from the east coast of Africa to the west. There was unrest on both coasts and the first incident in Marx's command of *Barossa* came shortly after his arrival at Sierra Leone. It centred on the trouble in the Brass River, where the rebellious natives, under Chiefs Brohimie and Nanna, were fortifying the creeks against the naval brigades. On 3 September 1894 Marx received official orders from Captain Francis Powell, Senior Officer, West Coast of Africa, to complete with coal and provisions, lay in a supply of ale and porter and proceed with despatch to join him in the Benin River – via Focados and the creeks. These official orders were written by Captain Powell from Phoebe on 3 September. They were also accompanied by a desperate handwritten note from him, written on the same day,

> *Come as soon as you can and help us…we are in a mighty tight place…bring some rockets if you can…anything that might be of assistance. The rascal [Chief Nanna] lives in a perfect network of creeks and ditches and has them all defended by cannon, 3 to 12 pdrs, he also has machine guns and lots of rifles. Altogether it is a tough job and we shan't crush him without considerable loss of life.*

Despite the urgency Powell had managed to add a friendly note,

> *...hope you have had a good time at home and are ready for a*
> *good spell on the Coast. You will probably be able to get a plan*
> *of the Forcados from one of the mail steamers we came in on the*
> *top of high water and took nineteen feet. The creeks leading to*
> *the Benin river have plenty of water but you ought to have a*
> *plan of them or you might take the wrong turning; all the mail*
> *steamers have plans. Bring our Canteen gear and any other stores*
> *there may be for us.*

Unfortunately this letter, written on 3 September, did not arrive in
Barossa until 2 October, so *Barossa* could not get there in time to relieve
Powell and join the battle. A fact much regretted by Powell and Marx
– 3 October Powell to Marx:

> *it is a great pity we couldn't have all the ships of the Division on*
> *the spot and done the job ourselves instead of the Admiral*
> *coming up from the Cape on Philomel...*

Rear Admiral Bedford had arrived in Benin, and with the backup force
from *Phoebe*, *Alecto* and *Widgeon*, the natives were defeated. A masked
battery across the creek, stockades, guns and stores were destroyed.
Brohemie's and Chief Nanna's towns were shelled and taken. Nanna's
personal treasure, amounting to £324 in British money, was captured,
but he himself escaped through the swamps. The Vice Consul rubbed
salt into the wound, when he regretted that Marx 'should not have
arrived in time to assist in said operations'.

However, Marx was able to assist and bring himself to Admiralty
notice, in the complicated matter of the grounding of the French ship,
Ardent, in December 1894. To cut a long story short, Lieutenant
Commander d'Agoult of *Ardent* had run his ship aground in the River
Niger. He had declared that he had a right to enter the river and explore
any of the creeks. The Niger Company disagreed and d'Agoult had

taken umbrage. He believed 'free navigation rights of the river had been infringed', so when his ship ran aground, in a fit of righteous indignation, he refused to take any help from the company and it was not until Marx arrived with food, quinine, a mosquito net and equipment to get the ship off the bar, that d'Agoult was saved and the ship floated off. D'Agoult had refused to ask Mr Bedford of the Niger Company for help and Mr Bedford would only agree to help if d'Agoult asked. The schoolboy quarrel was saved by Marx's ability to work with both sides. It was an example of the new tactful, diplomatic skill that he was to show in his work as a captain. He had a general, understanding friendliness that was able to defuse personal confrontation. Lieutenant Walter Cowan remembered how Marx got all his men to assist in pulling the French ship free before he, and his 'merry men', returned to the ship.[7]

With the departure of Powell, Marx became the Senior Officer on the station in the absence of Admiral Bedford. Events were hotting up again and more trouble was brewing in the Brass River. A factory belonging to a Mr Grasby of the Royal Niger Company had been looted and destroyed by natives. Marx had been given orders to assist the Consul General in restoring order, though Bedford insisted that no boat expeditions were to be undertaken without his authority, and whatever happened, every step should be taken to protect the health of the men. Preparing for possible trouble, Marx's first move, at five p.m. on Sunday 10 February, was to cross the bar and moor *Barossa* off the factory. He had the *Widgeon* moored a little further up. The Vice Consul, Mr Harrison, arrived to see him, and Colonel Boisregor who was commanding the protectorate troops came and said that he had divided his men between the Consulate and the Telegraph station. He asked that *Widgeon* might be moved further north to cover the factories between the Telegraph station and the Consulate. Marx told him that *Barossa* would be responsible for the stations from the Consulate to the sea. He organised a watch at the guns of both ships and prepared to land men if necessary. He had *Widgeon* work her searchlight every half hour, and *Barossa*, hers every hour. He took distances from both ships of all the important points so that the ranges might be accurately known.

Next day he went round the area with the Vice Consul to get some idea of the direction of roads and the nature of the country. He went to Mr Grasby's factory and examined it and also visited Mr Spiff, the native trader. He then visited the local mission station and saw the missionary who gave him details of the locality and said it would take three hours to get to Nimbe in a steamer from Brass and about five hours in a canoe; Little Fishtown was about two and three quarter miles inland; there was a good road to within 400 yards of the town, after that open scrub country with a swamp difficult to cross at high tide, though there was a native crossing of logs that might be passed fairly easily at any time, then a native path through plantations into the village. He said Mr Kindersley of the protectorate could give much important information about Great Fishtown, he himself had seen the people from there busily fortifying their creeks recently. Marx asked Mr Spiff to take him around the native Tua Town but he was too scared, saying that the people were all frightened, they had gone into the bush and the town was not safe. Good roads were of the utmost importance and Marx was pleased to find 'a capital road extending from the Telegraph to the Mission station', and a good road to Fishtown. In the evening he wrote to Colonel Boisregor advising him to remove the gin from outlying factories and put it under guard of the soldiery. He considered it 'great temptation for the natives to loot these undefended places'.

On the evening of 12 February he went in Captain Dundas's launch, to Akassa, where he conferred with Lieutenant Commander Henry Tottenham and Mr Bedford of the Niger Company, who told him that, by destroying and burning of villages by the soldiers, the surrounding area was gradually being reduced to order.

However, on 13 February, the Consul General arrived in *Evangeline*, bringing more soldiers and saying that he was worried by the number of men in full war paint appearing in Tua Town. Next day he sent for Marx and told him that he had received information that the town might be attacked that night. Marx carefully altered the disposition of *Barossa* and *Widgeon* so that there would be no accidental 'friendly fire' and they waited in anticipation. Nothing happened that night.

Tension increased but it was not until 20 February when Admiral Bedford was ready to mount a naval brigade to deal with the natives, that action began. His force consisted of a landing party of 150 bluejackets and marines from *St George*, *Barossa*, *Widgeon* and *Thrush*. The *Widgeon* and *Thrush* began operations by shelling the scrub on the riverbank below Nimbi, the capital of the Chief, Koko, who had been responsible for the attack at Akassa. The enemy attacked in war canoes but when three were sunk by machine-gun fire, the rest backed off. On the 21st, stockades near the shore were blown up, and on the 22nd, Nimbi itself was shelled. As the boats advanced, they took heavy firing from a concealed battery and some men were killed, but the town was taken and burnt. On the 24th, *Barossa* and *Widgeon* bombarded Fishtown. Shortly afterwards, Marx received a pencilled, scribbled note from Bedford,

Dear Marx,

Have got back into the river after a pretty stiff day's work. They are being troublesome people and stand a lot of hammering. Poor Taylor, my senior Lieutenant was killed and two men, half a dozen wounded.

Please make arrangements for the funeral tomorrow. I shall be down in the morning.

On 2 March, Bedford ordered Marx to be in telegraphic communication, should the situation alter for the worse. However, he was sufficiently confident of matters to turn his mind to other things, and also asked Marx to get for him three complete sets of local stamps and told him, '...*there are any number of quail just now at St Thorne and as by this time you must have slaughtered all ship's bullocks, you will want some sport to keep your hand in.*'

On 8 March, as things quietened down, the Consul, MacDonald, sent orders to Marx:

1) All canoes containing more than four people to be stopped and sent to the Consulate

2) An armed canoe with cannon in the bows or containing armed men to be immediately fired at.

3) Any canoe carrying a white flag to be sent to Consulate.

4) With the exception of instructions contained in Section 2, no one is to fire unless fired at.

It seemed that order had been restored. But life after the Brass River raid was again made difficult by cases of fever aboard *Barossa*. MacDonald hastened to assure Marx that in view of this, he thought the settlement was now sufficiently provided with protection and that the government would not be requiring his further aid. There was the usual concern of the civil population over fever on a ship. Infection must not be brought into the town and panic must be avoided, at all costs. Before the funeral of Lieutenant Chatteris was held on 8 March, there was an argument as to whether or not the Navy Marines should provide a firing party. MacDonald feared possible infection, but Lieutenant Hill thought 'our Marines ought to land...'. The Navy prevailed and MacDonald had, perforce, to thank Marx for 'the kind assistance you have given in rendering the last rites to the late Lieutenant Chatteris by furnishing a firing party and in other ways.' But when there was a second death ('poor Leishmann passed away...consequent on malarial fever') he worried that the second death, 'occurring so soon after poor Chatteris', would have a bad effect on morale in the ship and more particularly in the town.

I do not propose hoisting the Consular flag, half mast. I have sent round to the Agents, to ask them not to hoist flags at all. I also do not want a firing party. The funeral will be carried out by the Officers and men of the Protectorate Force. I should like to have kept your men in ignorance but it appears the Barossa's carpenter was sent for early this morning — could you get hold of him and tell him to hold his tongue. Poor Leishmann had, so the doctor says, a weak heart and it might not be a bad thing to say that he died of heart disease. These are small things perhaps, but I know soldiers are very much influenced by small things and I suppose sailors are the same...

Matters were alleviated for MacDonald by the quietening of the natives. He wrote to Marx, '...*the chiefs here have shown a decided inclination to cave in...*' but he still wanted the presence of a Navy gunboat retained in the area,

It would be an assistance to the settlement of matters in these Districts if HMS Thrush proceeded to Degema and stayed there for the night, large numbers of refugees from Nimbe and Fishtown are now in the Degema district.

He offered an inducement: *Barossa* could coal at Degema, where '...*the coal may not be so good as at Fernando but the facilities for coaling are much better. The coal would be put on board by Government Krooboys and the bluejackets would not be exposed to the sun and rain. Cost price, 35 shillings a ton would be charged for the coal.*' In the event, *Barossa* continued to coal at Fernando Po.

The trouble at Brass River was finally over: '*I hope next Sunday to have most of their canoes and a good deal of their loot here,*' wrote MacDonald. Bedford wrote to all officers and men who had taken part in the action. He expressed his

...high appreciation of the zeal and devotion to duty exhibited by them during the exceedingly arduous work they were called on to perform.... It was short, but full of difficulties and discomforts that have been successfully overcome and cheerfully borne.... I am very proud...to bring the services of the officers

and men…to the favourable notice of the Lords Commissioners
of the Admiralty.

Bedford told Admiralty that Marx had been 'most zealous in making arrangements for defence of Brass, did good work examining the Fish Town Creek'.[8] Their Lordships replied by promoting Lieutenant Tottenham to Commander, and Marx to Captain on 30 June 1895. There was another final, useful outcome from Marx's experience on the Brass River that Their Lordships appreciated:

Dear Commander Marx,

Your letter from Simon's Bay, dated 9th April, contains much useful information about the creeks of the Niger Delta. I am always grateful for any remarks and information which will help us to improve Admiralty charts and publications, which are still sketchy in several parts of the West Coast of Africa, especially in the region of the Niger, and I am therefore very much obliged to you for the trouble you have taken in the matter,

Yours truly,
W. J. Wharton
Hydrographer

Marx was well poised now for a successful captaincy. He would not have long to wait. The diverse squadrons of the New Navy were rapidly expanding to cater for the needs of a growing empire and the Pax Britannica was absorbing an increasing number of captains as well as lieutenants.

1 ADM 196/87.

2 The Boer War debacle and the subsequent Boer War debate led to a drive for 'efficiency'. See Searle, *Efficiency*, ch2, passim.

3 R Kipling, *Fringes of the Fleet*, p3.

4 F Dodd, *Admirals of the British Navy* (London, 1917). Introduction by E V Lucas.

5 Chambers, *Salt Junk*, p22.

6 Admiral of the Fleet, Lord Chatfield, *The Navy and Defence* (London, 1942).

7 See L Dawson, *Follow the Sound of the Guns*, a biography of Admiral Walter Cowan. Cowan also records a lighter occasion when Marx had his merry men hopefully digging for Captain Kidd's buried treasure on the Isle de Los, pp22–24.

8 ADM 196/87.

Eleven

Captain (1895–1906)

'I consider your advance for Mwhele...
most ill advised...'

On 26 July 1895, Marx achieved the coveted rank of Captain. He had done well. The average number of years taken to reach Captain from Commander at this time was seven.[1] Marx had done it in six. He was fortunate in that he had been brought to the favourable notice of Admiralty due to his activities on the coast of Africa and the French government had expressed their appreciation of his work in relation to *Ardent*. The New Navy, now in being, was also providing greater promotional opportunity generally.

Whatever the elevation of official rank, Captain Marx remained doing the same duty as previously – Commanding Officer of *Barossa*, now on the Cape of Good Hope station. There was no time to go home and celebrate such a significant official promotion. *Barossa* was in demand. Trouble had now flared up again on the east coast around Mombasa, centring on the activities of M'buruk-bin-Rashid, another local chief who would not submit to the authority of the British. Rear Admiral Harry Holdsworth Rawson, CB, had succeeded Rear Admiral Bedford in the area and his first task was to deal with the trouble. He told Marx that he hoped to meet Mbarak (sic) in Mombasa, but 'if he did not come in' he would make arrangements for a punitive march on the Chief's stronghold at Mwhele. He did not come in. Rawson prepared to mount a naval brigade.

Again, Marx found himself in an organising, rather than fighting role, as with the Lamu expedition; an acknowledgement of his senior position but doubtless still frustrating to a man of Marx's temperament. The expeditionary force consisted of 400 men from the cruisers *St George* (flag), Captain George Egerton, *Phoebe*, Captain Thomas MacGill, *Racoon*, Commander Powell Underwood, *Barossa*, and *Blonde*, Commander Henry Festing. They had two Maxims, a seven-pounder gun and a rocket tube. They were accompanied by sixty Sudanese and fifty Askari troops. General Lloyd Matthews (RN, retired) commanded the Zanzibari army. They started inland from Mombasa on 12 August with 800 porters.

Rawson's orders set out detailed requirements for an expedition of at least ten days and Marx was put in charge of base camp supplies and logistics. On 13 August, Marx landed his ship's company at the village of Shimba. They constructed a jetty to enable equipment to be landed and built a protective zareba (Sudanese word for a cattle pen). Rawson had given instructions for its garrison: twenty men from *Barossa*, plus three petty officers (POs) and two carpenters, *Racoon* was to supply the same numbers. On the 14th, Marx got all the stores into the village and fifty porters arrived. On the 15th, he disembarked his landing party, and ammunition was sent up to Rawson as requested. The difficulties of the next few days, told in his report to Rawson on 22 October, show something of the demands such background work entailed:

> 16 August
> On Friday the porters returned…taking with them the sick you had left at Shimba. In the morning we heard you firing (Rawson and his men were repulsing an attack at Nololo) and I took a patrol to your old camp next to us and saw several runaway porters, but could not catch them. Two came into my camp later and I made a prisoner of General Sir Lloyd Matthews guide whom I found in a neighbouring village and who confessed

to having run away. Later on the Chief of the village came and asked me to allow the guide to go, and, as their Chief seemed an important personage and it appeared to me most desirable to keep on good terms with the natives, I let the former go.

17 August
On Saturday I took a patrol to your 2cnd camp from us and examined the country closely between the three camps but could see nothing of the enemy…

18 August
On Sunday hearing nothing from you and many letters and telegrams having accumulated…I started with a small patrol for Mwhale but half an hour from your 2cnd camp from Shimba I met your letter ordering me to take back the men to their ships. (Rawson and his Brigade had defeated Mbarak at Mwhele the day before, with a loss of 3 killed, including General Matthews, and 11 wounded. Mbarak escaped, but two of his sons were killed.) I got back to our camp in time to meet the porters who had brought more stores from Jimbo and whose number had increased by 28. I sent them back immediately with all the stores they could carry, remaining myself at the camp, to try and get more porters, so as to get back all the gear that day. I asked the Chief, by name Monchera, of the neighbouring village of Mour Macha to get me some men to help my transport. That evening he managed to get 30, and by sending round to all the adjacent villages, by morning he had collected 60.

Monday – With these I was able to transport all the remaining stores towards the Ships, until I met my own carriers to whom the loads were then transferred. I would venture to suggest that the valuable services rendered by this Chief be brought to the notice of the Consul General. We arrived about noon at Jimbo, and after embarking all the men and stores, left for Kilindini…

There being no executive officers available for transport service, I gave orders to Mr. Elliott, Paymaster: Mr. Smith, Engineer;

and Mr. Gerty, Clerk, to carry out this duty. It was performed with great zeal and care, Mr. Gerty doing the double journey of 24 miles for three consecutive days.

Tuesday, 20th August
Having borrowed 2 cutters from HM Ship *St. George* to assist in the embarkation of your force at Gaze, I left Kilindini...arrived at Gaze about 10 a.m. Captain McGill's division came in at noon and I embarked him and the *Phoebe*'s men, also the wounded.

Wednesday
As there was no moon, it was too dark to get to Kilindini that night, so I left early the following morning...disembarking the *Phoebe*'s men and the wounded. I returned to Gaze after 4 p.m.

In conclusion I would observe that I was ably assisted by Lieutenant Booty who took executive command of the men. The men behaved well and marched capitally. I also wish to mention for your favourable consideration the name of Fennel – P.O.1 Cl. And Torpedo Instructor belonging to HMS Racoon who was in charge of that Ship's half company.

If Marx expected wholehearted commendation for his efforts to please Rawson, he was mistaken. Rawson took great exception to Marx's decision to leave his camp and try and get letters and telegrams delivered to him:

I consider your advance for Mwhele – leaving your important post on which so much depended, and risking capture by the enemy (which would have complicated the whole situation) – as most ill advised, and entirely contrary to what I intended.

Marx was angry and felt he had been dealt with unjustly. He hastily scribbled a letter:

*I have the honour to acknowledge the receipt of your memo dated
August 24th 1895 which came addressed to the Commanding
Officer of HMS Barossa!! [he then thought twice about that and
crossed it out] censuring my conduct in bringing your telegrams
and letters on the Mwhele road and I much regret having failed
to win your approval.*

*1 – I would venture to point out that the risk of capture which
you suppose I ran was very slight as shewn by the result.*
*2 – That I could get no native guides and that I happened to be
the only officer who knew the country and therefore could be
certain of finding the way.*
*3 – That I had fair reasons from the news flashed the nights
before, to suppose that the information contained in yours and the
Consul General's telegram and letters was worth carrying to you
and that in all probability from the position of your camp you
had been unable to take them [as an afterthought Marx amended
in different ink] take the searchlight flashes in.*
*4 – That I knew you had been ambuscaded and that you had
attacked Mwhele but not the result of either [and then, another
afterthought] though I had little doubt on that matter.*

*– That at all events some of your porters and guides had run
away and on that score I was most anxious to render you any
assistance you might require. As I had seen 11 run away and
knew not how many more you might have lost.*

*– That it was of great importance to me to be as thoroughly
conversant with the state of the country as possible as my porters
whilst travelling were always open to attack and I could spare
them but a small guard.*

*In conclusion I would point out that I had left the camp in charge
of a capable officer, Lieut. Booty, that I should not have gone*

myself if I could have sent anyone else and I trust that if you
will consider that I made an error in judgement it was from no
personal motive or want of zeal in behalf of the matter in hand.

Whether the letter was ever sent, we do not know. One is reminded of one of the verses in 'Laws of the Navy' —

'They prosper who burn in the morning
The letters they wrote overnight.'[2]

One sympathises with Marx's Old Navy instinct for individual action. Is it too much to suggest that Rawson's condemnation of Marx's independent initiative reflected the coming New Navy thinking that orders must be obeyed at all costs. This was two years after the traumatic collision of *Victoria* with *Camperdown* (16 June 1893) which sealed the abandonment of Tactical Advice (movement with or without signals) in favour of fleets controlled by signals from central command and captains who simply 'did as they were told'. Their Lordships closed ranks and putting all their faith in central control, insisted that orders given by senior officers were always to be obeyed at all costs.[3]

However, there was a consolation. All men and officers involved in the Mwhele expedition between June and August were awarded a medal of the same pattern as the Ashantee medal with the date inscribed thereon but without any clasp, provided they had not been granted a similar medal for previous operations. In that case they could simply have 'Mwhele 1895' inscribed on the earlier medal. Marx could add this to his bronze and silver medals from the Humane Society.

By now, the constant sailing was taking its toll of *Barossa*. At the end of the month, Rawson asked Marx for an official report of her leaks. Yet, leaks or no leaks, *Barossa* was still needed. They had not heard the last of Mbarak. By September there was again unrest in the area but this time Rawson was reluctant to take action. 'The Commander in Chief does not wish men to be marched about the country at this stage,' Captain Thomas MacGill told Marx. Nevertheless, there was anxiety at Takaungu and Marx was told to send a lieutenant and about ten men to assist Mr MacDougall in the defence of that place. He was to see that the guard was relieved once a week: 'In relieving your guard at Takaungu march a considerable number of men up there and back again, in order to allay the fears of the natives.' ('The Grand Old Duke Of York'?) MacGill continued, '…personally, I cannot think there is any danger to Takaungu as it is stockaded.' But a pencilled note from MacDougall addressed to Pigott and received by Marx said otherwise,

> *The rebels are on their way…. They are contemplating a*
> *determined attack on Takaungu either tonight or the night after.*
> *A general panic exists amongst the natives consequently. Can you*
> *possibly send a European officer to assist me these nights, as I*
> *have to patrol the sentries every half hour during the night*
> *otherwise the Askaris will sleep. This is my third night without a*
> *wink of sleep. Cannot a gunboat show her flag occasionally?*

By the beginning of October, Marx had orders to garrison nearby Rabai but on no account to use force without explicit orders. Accordingly, Marx set out with fifty riflemen, fourteen seedies [?] and in all a total of seventy-six officers and men to protect the town. He found that a letter he had sent requesting information had not been forwarded, but when he arrived, he found Mr Smith, the missionary, very welcoming. Mr Smith put a schoolroom at the disposal of the men and other rooms for the officers. The missionary was a great help. He had total mastery of the language and was familiar with the manners and customs of the natives. As we have seen, these missionaries were invaluable aids to the Navy and to imperial government.

Marx sent messengers to various places and received enough intelligence to satisfy himself that Mbarak was moving south on his own road. He felt he could fairly calculate the times when Mbarak would pass certain water holes. He decided to pursue him with a force supplemented by twelve Askaris and twelve bowmen from Rabai, and to catch up with him at Mwach, a camping place on the McKinnon Road, about seven miles away. When they reached the camp, he took the novel step of removing the clothes of the bowmen and having reduced them to their native attire, he sent them out as hunters to find Mbarak. He believed Mbarak was due to cross the McKinnon Road seven miles further on, and since the district was uninhabited, Marx's arrival would be unnoticed. Sure enough, the bowmen returned to say that they had seen Mbarak's party of some 500 crossing the McKinnon Road and that they had talked to them and narrowly escaped being made prisoners. A buck had crossed the road and in the confusion they escaped.

The prospect of action was now getting nearer. Marx recounted events:

> I immediately started for Mbarak's road, reaching there about 3 pm, and having chosen a secluded spot, zerebed myself, and as the sun set, put out all fires and lights and sent the men to bed. Mr. Dick, who had accompanied me from Rabai as a volunteer, went out patrolling to the South and returned at 8 pm with a report that he had seen Mbarak's camp fires some 4 miles off.

> We again started at three a.m. and by 4.30 had arrived in a position from which we could hear the cocks crowing, the women talking and smell the fires of Mbarak's camp. We spent the next hour in vainly searching for a way to get at the camp through the bush which was so dense that we could not penetrate it. At a quarter to six, it being then broad daylight, and being unable to find a way in, withdrew the men for a short distance to a more open space and awaited the arrival of 150 bowmen and 30 Guns, which I had written for to Rabai the previous night. They travelled their 17 miles very quickly and coming up about a quarter to six, I organised them into divisions, Mr. Dick taking charge of the guns. To all of them I gave strict orders to lie down in case of any firing. I then started again for the Camp, which we soon found and advanced in lines firing

volleys whenever there was any stand made, our friends in front obeying my orders to lie down very implicitly. The enemy's fire was considerable at times but badly aimed. We soon reached the camp and found that Mbarak and his party had, in their haste, forgotten their cattle, cooking Pots, and food with which the road was strewn for the mile and a half which we followed, at the end of which time, I saw the last of the enemy disappearing over the top of the opposite hill at a distance of about 1500 yards. Fortunately on our side there were no casualties but the enemy are reported to have had three killed and five wounded.

The men by this time being practically tired out, we collected the cattle, burnt the grain, destroyed the houses and returned to our camp which we reached about 11.30 a.m. We remained there until 4 pm and then marched to a place called Mbarak's Old Camp, (a distance of 3 and a half miles) where we remained for the night: the following morning we returned to Rabai, a distance of 10 miles, arriving there about 8 am. To ensure the Rabai people remaining firm to our side we gave them the 20 sheep and 2 Oxen we had captured to make a feast.

But still they had not got Mbarak. On Friday 4 October, some natives from Drohuma came in, saying that Mbarak had again crossed the McKinnon Road and was now going north. Knowing that if this was true Mbarak must be making for another water hole, Mr Dick (volunteer scout) started at midnight with thirty-three Rabai bowmen and fifty-four guns and his own caravan porters. They found nothing and it seemed the information was false. Mbarak was going south. To Marx's disappointment, it seemed likely he was now forty miles away.

There was still great unrest in the area. Mr Bradbridge (a consular official or company man) wrote to Marx saying that Freretown and Mombasa were threatened by Hammasi Khombo, another local chief in league with Mbarak, and that Marx should order *Swallow*, stationed in the area, to attack him at Mtwapa. Marx, mindful of Rawson's earlier orders, declined to do so. Marx also received anxious letters from Mr Carthew, missionary at Ribe, stating that Hammasi Khombo was collecting men to attack Ribe and Freretown. On 5 October Marx went to Ribe and collected 130 bowmen and twenty guns and organised them for the defence of the settlement. He lent them his Corporal of Marines for a day to show the natives how to throw up earthworks for the defence of the mission. Two days later he sent Lieutenant Hill, who had already proved his worth in the attack on Mwhele (he had captured one of Mbarak's standards) with eleven men and provisions for six days to garrison Ribe. On the 10th, a message came from Hill saying that there was firing in the neighbourhood and he needed assistance. At last a chance of action! Ready for a fight, Marx marched to within an hour of the settlement and camped awaiting imminent developments, prepared for attack. But nothing happened. News then came from Lieutenant Hill that there was now apparently no chance of an attack on Ribe, so Marx had no alternative but to return to Rabai. Next day, Captain Harrison arrived with 130 Askaris and Marx, having given him all the information he could, advised him to garrison Kaifa Fungu, and started his return journey to Zanzibar. Another brush with Mbarak had been missed.

Marx was at pains to tell Rawson of his appreciation of the work of Mr Dick in hunting so tirelessly for Mbarak and enabling Marx to get so close to him. He also commented on the aid of Reverend A Smith, the missionary who had been so helpful. He thought 'it would be a graceful act for these gentlemen to receive some recognition in the way of a letter of thanks.' Marx was also at pains to tell Rawson he had recovered all the expenses connected with the expedition from the British East Africa Protectorate. Presumably, he was now back in Rawson's good books. An easy battle at Mwhele on 16 February 1896 saw the end of Mbarak's rising. He and his allies had run out of steam. Marx was not involved. By then, *Barossa* was elsewhere and Marx was looking to a new commission.

There was a brief spell in England during 1897–98, while Marx attended another voluntary course at Greenwich College – a short bonus for family life. In the event he was awarded an honorary certificate in physics, steam, navigation practical and theoretical, marine surveying, naval architecture and compass adjustment, and received a letter of congratulation from Admiralty. This success was followed by his appointment to another third-class, twin-screw, protected cruiser, *Proserpine*, in September of 1898. She was the biggest of Marx's cruisers: Pelorus class, with a displacement of 2,135 tons, she had sixteen QF guns, three machineguns and two torpedo tubes. She carried 224 men and was destined for Jamaica on the North America West Indies Station. However, while en route for Barbados, at St Vincent, she had trouble with her boilers. Marx ascribed the defect to the incompetence of his chief stoker, but in fact all this class had problematic boilers. *Proserpine*'s commission took in Barbados, Bluefields in Nicaragua, Bermuda, San Domingo and Venezuelan ports.

The chief incidents of note in the new commission arose from the revolutionary situations in Nicaragua and Venezuela in 1899. In April of 1899, *Proserpine* was at Port Simon in Nicaragua in company with the American USS *Detroit*. Local trouble had arisen in nearby Bluefields, over payment of custom dues demanded by the rebel government. The British Vice Consul had cautiously paid some of the dues, declaring the rebel government a de facto government, but after the arrival of HMS *Intrepid* under Captain Burr, refused further payment. The Americans had refused to pay anything. The rebels became more demanding, taking action against American merchants and seizing their goods. The unrest developed into street riots between the Jamaican Negroes of Bluefields and the Nicaraguan soldiers: men were wounded, one man was bayoneted, another shot and had to have his leg amputated; there were stabbings. The British and American governments decided to take over. Captain Marx arrived in *Proserpine* to see what needed to be done.

This was the height of the 'send a gunboat' era. A gunboat captain's first duty was to protect the safety and interests of British citizens ashore. With the American and British ships in harbour things quietened down.

Marx was expecting the Consul from Greytown to arrive and settle matters. Typically pre-emptive, he decided to sail to Greytown, and fetch the Consul. But at Port Simon, where he was coaling before leaving, the Vice Consul arrived and told him there were rumours of Bluefields being attacked again: forty-five Nicaraguan soldiers and two guns were being sent down. Marx then got in touch with the Consul, Bingham, who tactfully suggested that the guns and soldiers were probably meant as a guard of honour for the returning President who was to arrive in a few days. Marx saw Captain Merry, the American minister and together they set about calming the situation. Marx went to see Colonel Torres and General Estrada of the de facto rebel government and castigated them for the bad discipline of the Nicaraguan soldiers. They did not deny it, but said the men were drunk at the time. Marx said that was no excuse, and told them 'it was very unusual in a civilised society to provide drunken men with ball cartridges and ammunition'. He asked that orders be given to remove the ammunition. They agreed but Colonel Torres (a butcher by trade) and General Estrada (a carpenter) said it was the custom to carry knives; if they were taken away, other knives would simply be secreted. Marx agreed to them being kept. The American Commander Symonds said that if he found General Estrada in the streets, he would clap him in irons on board the *Marietta*.

An inquiry was held and Francis Rose, a man who had been stabbed, declared he and the soldiers were so drunk, none of them could remember what had happened. Marx, having interviewed various men, decided there had been, in modern terms, a race riot between Nicaraguans and Jamaicans. 'Men had been arrested and ill treated and put into gaol for a night simply because they were coloured.' The inquiry seems to have been something of a fiasco. Marx thought 'there was little that would be admitted as evidence in an ordinary court of justice.' Much of the evidence given was false and faulty but, backed by the British and American ships, it succeeded in restoring peace, though the Nicaraguan soldiers still kept their arms.

Marx satisfied himself that the British citizens of the area were content and nothing more needed to be done. Commodore Henderson said that British merchants were content and prepared to pay double dues because they did not want to get on the wrong side of the insurgent General Reyes and his 'Rough Riders'. Clowes in his *History of the Navy* refers to the unusual aspect of British and Americans working together to make peace. Some of that was undoubtedly due to the tact and initiative of Captain Marx.[4] They continued to be evident in his commission that year as the revolutionary element in the area continued. He enjoyed developing his initiative and his diplomatic skills as well as his military ones.

After having satisfied himself that the two British citizens in Sanchez were safe, Marx sent a report on the state of San Domingo and Sanchez in the wake of another popular revolt and the murder of the President. It was addressed to Commodore Henderson at Jamaica in August of 1899, showing his concern to elicit from the rebels an assurance that British rights and interests would be upheld, which he did through the British-owned railway company. Telegraphic communications were difficult and Marx's diplomacy was at first hand.

In October of 1899, Marx was at La Guaira in Venezuela where again there was revolution. On 21 October, he wrote to Mr Haggard, the Consul, of his concerns at the unrest in the city of La Guaira, but Mr Haggard assured him that all was quiet in Caracas and he did not expect trouble. However, 'in view of the general anarchy all round' Haggard agreed with Marx that a visit to Tucacas was advisable. It was an isolated town and he thought that 'British subjects should have the encouragement and if necessary the protection afforded by another visit from an English Cruiser'. There was nothing so comforting to a British citizen and supportive to a colonial governor as a British naval gunboat in harbour.

When Marx arrived in Tucacas he found it was

> ...closely invested by the insurgents who have all the hundred miles of the English Railway, except 400 yards which passes through the town in their possession.

The employees of the Company are entirely cut off from their headquarters. [A number of] their houses show considerable signs of the late fighting. I offered to take them and their wives away; but they prefer remaining at their posts. So having given them some hints as to the precautions necessary to stop stray bullets, we returned to the ship, weighed and proceeded to La Guaira.

On the morning of 20 October, the President, Andrade, suddenly disappeared. Marx telegraphed the news to Admiral Bedford. At two in the afternoon, the President arrived in La Guaira with about 1,000 troops, having marched over the mountains from Caracas. He started embarking them on board the Venezuelan squadron of gunboats. Marx told Bedford that matters were becoming 'very disturbed on shore'. Captain Marx approached the American, Captain Hemphill of the USS *Detroit*, and together they worked to promote peace: 'Fortunately, seeing that the *Detroit* and ourselves were prepared to act promptly and in complete accord, the town was kept quiet during the night, only a few stray shots fired.' The soldiers quietly disappeared.

But by 23 October matters had escalated and there appeared to be a danger of fighting breaking out in La Guaira. There were three factions, as Haggard later explained to the Foreign Office:

There were three parties in the fighting
1) That in possession of La Guaira (i.e. the Custom House which provided the sinews of war); the provisional government party represented by General V Rodriguez who had constitutionally inherited his right to government by the extraordinary flight of General Andrade
2) The party of the conqueror General Castro who, at La Guaira at all events, had not yet recognised that right as superior to that of conquest; and
3) That of General Hernandez who still has a large following. The fact of the non-recognition within ten miles of the capital of the solidarity of these three parties who are nominally at all events united in Caracas, is to my mind pregnant with possibility, specially that of dissention between the parties of

Generals Castro and Hernandez who are supposed to be so united as to have become almost identical.

The three parties looked in danger of imminent conflict. Marx sought out one of the aggressive factions. According to Haggard, he 'gave judicious advice to one of the bands about to attack the town'. Perhaps he reminded them of the retribution which Her Majesty's Navy could bring down upon their heads. He then took an overt political role. He wrote to the Consul advising him on management of the town in the event of further trouble, telling him, '*it is of the utmost importance that the Flag of the Consulate shall not be made to cover the property, or person of any belligerent whatsoever, and I look to you to maintain absolute neutrality*'. Peace prevailed. Marx had stopped the spark from igniting the bonfire, and it brought accolades of praise from Venezuelan and British governmental sources. The Marquess of Salisbury expressed his appreciation of 'the tact and discretion [Marx] displayed in the protection of British interests'. Ewan MacGregor expressed 'the satisfaction of their Lordships at the tact and judgement which Marx displayed in carrying out the duties devolving on him during the troubles at La Guaira.' Mr Haggard recorded,

> *...the high sense felt among the English community here of the value of the services rendered by Captain Marx and Her Majesty's Ship, Proserpine, during the late anxious weeks — to these...to a great extent all events attributed, not only to the quiet at La Guaira but also the fact that public order has not been disturbed in Caracas itself during an unusually long and acute period of tension...*

Marx had enjoyed himself. It was not long before he received another letter of congratulation from Admiralty. It was an appreciation of 'the valuable report on Martinique' prepared by him in the following year.

The final incident of any note, which also earned Marx some commendation, concerned the grounding of the *Carinthia* in May of

1900. It was a steamship carrying cattle. The first notification came when the Captain, anticipating boisterous weather and finding his ship dangerously bumping, even in a gentle sea, asked Marx if he would take the cattlemen off the vessel. Marx replied with regret that he was unable to take the cattlemen and told *Carinthia*'s Captain to land them under charge of the Consul. The bad weather came and the *Carinthia* ran on to the rocks. The ship filled with water, 'holds abaft forepeak to Engine' were flooded. The situation was dangerous. Marx decided to use his men and boats to get the mules off before they were drowned. The *Proserpine* and another ship, the *Valencia* tried to take *Carinthia* in tow. It failed, and a salvage vessel had to be called, but Captain Campbell of *Carinthia* was grateful and impressed by Marx's assistance:

> *Without your valuable aid many more of the mules would have been lost. Your personal advice and assistance has been most welcome under the most trying circumstances.*

In July, Marx was ordered to Colon, 'with moderate despatch', to keep an eye on two Colombian vessels that the Colombian government said were pirate ships. Marx asked the Governor of Trinidad whether they had committed depredations against British property or British citizens. He was told they had not, so he decided, reluctantly, he was not needed.

The work of this captaincy although successful and rewarding to a man of Marx's temperament and ability, had taken its toll. On 27 October 1900 Marx was invalided on full pay and granted a passage home on *Pearl*. He was on the sick list until October of 1901. It is not known what the illness was. There are no diary details and we can only assume that it resulted from the hard work of the last five years in difficult conditions, perhaps even now exacerbated by his earlier proclivities – Colon was a notorious red-light district! But the respite at home, for whatever reason, marked the end of Marx's years as a gunboat captain. They had served him well, giving him a chance to demonstrate his organisational ability and diplomatic skills, as befitted a senior captain. It also marked the end of Marx's time in the dispersed fleets of the empire. Henceforth, he would be a captain in the armoured cruisers and battleships of the big fleets of the New Navy.

1 Jones, ibid, vol 2, ch10.

2 'Law of the Navy' – a popular poem. Author anon.

3 See Gordon, *Rules of the Game*, especially chapters 10 and 15.

4 See ADM 1/7406 and ADM 1/7406 249180.

Twelve

New Navy Captain (1901–1906)

'...wants practice handling ship and fleet...'

Captain Marx was on the sick list until October of 1901. By 1901, the New Navy, expansionist, centralised, steam-turbine battle fleet was established. Destroyers and new armoured cruisers, battleships and pre-dreadnoughts were the mark of this New Navy. Unfortunately, these significant years for Marx's career are years in which we have none of Marx's personal papers or diaries to draw on. It is possible that they were burned in a fire or lost in a burglary, according to family memory, but it means an understanding of Marx's life in the next few years depends on official reports and knowledge of his character.

When he rejoined the active list, Marx spent two months in the first-class protected cruiser, *Grafton* and then five months in *Warspite*, a relatively old armoured cruiser, flagship of the Commander in Chief Pacific. Marx had to acclimatise himself to the New Navy. It was difficult for a captain who had spent all his life in the dispersed fleets of the Old Navy to adapt himself to the rigours of the New. Marx had been off the active list for a year now, though on full pay, and when he returned, the big, centralised fleets of the New Navy were unfamiliar to him. After his exciting life in individual, autonomous gunboats, prowling the far-flung coasts of empire, the return to a large, centralised, home fleet was perhaps difficult for a man of Marx's temperament. Or did he relish the new challenge? His first commission came in one of the New Navy cruisers. In July of 1902, he was appointed to *Hogue*. She was in the Channel fleet, under Admiral Beresford, a new Cressy class, first-class armoured cruiser, completed in 1902. She was the fastest of her class, displaced 12,000 tons, held thirty QF guns and two torpedo tubes, and she carried 760 men. Marx was her first captain. It was a good appointment – but there were setbacks. An inspecting officer judged *Hogue* to be only 'fairly satisfactory' on examination, and the cruiser was involved in a subsequent collision with a sailing vessel, the *Mary B Mitchell* on 30 January 1903. At the subsequent court martial Captain Marx was found guilty of 'Negligent performance of duty in allowing *Hogue* to collide with 3 masted schooner in Weymouth Roads' and was admonished to be more careful in future. It is instructive to compare the type and size of *Hogue* with Marx's last command in *Proserpine*: *Hogue* had four funnels, thirty Belleville boilers and carried 760 men. *Proserpine* had two funnels, sixteen boilers and carried 224 men. Perhaps it is understandable that Captain Marx may have had trouble in managing the change.

However, the adverse comments do not appear to have done him too much harm since in the August of 1903, Marx received the MVO (Member of the Victorian Order), presumably for performing escort services to the Royal Yacht and in May of 1904, he preceded Beatty as Captain of another brand-new first-class armoured cruiser, *Suffolk*, a member of the *Monmouth* class. This was a short-lived appointment, just six months, from May to October of 1904. It seems not to have been a demotion, because Marx was then offered the captaincy of the first-class battleship, *Mars*, in the Mediterranean fleet, and in March of 1905, he was appointed ADC to the King. Surely now Marx must have felt that he was heading for the top. *Mars* was one of the *Majestic* class, the largest class of battleships ever built, entering service in 1897 and displacing between 14,560 and 14,890 tons. She had four BL guns, thirty-four QF guns and five torpedo tubes. She carried 672 men. The well-known exhibition painter, Arthur Burgess, produced an impressive painting of *Mars* for Marx. His future looked good.

However, there was another setback. In an inspection report of 29 May 1905, referring to *Mars*, Vice Admiral May[1] said,

> On the whole satisfied with efficiency and cleanliness of the Ship, efficiency of machinery and cleanliness of Same and Boiler Rooms not favourably reported on. Their Lordships cannot acquit Capt. Marx from blame for having so important a department of his Ship in an inefficient condition.

Admiral May was very 'New Navy': 'scientific', punctilious, ambitious and perfectionist. He had not had the small-fleet, gunboat experience of Marx. Perhaps he placed more emphasis on machinery and boiler rooms than the cavalier Captain with his Old Navy experience. One could hardly imagine two men with more contrasting temperaments – Marx was never of the 'spit and polish' brigade. But again, the adverse report does not seem to have hindered him. While Captain of *Mars*, he went with Admiral May and the fleet to Brest, from 10 to 17 July, 1905, to promote the 'entente cordiale'.

> A party of 109 officers from the fleet, selflessly responding to their admiral's call for volunteers and headed by May himself, visited Paris for four days at the invitation of the French government. The captain of *Mars* was well to the fore in this expedition, which was given over to unrestrained junketing. The British naval officers, who were all accommodated at the Hotel Continental, ordered whatever they liked at the Hotel, all expenses being borne by the French, and carriages were placed at their disposal any time they were required. They were divided into groups, and escorted by French naval officers to dinners and theatres. Marx must have encountered many temptations along the way, and if he was still inclined to indulge his ancient taste for 'la grande horizontale,' he had an unparalleled opportunity.[2]

The Legion of Honour, in several gradations, was given by the French Foreign Minister at a dinner and reception on 16 July to both Royal

Navy admirals, the Commander in Chief's staff and all commanding officers of Her Majesty's ships at Brest. Marx's name appeared fairly high up in the list.

Marx continued to go up the ladder and presumably to enjoy good relations with the influential Vice Admiral May, regarded by some as a future First Lord,[3] who after having completed four years as Controller, took up command of the Atlantic Fleet at the beginning of 1905. On 17 August 1905, Marx was appointed to HMS *Dominion* in the Atlantic fleet. May was in *King Edward VII*. *Dominion* was another new first-class battleship of the *King Edward VII* class, launched in August of 1903. She was one of the penultimate group of British dreadnoughts, displacing around 15,585 to 15,885 tons. It was Marx's biggest and most prestigious command yet. The ship had eight BL guns, thirty-eight QF guns, four torpedo tubes and carried 777 men. He was her first captain. It was a plum job. In January of 1906, he was entrusted with the mournful but prestigious task of bringing M Prefontaine's body back from France to Canada. M. Prefontaine had been a Canadian government minister. This combined British and French ceremony was part of the government's interest in promoting the 'entente cordiale'. There was a ceremonial delivery of the body to the British at Cherbourg with a French naval farewell. There was bad weather on the return journey to Halifax, and significantly, in view of May's uncomplimentary inspection report earlier, Marx stated that *Dominion*'s engines, 'thanks to the care and attention of the engineer commander, have worked smoothly without a hitch…'. The body was landed and Marx, together with four of his officers, was invited to attend the funeral at Montreal, travelling by special train. He arrived back in Portland after grappling with 'the usual weather' – a favourite phrase in his reports (as one wit annotated, 'what is that?'). On 8 March 1906, Marx was gratified to learn that he had been promoted to Rear Admiral.

However, Marx was never to fly his flag at sea as Rear Admiral. Seven days later, on 14 March 1906, he learned that he was to be superseded by Captain Charles L Kingsmill, erstwhile Captain of *Majestic*. Despite being on the active list until his retirement on 8

September 1909, at the age of fifty-two, he was not employed again in active service during that period. From 1906–07, he attended war and signal courses at Portsmouth and no doubt expected and hoped for a further appointment, but none was forthcoming. There is no evidence in diary or memoirs to indicate his own feelings on the subject. He was never a man to feel sorry for himself – he had overcome that in the early days of his naval career – but he must surely have been bitterly disappointed.

The obvious question is, why did a man who got so far up the ladder, who seemed so suitable and experienced in so many ways of the service not receive a flag appointment at sea at the end? Perhaps the answer is to be found in these comments as to his suitability from Rear Admiral Beresford[4] and Admiral Sir Compton Domvile:[5]

> Charles Beresford, April 1904
> Recommended for advancement. I do not think Captain Marx will ever handle a fleet well, but all his other naval Knowledge is excellent.
> March 1905
> A Zealous Good officer good judgement, fairly sound physically wants practise [sic] handling Ship and Fleet
>
> Sir Compton Domvile, November 1904
> I have had few opportunities of seeing Capt. Marx: what I saw of him I liked very much. I should say he is not physically strong.[6]

At this time Marx was fifty-two and had not had much practice in handling a battleship, let alone a fleet, and the demands of New Navy fleet-handling presented a considerable learning curve to a captain versed in the work of the Old Navy. Perhaps it was too late for battle fleet advancement. Nor would he achieve active Admiral rank in a New Navy valuing the virtues of bureaucratic and administrative skill.

The comments about Marx's physical health are interesting. The prospect of war was on the horizon and physical fitness was important for fleet commanders. It is possible that Marx appeared suspect in this area. He had had periods of invaliding from the service and in his later world war diaries often alluded to bronchial trouble.[7] However, he did lead an active life until he was eighty-seven!

Perhaps too, over Marx's career there had always been a general perception on the part of authority that there was a certain off-hand carelessness about him, an unwillingness to linger over detail. A brief note from Marx in *Hogue*, to report his arrival at Gibraltar, betrays this casual approach: he gives times, but not dates for departure and arrival; a small thing but perhaps indicative. He was criticised by Admiralty for his unsatisfactory safe-custody arrangements as a result of the loss of a confidential book aboard *Suffolk*. He was also criticised for the very unsatisfactory results obtained by the twelve-inch guns during a heavy gunlayers' test on *Dominion* in 1905. One mustn't read too much into this however, many a successful war commander had small accidents and misdemeanours to his name, and *Dominion* was one of the last pre-dreadnoughts of the *Edward VII* class, known as the 'Wobbly Eight', because of their difficulties in sailing in a straight line, in which even Admiral May had trouble with his guns at first. But knowledge of Marx's character over the years might lead us to suppose that he liked to kick over the traces from time to time and that did not always endear him to Admiralty.

There is also another point to be made. Marx was contemptuous of Jacky Fisher who became First Sea Lord in 1905. He was never even a small fish in the 'fishpond' (Fisher's circle of 'affishianados'). At the very time when a good relationship with the new First Lord might have meant advancement to Flag Admiral at sea, Marx was demoted. It may have had some significance but it seems most likely that Marx's failure to go any further in his career at sea was simply due to the fact that he had not had enough New Navy ship experience and that the increasingly professional, bureaucratic, centralised Navy of the big battleships did not suit his temperament. As it was, Marx retired from the Navy on 9 September 1909, was promoted to Vice Admiral (retired) on 22 July 1910 and Admiral (retired) on 4 June 1913. He could not know that the Navy had not finished with him yet! His brightest hour was still to come.

---

1 Admiral of the Fleet, Sir William Henry May GCB, GCVO.

2 ADM 1/7805.

3 By Lord Selborne in particular, First Lord of the Admiralty, November 1900 to March 1905.

4 At the time, Rear Admiral Charles Beresford was Commander in Chief of the Channel fleet.

5 Rear Admiral Compton Edward Domvile KCB.

6 ADM 196/87.

7 Dr Walford Gillison suggests he may have suffered from TB and recovered, leaving a weakness.

Thirteen

From Admiral to Captain
(1914–1917)

Auxiliary Patrol

In 1914, war broke out. At last, Admiral Marx got the opportunity he had always been waiting for, a chance to show what he was made of, a chance to take part in 'the real thing', the biggest action of all, World War One. But was he now too old? When most of the Grand Fleet commanders of 1914 were in their forties or early fifties, a retired admiral of sixty-three and very much of the old school, was not an attractive proposition for Admiralty. Their Lordships were reluctant to employ a man who had not served afloat since 1906. Marx had to find a way to make them take notice and he did. Not only did Admiralty take notice, the country took notice. Marx camped out on the steps of Whitehall and refused to take no for an answer! *Punch* captured the spirit of the occasion in verse:

> So he hied him up to London for to hang about Whitehall
>   And he sat upon the steps there soon and late,
> He importuned night and morning, he bombarded great and small,
>   From messengers to Ministers of State
> He was like a guilty conscience, he was like a ghost unlaid,
>   He was like a debt of which you can't get rid,

217

Till the Powers that Be, despairing, in a fit of temper said,
'For the Lord's sake give him something – and they did.'[1]

Admiralty could not withstand the general adulation of the public and decided that Marx was more of a nuisance outside the service than in it. Also, he made it clear that he was willing to surrender his admiral status and serve in a junior post. Marx was not alone in offering to serve in this way. There were other senior naval officers who because there were no openings in their own rank, offered instead to accept temporary commissions in the junior grades of the Royal Naval Reserve (RNR). The spirit of Marx and these officers in suggesting themselves for appointments, in no way compatible with their rank, was warmly applauded by *The Times* whose naval correspondent praised this '...fine example of patriotism and self abnegation'. Their Lordships soon overcame their initial objection to employing these men and Marx was gazetted Captain, RNR, in September of 1914.

In 1915 we return to Marx's diaries. He kept them until his final retirement in 1918. This time, much briefer, more spasmodic entries, a small torchlight on his personal life as compared with the searchlight of earlier years, but they are particularly interesting in relation to his work during World War One. They show the often boring and gruelling nature of this work in the RNR. But the constant possibility of meeting with a submarine, of excitement, action and authority, made up for it to a man like Marx. Nor should his genuine willingness to serve and sacrifice himself for King and country be underestimated.

His first appointment was to the trawler, *Stephen Furness*, but in November he transferred to the 450-ton, armed yacht *Agatha*. Retired Admiral Algernon De Horsey (known to some as 'De Donkey' in his active days),[2] apparently took over the *Stephen Furness*. *Agatha*, which had been completed in 1905 and offered to the navy by her owner, Sir Walter Greene, carried two six-pounder guns and was attached to the Cromarty Auxiliary Patrol. Her brief was to carry out routine anti-submarine patrols and examine shipping in an area of the North Sea that stretched from Wick in the north, to Kinnairds Head in the south and covered the important base of Cromarty.

By January of 1915, *Agatha* was hard at work:

> stopped Alice Taylor which ship gave us much trouble, having to fire twice at her. Made Captain come on board, his name was James Ross.

On the 18th, Admiral Edmund Pears, Commander in Chief, came on board and decided that *Agatha* should refit. Eleven men arrived to deal with her defects. This seemed a good time for wife and daughter to pay a week's visit. Marx reserved rooms at 37 High Street but Lily wired to say that she was too busy, only Con would come. Marx used the time for 'hardwalking, I am out of condition'. Perhaps his lack of condition presaged illness. In February he described himself as 'Very seedy', still one of his favourite words.

It was at this time, at the start of his new temporary commission, that he appears to have taken matters into his own hands and inserted in the personal column of *The Times* the following advertisement: 'Wanted, an honorary, that is unpaid, SUB-LIEUT for one of H.M. patrol yachts: must have sea experience – Box0.672'. It was an initiative, typical of Marx but perhaps not appreciated by all at Admiralty.

The time of refit at Cromarty was made pleasant by the visits of his dear daughter Constance, and the pleasure at being more in the centre of events. He heard news of military exploits and was able to discuss them with senior commanders. He called on Admiral John Jellicoe, commanding the Grand Fleet, and Rear Admiral C Madden, Jellicoe's Chief of Staff. He saw Commodore First Class and Captain of the Fleet, A F Everett and Rear Admiral A Leveson, who was Director of Operations Division, Admiralty War Staff. He was cheered by Vice Admiral David Beatty's success in the North Sea and the sinking of the *Blucher*. When *Iron Duke* and the other ships came in, 'all over the dockyard men knocked off for them' in tribute. Marx felt again at the heart of events. His inferior work seemed more meaningful. When he heard that *Achilles* had narrowly escaped being torpedoed he rushed some men out in the trawler, *Hunnack Joliffe*, and for a couple of days tried to raise a submarine, but none were forthcoming.

Marx received an answer to his advertisement for a voluntary sub lieutenant in the shape of Sub Lieutenant Oates, who arrived on 10 February. He arrived to a chaotic state of affairs, despite so-called refit, the furnace was leaking and the boiler useless. With difficulty the ship had to be towed round to Inverness and when Sub Lieutenant Millen let the ship drift out of her course, Marx reported that it was Oates who 'saved the situation'. There was no tug to take them into dock, they had difficulty in turning and when they got to the lock gates, they were too late to get in. It was frustrating waiting to have the boiler fixed, and to add to his troubles Marx became ill and again felt 'very seedy…extremely seedy'. Possibly 'flu – there was a lot of it about. The doctor was called and a prescription seemed to do the trick. It is interesting to note that in his later diary Marx showed a tendency to hypochondria, always recording any ill health, even a cold: 'it has reached the runny stage'. Perhaps this bears out Dr Halliday Sutherland's account of a visit that took place on board Marx's yacht, possibly at this time. Although the account takes some poetic licence, it rings true in many ways:

> A British armed yacht, flying the white ensign, entered the Haven and I was instructed to see the sick on board. I was warned to mind my 'ps' and 'qs' because her Captain was 'pukka RN' and 'one of the old school'. On the yacht I was received by a short, square-built old gentleman with four gold rings and the curl on his sleeve. He had white hair, a red face and fierce blue eyes – and I appraised him as a regular quarter-deck brawler.

When Dr Sutherland went aboard the yacht, he found the Admiral had been treating the sick men and in his enthusiasm had been treating men who were not ill at all. Afterwards at a tea in the Admiral's cabin, Sutherland describes the Admiral indulging in a pleasant monologue:

You're at the hospital ashore? Well, the beach is alright, but not in war. That's the time to be afloat! When war was declared, I told my daughter, I'm going afloat. She's a most sensible woman, and of course she agreed. Impossible to sit through a War talking to old fogeys in the club! There were difficulties at the Admiralty – too old! By God, sir, would you believe it that one man said that to me! He didn't repeat it. And that it was impossible for me to fly my flag at sea. Who the devil wanted to fly my flag at sea? I told them I'd go with the rank of a post captain in any craft they gave me. And I threatened them. Suppose I'd joined up as a rating, eh? That would have given the service something to talk about!

They gave me this yacht as a submarine-chaser. I've made her shipshape. There's a useful gun on the fo'c'sle and two depth charges aft. If the submarine submerges before you get her with gunfire you sail over the spot and let go the depth charges. At three fathoms they automatically explode. You know all about that? These are the new ideas, but if they don't work I've still got a shot in my locker. The old way – ram the submarine. Run her down, sir!

Whatever the imaginative and exaggerated slant on the conversation, he captured the essence of the man and his work in his book *The Arches of the Years*, written later.

It was early days and *Agatha*'s boiler continued to cause trouble and the engines were problematic, it seemed they had not been properly worked. When a fisherman reported a submarine sighting and they sailed out to find her, there was trouble with the engine, which prevented them from further action. It was all a far cry from the efficiency of an Atlantic fleet battleship. Personnel too, presented problems,

Enquiry re the sale of a Baker's gift of tobacco to the fleet by the ship's steward of the Stephen Furness. A Powell, our steward, had been selling them at 2½ pence a piece on board here and Henderson, a fireman, had written to the donor. As far as I see Powell had bought them fairly, but it is a disgraceful proceeding.

Oates also proved to be a worry as officer of the watch,

> John Main came and told me that a vessel was coming in. I
> said, 'tell the officer of the watch I want him. He said that he
> did not know where he was and I sent him forward to find
> him... . Mr. Eason said he could not find Mr. Oates. I then
> called out down the after ladder for Mr. Oates and sent John
> Main to his cabin and after 10 minutes Mr. Oates came up. Mr.
> Oates, when questioned by me the following morning said that
> he acknowledged being below, that he was not asleep, that he
> was unpaid and had taken advice before he joined and that he
> had been told he was not answerable to naval discipline, that
> he was unpaid and that he had been given the same work as
> ticketed men, and that it was not fair. I showed him the
> advertisement which he had answered and told him that he was
> answerable to naval discipline and showed him the Printed
> Regulations and the Articles of War. He asked me if I would
> apply for him to be paid and I told him I would consider the
> matter. He also told me that his friends whom he had consulted
> told him he was not answerable to naval discipline, not being
> on the books. I assured him this was a mistake.

Later Marx questioned John Main as to the state of Oates's cabin when
he went down. Main said that it was in darkness when he answered,
and Mr Oates, when he did come up, was adjusting his dress.

The work of patrolling went on; searching for submarines and
stopping and searching any dubious vessels. On 3 March Marx
overhauled the *Princess Royal* who would not stop for a sound rocket
and three shots. She had no colours, her name was painted out and
when hailed, she 'put on coal'. Marx ordered his ship to fire at her boiler.
She stopped. Later, when her Captain realised the true situation, he
came aboard and apologised. After all, they were both engaged in the
same cause.

But there was plenty of opportunity, in between patrolling, to pay visits at ports. It was an unusual but satisfying social life with its own intimacies: occasional visits from family and friends, meetings with old naval comrades. Marx enjoyed it.

> Went to Invergordon. Got a drifter and went to Orion to see Leveson who was kicked out by Jacky (Fisher) as well as Sturdee.[3] Met Capt. Leake of the Pathfinder, a funny chap who was so precise that he argued with Leveson if the Pathfinder took 4 or 6 minutes to sink after she blew up. Also Leveson said that he had had a knock on his head and he corrected him. Also there was an argument if the Butcher was on the after gun platform with him when she sank. He got quite warm and said that only the Captain of the QDK was there...

> At Inverness...met the Provost Burney, he told me that Adl. Moore[4] had been superceded in Beatty's squadron for not firing on the second ship when told to do so.

> Met Sir Robert Arbuthnot...lunched with Sir Robert.[5]

> Called on Sturdee who gave me much useful information re many things, notably his action also's want of action.[6] He also gave me 10 rifles, so we are not as badly off as we were.

> had tea with Leveson. Met Sir G. Warrender[7] who looked older and was deaf, but it was a ray of sunshine seeing one's old friends.

Despite the pleasure of renewing old activity and social life, there was the constant problem of trying to maintain an efficient anti-sub patrol with substandard boats that were constantly in need of repair and ships' companies that left much to be desired. Marx had six armed trawlers under his command and the skippers did not always appreciate the attentions of this Old Navy Admiral, 'exercised the unit in right angled manoeuvres'. The mind rather boggles at the thought of six armed trawlers doing right-angled manoeuvres.

Personnel was a constant problem and one imagines the difficulties that could arise with this ambitious and sometimes less than emollient Admiral.

> Found grave fault with Puffin's Captain about his losing me in fog, about his not having made the alterations for the efficiency of his ship that I had told him to make on Tuesday (18) and also with the general slackness of his ship. Lewis Powell could not be got to the gun to learn to fire it, as he said he was nervous of guns. Gleven RNR said he had a pain and could not go aloft. It is not much of a company.

The men on the fishing trawlers also resented being asked to work with substandard equipment and in accordance with Royal Naval regulations. On one occasion, when Marx signalled for some of the crew of the *Grenadier* to put to sea, they refused and Marx arrested the mate of *Grenadier* and put him on the *Stephen Furness*. He sent Sub Lieutenant Ryan to take his place and sent a carpenter 'to inspect their boat and oars, which was their reason for refusing. The carpenter reported the boat was in poor order and had but one oar.' Admiral De Horsey sent the mate back to *Grenadier*. Presumably he did not appreciate Marx's high-handedness. However, he did send *Grenadier* to Inverness for a new boat.

The men concerned in this mini-mutiny, Bremner, Swanson, McCloud, took their service clothes and left the ship. Marx would have liked to put them under duress but since they were discharged from the Naval Reserve by the Registrar, and they had refused to sign articles and refused to do duty, the Registrar said Marx could do nothing unless he could argue military reasons for keeping them. A few days later the men of *Teal* also refused to come off, though ordered to do so. It must be remembered that some of these erstwhile fishermen and merchant seamen were volunteers.[8] It made it doubly difficult for their naval commanders.

The heavy weather in the North Sea also took its toll of personnel and ships. The men were often seasick, presumably sailing in weather they would not normally have fished in. Marx had to send Donaldson, the new signal boy, ashore with a broken blood vessel in his stomach through seasickness.

> Went in, found a whole gale blowing. Went alongside the collier...rolling hard...shoved off and anchored near a steamer ...nearly collided. Mr. Ryan on watch told me too late to do anything. I slipped the cable...tried to pick up the buoys...but the ropes carried away and so bent the cables. It was blowing a hurricane.... The Grenadier and another drifter were blown ashore.

But the main purpose of the work remained, so far as Marx was concerned, to sink a submarine. There were many rumours of sightings and many times they went out with high hopes, only to find nothing. Once they thought they had gone across the top of a submarine, 'it felt like the ship was rubbing across a chain'. In hopes, Marx let off a depth charge: 'A piece of old wood came up, it looked like wreckage, it was black.' But nothing else floated over the area. Another false alarm. Hunting submarines also presented other dangers,

> At 1 am I came across the 2cnd Division of destroyers, about 6 in number. Had quite a lively time in the dark...

A *lively time* was meat and drink to this retired Admiral. He could have echoed with Roger Keyes in the *Dover Patrol*, Kipling's words:

> With the sky above and the mine beneath, and a gale with its blast so keen,
> We laughed, m'lad and we chaffed m'lad, as we hunted the submarine
> With the sky above and the sea above, and a void where our ship had been,

It's our pride, m'lad, to have died m'lad as we hunted the
submarine.[9]

Shortly after the false alarm, Marx had a fall on deck and injured his
arm. It continued to hurt him and he was ordered to Haslar, the naval
hospital at Portsmouth, to have it X-rayed. Apparently it was not broken,
but Marx enjoyed the attentions of a masseuse who managed to make
him feel better. He had no wish to stay at home longer than necessary,
though it was good to see daughter Conny, now working as a nurse.
Conny had left home quite young, in about 1908, and trained as a social
worker, working in a Chelsea slum. Subsequently, she worked for the
Red Cross, was a founder Women's Royal Naval Service and one of
the first hospital almoners. Marx went to the United Services Club where
he met Commodore C F Lambert, Fourth Sea Lord, 'who was not genial.
Asked for a faster ship and he said it should be noted. Not likely to
get one.' It is likely that many at Admiralty regarded Marx simply as
a nuisance.

He got back to *Agatha* to find the boiler needed re-riveting (there
was always something!) and that instead of being eight days out and
four days in, it was to be twelve days out and four days in. Submarine
activity was increasing. There were some false alarms but no submarines
were found. He appears to have had various 'run ins' with Captain H
L Dicks, Senior Naval Officer at Cromarty, who complained to Admiral
Pears[10] in 'a bitterly malignant letter', that Marx was always neglecting
his duty. Perhaps some resentment and jealousy towards the old Admiral
was evident. Marx went to see Admiral Pears about 'the vindictive attack
made by Acting Captain Dicks' and was pleased to think he was
successful in getting Pears to see his point of view, 'getting him on
my side'. Admirals tended to stand together unless personal resentments
or genuine disagreements arose.

On 2 June Marx said goodbye to Pears and handed over *Agatha* to
his successor, Commander G Whall. He had hoped to command the
yacht *Atalanta* but Admiralty wanted him to have a different ship and
sent him a mollifying letter from the Yacht Patrol Office,

We have an even better yacht for you than Atalanta – a Russian
vessel called the Iolanda.... I hope you are enjoying your
holiday after all your strenuous labours. H. S. Lecky

Marx was appointed to *Iolanda* on 24 June 1915 and went aboard on 2 August. It was the usual business: 'engines worked well, telephones, steering gear, telegraphs, badly...condensers choked with weeds from the dockyard...'. Guns had to be tried, 'broke a good deal of glass and shutters, and the measured mile tested, got thirteen knots'. Repairs were needed. They sailed to Milford Haven and repairs were carried out. Condenser crank heads and water pipes were mended. Marx found it all very irritating. He was annoyed when the shore Paymaster made a signal that the Assistant Paymaster was to go ashore – 'confounded cheek'. And the new crew was not impressive: 'our men came off very drunk and kicked up a row. Gisborne left and very glad I was to see the last of him.' The stay at Milford was only brightened by a brief visit from Lily.

When *Iolanda* was ready, she put to sea for the usual routine of patrolling and searching for submarines. Marx felt that they were always just missing them:

> Sept 24th passed over a submerged obstruction probably a submarine. I was in bed asleep. Davies, Chief Engineer...a stoker and Baker...Hill and Cock felt it. Dropped a Dan buoy with 40 fthms of line...no more luck principally due to Chief Engineer writing a long report instead of screaming up the telephone.... It is too sickening.

Marx started to feel depressed. 'Have a filthy cold...'. The cold developed into bronchitis. 'I can't get my throat right.' He decided to go home for a week. Perhaps they were all feeling the strain. Perhaps he had been pushing too hard. Marx arranged three days' leave for each watch before leaving and when he returned he was at pains to promise the men as much leave as possible in the future.

A severe gale in October caused trouble and made Marx again lay down the law:

At 11.30 a sea came on board and smashed the shutter of about ¼ inch thickness on the Stoker's bathroom, also the Chief Engineer's cabin. I sent the boatswain round to see everything correct at 11.30 pm. He repeated that everything was alright though he had seen the broken shutters…in the morning saw the Boatswain and explained to him that he ought to have reported the broken shutters. Went round the messdecks and found them filthy. Sent for Chief Engineer and the second, gave them orders that men were not to go on their messdecks dirty, that I should give them one month from today to get the ship efficient as a steamer. Pointed out that we had been four months in commission and had not been able to have a full power trial. Many men sea sick and three officers out of six.

In November *Iolanda*, leaving Milford Haven with new sailing orders for Gibraltar, encountered a worse gale:

Nov. 12th – the ship rolling heavily, the men seasick and unable to keep steady, taking in much water. Thank God I boarded up the main deck windows. Marten, QM nearly washed overboard taking the log. The lifeboat starbd side damage, lifted on to her rail. A large quantity of water got into stokehold and engine room. The ash shoot broke, letting in large quantities of water. The 2cnd engineer had not made the bunker lids tight and 8 am I almost made up my mind to run for Vigo as they reported water gaining on pumps.

Nov. 13th – weather improved…wind shifted…have had to keep our nose to the mountainous sea. The ship had over 150 tons of water in the stokehole which the pumps gradually got out and the engine room was cleared. Bent fore and main stayside and fore trysail. …the steam pinnace which was on deck was washed into the sick house and badly smashed. The two lifeboats starbd. side were more or less damaged before I could get them on the rail.

It had been a narrow escape.

There were also problems with the crew. The Coxswain, Wright, was suspected of stealing alcohol:

Some four days ago a bottle of John Jameson was opened for lunch, at dinner Unwin poured out same from the bottle, but it was evidently watered. I had it put back in the drawer, on the following morning some of it was gone. I consulted Wilde [the doctor] who advised sulphate of zinc to be put in to make the thief sick. On the three next days the bottle became emptier and emptier. On the 17th Wilde suggested a double dose of sulphate of zinc and quinine. Fulcher [Sub Lieutenant] put it in this morning, more was gone and I also found a bottle in my cupboard which had had whisky in it, which also had a Polgrun cork and which had been kept in my after cabin. The evidence was so strong that, in spite of Wright taking his dying oath that he had not touched it, I dismissed him.

Gibraltar was a welcome relief. Marx dined with Admiral Currey, and Captains Goodrich and Kirby.[11] He visited the Moseleys and joined the club and the library. He lunched with his friends, the Wooleys, and heard all the local news. Unfortunately, his time at Gibraltar was cut short by orders for Algiers. On the way they passed 'a dead sailor in a lifebelt…poor chap he must have been dead some 20 days'. He went into Allboran and Alhucemas Bay, looking for submarines. At Oran, where he went for water, two of the officers of the Lincolnshire Yeomanry came on board. They had been wounded on board the *Mercian* when it was attacked by a submarine. The captain lost three boats and twenty or thirty men by being lowered by mistake. They had 20 men killed and 50 wounded by shellfire as they did not use their rifles or their machine gun first. After they did, the submarine cleared off. How they could have been so stupid I can not understand.

Marx longed for a chance to show his mettle against a submarine. He was pleased to see that *Iolanda* was steaming a little faster than her usual thirteen knots, now. The weather was good. He organised rifle aiming at a towed target (shades of the Old Navy) and there was some relaxation ashore. Life was pleasant though still no submarines.

Dr Wilde and Sub Lieutenant Fulcher went out fishing in the starboard lifeboat by themselves without a crew, which was against Marx's orders. Laird went out to look for them in a dinghy but the sea was too heavy and he returned to tell Marx,

At 8.30 Laird came and told me that he had been out in the dinghy looking for them and had to come back because of the sea. Having slanged him for doing so, I sent him to ask Adl Pradier to send a tug out to look for them which was done but they were not found. At 6 am I weighed and went to look for Fulcher and found him after an hour, both he and Wilde much done. Pradier came on board and said that he had not been told the night before or else he would have sent every ship in the harbour to look for them, and asked the two culprits to lunch. I went too and we had a big formal French meal. It was rather amusing.

Then it was back to Gibraltar, more socialising and cruising in the area until the end of the year, which gave Marx 'the quietest Xmas I have ever seen'. At Algeciras in January, he got a rangefinder, which was 'a great comfort…'. He tried to teach the men the use of the rifle, 'but it seems almost hopeless. No one to teach except myself and I impatient.' After going backwards and forwards on the beat there was a break for a little rest and local exploration, always a delight to Marx. 1916 started with a visit to Granada and the Alhambra with Dr Wilde and 'the impression I carried away was one of the great beauty of the Moorish architecture and decoration'. He visited the Gypsy quarter which, 'for pure filth beat anything I had ever seen'.

There was re-fitting at Gibraltar, so a chance for a longer spell of socialising; gossiping over Admiral Brock's engagement, 'as he has been engaged before it is a question if it comes off' and dining with old and new friends.[12] Then it was a return to 'the dull, unspeakably dull' routine of patrolling in the Med. He received a letter from his son George who had joined the Navy and was now a torpedo lieutenant on *Zealandia*. George was also finding life tedious and commiserated with his father:

> *30 March 1916*
> *Have you had any more adventures? It was very sad not hitting that fellow harder. I met a Comdr. Barrow who was your sub in the Proserpine and Petrie a lieutenant who was a Midshipman in the Dominion. We had a small excitement but nothing came of it. We actually saw a mine...wishing you better luck next time.*

Marx took pains to make friends with locals at places where he felt he might need to land sometime. Tobacco was a good sweetener. He still felt he probably hit a submarine occasionally but was that wishful thinking? He became increasingly frustrated. In May, there was an altercation with Admiral Currey,

> I explained to him the impossibility of protecting the trade route if we did not examine the ships that passed. He then stated that it was impossible for ships to pass either the straits of Taranto or Gib and that it was his wish that the East and West going traffic should not be interfered with...I have made my protest and hope there will be no evil consequences.

His hopes were of no avail. It seems there were consequences. When he returned from patrol into Gibraltar, four days later, he found he had been superseded by Chisholm Batten.[13] It looked as if his attempt to do something positive for the war effort had ended in failure and ingratitude. He must return to England. But all was not yet lost. When he returned to England he would find a new future awaited him and perhaps he could get to grips with the German submarines at last.

---

1 For full text see Epilogue.

2 A comment of Captain Clayton to his wife.

3 Vice Admiral Sir F Sturdee KCB, CVOCMG was engaged in action off the Falklands against Admiral Von Spee when several German ships were sunk in December 1914.

4 Admiral Sir Archibald Moore who moved his flag to *Invincible*.

5 The feisty Rear Admiral Sir Robert K Arbuthnot, who spectacularly steamed his flagship *Defence* across the line of battle at Jutland and was killed.

6 Admiral Sir Ernest Troubridge was accused of cowardice for failing to chase and attack the enemy ship *Goeben*.

7 In 1915 Jellicoe defended his retention of the 'deaf and absent-minded' Vice-Admiral Sir George Warrender on the incredible grounds that he was 'excellent as a squadron admiral in peace'. Gordon, ibid, p565.

8 Conscription did not come in until 1916 and then it was mainly into the Army.

9 Roger Keyes, *Dover Patrol*, vol 1.

10 Rear Admiral E Pears had just relinquished command of the training service.

11 Admiral B Currey, Senior Naval Officer, Gibraltar, October 1915.

12 Admiral Sir F Brock, Senior Officer at Gibraltar, September 1912 to October 1915.

13 Captain Alexander Chisholm Batten noted for a brave sea rescue at Vernon.

Fourteen

Captain of a Q Ship –
August 1916 to September 1917

'...at last we get one...'

Marx's diary was not resumed until the end of August 1916. But he had not been idle. These were momentous days. The submarine menace was increasing as Admiral John Jellicoe, the Commander in Chief, Grand Fleet, had feared, and 'in September, the submarine "season" started again and continued until the end of the war...'.[1] Jellicoe decided on a new attempt to deal with the German U-boats. It was a strategy that provided Marx with the ideal job, one that called for all his initiative and courage and gave him the challenge he longed for. He was offered a Q ship, one of the new, so-called 'mystery ships', a decoy ship for German submarines: its task, to pretend to be an innocent merchant ship and tempt the submarine into attack, whereupon the mystery ship would open fire and hopefully surprise and sink the sub. As Rear Admiral Gordon Campbell, the great hero of the mystery ships, said, 'I think the independence of the job was one of the great attractions.'[2] Marx's headquarters would be at Queenstown under the command of the dedicated Admiral Lewis Bayly.[3] Berehaven was the local base so long as dockyard assistance was not needed. Bayly had a reputation as a martinet, but as Campbell said, he was also 'of the type that always allowed the man on the spot to do what he thought best…', an Old Navy attitude which suited Marx admirably. Also between Marx and Bayly there was the friendly relation of equals. Marx would often stay with Bayly socially.

Marx's ship was to be the converted sloop, *Aubretia*, one of the *Flower* class, and known to the initiated as *Q 13*. (A newspaper article refers to him looking for the enemy from aboard HM Armed Yacht *Beryl*, owned by Lord Inverclyde, before taking *Q 13*.) While at home waiting for *Aubretia* to be refitted, he decided this time to try for a volunteer of his own choosing,

Dear Admiral Marx,

I can't tell you how delighted I was when we returned yesterday and received your wire asking me if I would volunteer, only of course I said yes and am now counting the days till I get a passage home. I expect I shall have to wait to hear till my relief is sent out but I promise you I shan't waste much time in joining up as soon as I return to the dear old country. Its really awfully kind of you asking for me and I promise you I will do my very best to give every satisfaction. I'm so excited at sailing under your command again. I had really given up all hopes of ever getting with you…

The letter is undated and incomplete, but was apparently from one Lieutenant Tod, who had been under Marx previously. On 20 August, Tod came to stay at Clatford Lodge and Marx reported that he 'accepted the billet'. Together they went to Blythe to see the *Aubretia* refitting. They put up at the Great Station Hotel, Newcastle, on the way and Marx met Captain Brandon:[4] 'keen, liked him…, and Commander Pitcairn,[5] as white livered as ever'. Pitcairn had left the service and joined Marconi. Marx met daughter Conny again and they went to the cinema together and saw 'a truly awful film…'.

The first sight of *Aubretia* was 'a great disappointment':

Went over her, not much catch, badly arranged, lunched with firm. Ship's company a queer lot. Eng Young seems sharp. Mr. Park my bowman in Blanche. Not at all satisfied. No accommodation for me.

Marx returned home depressed. He cheered himself with visits to friends and family, and waited for his ship to be ready. The date had already been postponed for five days and he was impatient. He went down to the ship on 6 September. He saw Sub Lieutenant Robinson who had joined and gave him a week's leave. The advance party came and joined and Marx was relieved to find them 'a good looking lot'. Some stores came in and he felt that things were getting on – but not for long. Five days later he went up to Blythe to get the ship ready, as ordered by Admiralty, 'in all respects for sea and weather', and was annoyed to find Crozier 'quite unsatisfactory and the ship not progressing at all well'. However, Captain Brandon, the man he had admired at Newcastle, came and woke things up a bit. He came on board with Captain Blatchford, Admiralty inspector, 'and thank goodness they did as I could get nothing done,' said Marx. Now that he was to be an innocuous and unknown 'mystery ship' Marx could not pull rank, but even so, matters were better after this visit. The rest of the crew of the *Aubretia* joined but still the impatient Marx was not happy, getting ready for sea trials with an extremely bad cold, and supervising the coaling of 127 tons from 6.30 to eight p.m., which was 'very badly done', made him feel irritable. He found the ship had a permanent list to port, 'I have been cussing Crozier as everything he promised has not been done...'. To add to his troubles, his new servant was late in arriving and he 'breakfasted on board very uncomfortably'. At length, the ship went out for preliminary trials:

It was very rough, but the trials were fairly satisfactory. The men got sea sick as the wind blew at force six. A gun misfired. The shot came down on the boat – splinters like long matches.

The ship was more or less cleaned up and was ready to go, but then another setback. Marx had trouble getting the certificates he required. It was not until 26 September that *Aubretia* got away. Then it was to sea, at an average speed of fifteen knots, around the Hebrides and to the Q-ship headquarters at Queenstown. On the way she was challenged by a destroyer and a motorboat – a novel experience for Marx, the erstwhile challenger. The guns were got out and loaded ready and the men were set their watches. They sailed into Queenstown where Marx met Admiral Bayly and got his sailing orders. He dined at the club and caught up with his old colleagues, MacDonald, late of *Proserpine* and Commander Noak of the *Dominion*. Bayly was a 'hands on' Admiral. When Marx had trouble getting his starting stores, Admiral Bayly brought them on himself.

The first destination was Plymouth. It was not always easy for an unknown and inferior 'mystery ship' to get into harbour, and it must have been galling for admirals and senior captains, used to being given every respect when their great battleships came into port, to find themselves seen as masters of irrelevant tramp steamers and sidelined when their little ships came into port, unable in any way to pull rank. Campbell described a typical incident,

> Going round a corner in a hurry, I unfortunately ran into a party of bluejackets, one of whom was carrying a 'mess kettle' of rum. I collided with him and some of the valuable contents were capsized. I have never been called such names in my life as were hurled at me then. My first impulse was to put the man under arrest for insulting his superior officer, but realising I was only the skipper of a dirty tramp, I doffed my bowler hat and offered my most humble apologies...

Campbell was only a lieutenant commander, for a senior admiral like Marx to allow himself to be treated as an insignificant nobody was heroism in itself. Bayly paid tribute to Marx's Old Navy method,

I was amused to hear of your going up harbour at Plymouth

without permission: ships that have been there tell me it is as much as they can do to get themselves taken any notice of at all when they arrive there. I believe the neutrals carrying for us are given routes. The whole system leaves much to be desired.

At Plymouth, Marx had trouble with his new crew, the men came off leave very drunk. As usual Marx decided to keep 'a tight ship'. An example had to be made. One stoker was arrested and given thirty days' detention. He took a badge from the Petty Officer and reprimanded the Chief Petty Officer. As they left for the Channel, he was very disappointed in Tod, who 'got much mixed up... . It was thick and he must have mistaken Sturt Pt. for Portland Bill. I expected something but did not realise what an ass he had made of himself. Well, forewarned is forearmed but it is a nuisance to have a man who can not take a sight correctly or add up the log... .' He was mollified to find that the rifle firing practice they had off Ushant was yielding some improvement and they could outrun some other boats. When he was held up by torpedo boats on 20 October, he told them, 'I was from Queenstown bound to Portland with Admiralty stores...I increased speed and as they increased so did I and they could not catch me... .' The trouble with his crew continued: 'The wireless man Reed got sulky and gave trouble... .' Tod 'was again out of his reckoning many miles to the Eastward of the Lizard...Reed was very troublesome indeed and our shooting very bad.' But there was some excitement to compensate. There was an SOS from the *Siamese Prince* and Marx was told that subs were very active in the area 49.30 North and 11 West. It looked as if the little *Aubretia* could now be of use. However, it was not to be. Although he managed to get into Falmouth without arousing any suspicion as to his true nature and 'completely took in all the Customs and Examination Officers', he had a bad fall while getting out of the boat and broke three ribs. It meant going into hospital and then having to 'poke about at home' for a spell. To add to his troubles, he went down with 'flu at home and was in bed for three days with a temperature of 103 degrees. Lily followed and was 'rather worse', various servants also became ill, 'there was no dinner until very late...'. Then it was back to his ship at Queenstown with a bad attack of bronchitis but pleased to be going back to work at a time when the newspapers were full of articles about the increasing submarine menace. Marx pasted them into his diary. Surely now he would find his prey – 'the place reeked of submarines'. He received a letter from Bayly,

30 November 1916 – So very many thanks for your kind wishes, which are cordially reciprocated. The Admiralty ordered me to send a Q to cruise from Lizard to Ushant one day, and Ushant to Lizard the next, a silly way to do things, but they are my masters so I sent you. You will see that they have agreed to give Q officers and men submarine pay, and to call for volunteers, so you had better make a list out of those you want to get rid of.

Admiralty was waking up to the usefulness of the Q ships. The submarine menace was increasing rapidly and the country was now entering, as Marx put it, 'the new era of frightfulness'. Bayly commented on the increased pressure of submarines in February. On 26 March he sent a telegram to Marx, '*Q 13 is much wanted. She should sail for Queenstown.*' He was concerned that Marx should be happy with the performance of his guns. Anything that could prevent the attacks on naval and mercantile ships by German U-boats pleased Admiral Jellicoe, and the Q ships were now having a degree of success. To be effective, the Q ships had to change their disguise constantly. *Aubretia* completed her new disguise in Causand Bay and started to patrol Ushant to the Scillies, now as *KAI Danmark*, previously she had been *Jacy*. Names and disguises needed constant changing. On 16 May, *Q 13* was *Moldonado* of Uruguay. In July, she was painted a dazzle pattern. Marx wrote to Admiral Dare[6] explaining his technique for disguise:

I generally pitch upon the Nation that has been suffering most heavily from the marauders, and telegraph Lloyds for a list of

*that nation trading to England at that time and the ports with
which they are trading. I then pick out the one about our tonnage
with the shortest name. The flags are painted on the gun ports
which must fall down, ready to have a tarpaulin with a bar of
iron at the bottom to fall over them. The white ensign is always
kept bent on to the foremast head halliards in a bag hung bottom
up on the bridge rail. The iron flags I had hinged on to the side to
fall down when required used to get bent by the sea and were a
danger, as they looked like gun ports so they have been done
away with.*

Marx wrote at length to Dare giving him 'hints about the business'
of being a Q-ship commander:

*…it is a difficult thing…as everything one does successfully is
the result of common sense action at the moment.*

*As regards abandoning ship, in my opinion it is better to await
the order to send your papers on board as otherwise your
adversary may want to do a little target practice and commence
shelling hard as was the case with Q 7. I am afraid all this is
now obsolete as they will sink at sight.*

*The look out man being high up is sometimes necessary, a crow's
nest is generally out of the question, and a mast head man in a
black waterproof streaming in the wind is as good as a danger
flag: and that is why I am having a donkey boiler funnel fitted to
put him in — which will raise him above the bridge.*

*It is a moot point what projectile to use, Lydite or common shell.
I have so far used lydite for the sake of its explosion on the crew
but with the modern SM I have given orders that the guns are to
be kept loaded with lydite and the next rounds are to be common
shell for piercing armour, if any.*

*As to depth charges, mine are always kept ready at sea and I
have a third at hand in case of being wanted. A hand is told off
to put them at safe in case of the ship sinking so as to avoid the
fate of the Genistre.*

*There is one thing that I think ought to be pointed out and that is
that when engaging a submarine, a careful look out should be
kept on the other side. Sm. undoubtedly work in pairs, and it is
the hardest thing possible to keep men from being attracted to the
side where the vessel is being attacked.*

Q 13 also often found herself on search and rescue missions. On 11
January, looking for a submarine off the Casquets while disguised as
the Danish steamer, SS *KAI*, Marx 'picked up two lots of men' stranded
in the water. He always found the rescue work particularly distressing,
'the Germans are pigs!' so was delighted when, next day, he picked
up the submarine responsible. And, joy of joys, not only did he pick
up a German submarine – he blew it up! It was the moment he had
been waiting for! It had come at last! The entry was not written in capital
letters. Perhaps it should have been. It proved a crucial point in his
life, though not for the reasons he anticipated,

> 12 January – sunk a sub off the Casquets. Thank God after
> trying for 2 years and 3 months and having passed over 2, hit
> a third on my bow going 13 knots, been present when a trawler
> at 1000 yds has twice blown up her sweep on one, twice dropped
> a depth charge at another. At last we get one, blew her conning
> tower off.

On the same day he drafted his report to Admiralty,

> Sir,
> I have the honour to report that at 10.30 am today, Lieut.
> Campbell and Ldg. Signalman Robertson sighted an object in
> the water between 2 ½ and 3 mls off, 2 points before beam.

I was informed, and at 10.34 am making it out to be a submarine, the rattler was sounded.

10.38 am. The submarine fired a shell which passed over the after part of the ship. Of this I took no notice. In about 10 minutes another shell was fired passing ahead and beyond the ship. The engines were stopped and the engineer told to make as much steam blow off as possible. The submarine then signalled to stop, which we slowly answered and he fired a shot to enforce it. We then made Kai's number and he replied 'send a boat'.

At 11 am he fired a shell to hurry up boat as we were purposely delaying its departure. At 11.10 am Lieut. Tod got away in the boat and pulled to leeward, the sea being very considerable. The submarine being to windward, then advanced rapidly towards the port beam to 400 yds. 11.23 am the buzzer was sounded and Robert Jolley, Ldg Seaman, put his first shot (a 12 pdr) in at the bottom of the conning tower at a range of 250 to 300 yards. There was a very considerable explosion when the lyddite burst, which blew away the conning tower completely, scattering the four men who were on it. This I partly attribute to a bag probably containing bombs. Which had been brought on deck. The lifting of the conning tower was seen by captains of guns; Lieut. Campbell; Surgeon Prob. Millar, and Assistant Paymaster McKinnell, and I saw that the smoke was of two colours and of much larger volume than would have been caused by an ordinary lyddite 12 pr shell. Ch PO Marsh then put his second shot into the hull just before the place where the conning tower had been. Lionell Bradon, AB also put a 3 Pdr. Shell into the forepart of the hull. The submarine fired one shot which missed, after the guns were exposed. The black hole where the conning tower had been was plainly visible. The submarine began to sink, and the sea was covered with oil. The ship was steamed fullspeed to the spot where the submarine was seen to sink, which was clearly marked with oil and bubbles, two depth charges were dropped one set at 40 and one at 80 feet.

By the time the boat had been picked up, the oil had extended for quite 400 yards. A total of 8 rounds were fired at the submarine.

My officers and men carried out my wishes to my entire satisfaction.

A sketch was appended and a note to say that the submarine was sunk by the stern.

An eye-witness account from Petty Officer F Woodward, LTO was enclosed:

Sir,

On the 12 January 1917, I was ordered to let go both depth charges, the port charge being let go from the bridge. I slipped the starboard charge and went on deck to see the effect. A large column of water shot up on the outer edge of the disturbed water. I saw three objects with jagged ends. In colour they looked black, a lot of oil was about and a strong smell of oil.

An eye-witness account from various men

I am Sir your obedient servant...

Later Marx wrote a simpler, undated version to cousin Ethel,

I don't think I have told you of our action on the 12 January with a submarine, and it may interest you. About 10.30 am the officer of the watch and signalman saw something on the water, I was sent for and in about five minutes she was made out to be an enemy submarine on the surface. Of course, I was not what I appeared to be and as she was three miles off she opened fire and closed from 3 to 2 miles. Her shell passed over, we taking no notice. At 10.40 she fired again, another bad shot, but as their guns are more powerful than ours, we stopped and blew off steam. She then asked who we were and after a time I told her what I thought was good for her to know. She then made send your papers on board, so we leisurely lowered a boat, he hurried us up with another shell which also missed. It was blowing very fresh and our boat could not look at it and went away to leeward, the submarine being to windward. She had to come closer to close the boat. Meanwhile the crew of the submarine had brought on deck two bags of bombs for our benefit. It was very tempting to start in, but his wretched torpedo tube was trained on us. At last, when between three and four hundred yards off he altered his course and his tube no longer bore on us, so off went our disguise and the guns: the second shot hit his conning tower and all the 3rd and 4th shots hit him, tearing up his deck, and he sank in a most satisfactory manner. We then finished him off and I don't think he will commit any more acts of PIRACY. The number of poor devils they kill in cold blood is really enormous. Be discreet with this as it is not supposed to be good for you to know too much.

With best love, I am your affectionate cousin, JLM

Marx's devotion to his cousins, Edith and Ethel, was lifelong. It is hard not to think that there was still a lost love in that quarter.

After this, Marx went into Queenstown with a happy heart, 'saw Admiral who was friendly and asked me to stay. He wrote a very complimentary letter saying skilful seamanship and many other [good things].' Bayly also used Marx's attack on the German sub, and a similar experience of *Q 7*, to illustrate and confidentially inform other Q ship crews of 'the necessity of the most perfect discipline and organisation of the Q ships together with the danger of anything in her construction or design which would give her away'. Using Marx's information, he also described the nature of attacks on Q ships,

The submarine fires her first shots at long range: she gradually approaches and orders a boat to be sent to her, whilst the Q ship stops, blows off steam and gets boats ready. On the submarine's conning tower (this was seen by Q 13) is an Officer or rating lying flat with a pair of glasses watching every movement of the Q ship; and doubtless should the Q ship make any false move, should one man give the show away, the submarine could, with a slight movement of her helm, sink the Q ship at once with a torpedo.

The submarine approaches so as to get near enough to go on board and fix her bombs: the Q ships delays with her boats, etc. as much as she dares so as to get the submarine near enough to make certain of her guns hitting at the first round, thus giving no time for diving. As they close, the submarine gets suspicious; nervous of other ships approaching, or angry at losing time and so missing other chances; and opens fire at the ship (as with Q 7) at a longer range than the Q ship would wish. The Captain of the Q ship remaining hidden, has to decide entirely by himself when the exact moment has come to open fire, knowing that if his second shot misses, he not only frees the submarine to dive and bolt, but he has lost a great opportunity, and has given his ship away, probably had his ship's photograph taken.

Such a fitting as in one Q ship where the foremost main derrick is over the condenser discharge is quite enough to prevent the submarine ever approaching. No details are too small to be considered.

It was a happy time for Marx. He enjoyed dining and sleeping at Admiralty House. He always enjoyed good relations with Bayly and generally stayed there when he went into Queenstown. Marx noted that when Admiral Simms, the American Admiral, came into Queenstown, Bayly complimented him by flying the American flag from the Admiralty House staff – a blue square flag with three stars. 'A very diplomatic thing for Bayly to do.' Admiral Simms later recorded his appreciation of this graceful act. While staying with Bayly in January,

Marx met Commander Powell of *Q 2* who was there. Powell had been in the White Sea and just come back, 'he claimed a sub and got £200 (1/5 of reward)…'. He brought interesting news of Russia,

> Russians doing nothing…the railway is not open yet from the new Port which is up a narrow inlet…tons upon tons of necessities are going rotten and no attempt is made to get them away. The line is so bad that the trains always run off the rails and no one cares. He said it was hopeless. He got a torpedo under his engine room.

He spent several more relaxing days at Admiralty House, meeting various people. There was a touch of the old, relaxed Marx when he noted Miss Gubbins, 'a good worker, not much to look at'. He also noted the physical toll which the Q-ship work took of Bayly during the first half of 1917. Later, in June, he was pleased to see how much better Bayly looked, after a short holiday. But in February it was time to go back to patrolling off Ushant to find and sink more subs. It was not just the subs which were dangerous, the weather could be wild and treacherous. Caught in an easterly gale one day, getting dangerously close to the Bishops Rocks on the starboard bow, *Q 13* was lucky to escape unscathed, 'thank heaven it was clear or we should have shared the fate of Sir Cloudesly Shovel who lost his fleet on the Scillies'.

On 20 February Bayly received a letter from Admiralty, which he forwarded to Marx. It was the first intimation of trouble:

> *I am commanded by My Lords Commissioners of the Admiralty to acquaint you that they consider great credit is due to Admiral Marx and the officers and men under his orders for their action on this occasion but that the evidence of the submarine being sunk is not conclusive.*
>
> *His Majesty the King has been pleased to award the Distinguished Service Order to Admiral Marx, and the names*

of one officer and two men should be submitted for the award of
the Distinguished Service Cross and the Distinguished Service
Medals respectively.

I am to add that Their Lordships have approved the award of
£200 to the Q 13, and I am to request that this sum may be
distributed [among the crew] Admiral Marx being a
Commissioned Officer R.N. is not eligible to share. A report of
the distribution made should be forwarded to Admiralty.

Marx's pleasure at the honour of the DSO was destroyed by Admiralty's unwillingness to acknowledge the sinking of the submarine. He determined to prove them wrong.

Meanwhile, life continued in the usual manner. New disguises were undertaken and new submarines chased. Amidst the various incidents of false alarms and missed subs, there were frequent returns to Queenstown and in February Marx enjoyed the rare company of his son George, now a lieutenant in the Navy, who came in for a few days prior to his appointment to *Vernon*. It was while staying in Queenstown with Bayly in February that Marx was offered the chance of escorting Captain Nasmith[7] and his submarines to Canada, and trying for a German submarine off the west coast of Ireland. He left with Nasmith and the subs *E-32, E-54, D-7, D-3*, the night was very dark and the submarines were not good at station-keeping. They had to ease down to 9.5 [knots] which they improved later, but when it came on foggy they had to leave one of the subs behind because she got involved in 'a turn up with a patrol sloop. We heard the screams of the sloop on her siren. A ship, the *Araguaya* also made an SOS on seeing us,' but the other subs were safely despatched to their stations from Eagle Island on 20 February. In Canada, *Q 13* became the *General Walker* and had 'USA' painted on her outside and American colours were hoisted. Marx made inquiries as to whether America was at war yet and told, no.

Marx spent five days with the subs and then escorted them back to Queenstown, where Bayly met him and congratulated him on his DSO.

Marx makes nothing of his own honour in his diary entries but only records that he was 'delighted to be able to recommend Campbell, Jolley and Robertson, and that both of the latter are rather troublesome in consequence'. He had in fact recommended Temporary Lieutenant James Campbell RNR for his 'coolness, keenness of vision and aptness in suggesting methods of allaying the enemy's suspicion' and Leading Seaman Robert Jolley, Captain of the after gun, 'who had by his first shot, blown up the conning tower and managed the complicated method of screening his gun perfectly,' and Leading Signalman Johnson Robertson 'who first saw the submarine at a considerable distance when the visibility was far from good and during the time the submarine was coming, made his signals with great coolness, thoroughly entering into his part of deceiving the enemy'.

Not everybody was as matter-of-fact as Marx, about getting his decoration. Marx received a glowing letter from Fulcher, who had been his old Sub Lieutenant on *Iolanda*,

Wimbledon...1 April 1917

Dear Admiral Marx

Just a line to congratulate you on your latest decoration. I was most awfully pleased to hear the news and you really deserve it, may you live to get many more (Huns, I mean).

I am home now on ten days leave and rejoin the old ship on Wednesday.... I shall be dreadfully disappointed if I do not get a transfer to your ship. Admiral Batten is really awfully nice to serve under only just a little too nice and easy going, the ship has been just dead since you left and the crew want a good shaking up. I am sending six of them to Whale Island for 14 days gunnery course.... Williamson has broken out again to his old habits so I think this time he really must go. The Gibraltar patrol is really quite interesting now, we patrol the Spanish coast and often get a little Salvage work to do…. The Atalanta came in for £6000 salvage money but the poor old Iolanda seems to have no luck….they are fitting us with a small plane for scouting purposes and rigging a derrick on the mainmast for hoisting in and out… I think it is a good idea, I hope we shall have a little luck with them….the best of luck to yourself.

Yours sincerely, V. Fulcher

It was one of the few of Marx's later letters that have been preserved. There was also a letter, probably from Mrs Bayly,

27 March 1917

My dear Admiral,

Very many thanks for your letter which I got this morning and my best congratulations on your getting the DSO. I have been reading accounts of you in the papers today, and quite feel a sort of reflected glory in knowing you!

Lily also wrote a letter to tell her husband of all the congratulations she was receiving on his behalf. It casts an interesting light on life at home and on Lily's unusual and doughty disposition,

You say that you would like me to type my letters, so here is my first effort [one can see why, Lily's handwritten letters are almost illegible]. Mrs P.P. came yesterday, very sorry to miss you and full of congratulations…. Today I went in the dogcart to Rothsay to the Committee meeting, Mrs. Edmunds very full of congratulations. Dr. Farr sent you many congratulations and Louis said there was letter in the post doing ditto. I began to throw the coke that Loder brought in yesterday, over the fence into the place for it. You would have jeered at my efforts as it

was difficult to throw a spadeful so far and I nearly hit myself
with pieces that would hit against the wall and fall down the
wrong side. However, General Poore turned up so I had to go and
roar at him for quite twenty minutes. He was very sorry to miss
you and was very pleased at your success and honour. After he
went I returned to the coke and Berkley came and stayed as she
always does, till it was quite late, so you see that tho' I try to be
a woman on the land I am not quite a free agent.... I am
enclosing a copy, or rather the original document about St. V.
Please make corrections and say what I am to do with it and if it
is the sort of advertisement you want put in the Field.... I
think the Morning Post or Thimes [sic] would be useful
nearer the time. People are then looking for somewhere to
settle nearer the holidays. By the way, I must not forget to tell
you that Victoria was very congratulatory today...Mrs. Berkley
is sure that our tenant is going to marry Mr. Ellen, they have
been trysting on the Salisbury Rd and the other day, Mrs. H tead
with the Ellens and was very pink and gay. I sent your book back
to Mudies today...I also sent you gloves etc that were in your
drawer with collars, care of the Admiral Superintendant,
Devonport.... I heard from Con today, she seems very
flourishing and busy...there is no more news and besides, old
women bore you so goodnight and pleasant dreams of young
cooks. L.M.

When Marx heard that Admiralty was denying his sinking of the German submarine, he was horrified and sure there had been some mistake. He declared there could be no doubt that the conning tower was bodily removed by the violence of the explosion and the hole was clearly seen from the ship. Furthermore, bubbles were seen coming to the surface after she had sunk and when the depth charges were exploded on them a piece of the structure was seen to come to the surface. The sea was soon covered with oil.

*Under these circumstances I would venture to suggest that Their
Lordships may be asked to reconsider their decision and to grant
my Ship's Company the full reward of £1000 as in my opinion
they thoroughly deserve it.*

It was not only glory that a Q ship got when it sunk an enemy sub,
there was always the financial reward that went with it – *not* to the
Captain, but to the men. Marx was certain that there had been a
miscarriage of justice. To prove his point he provided Admiralty with
various submissions and eye-witness accounts of what had happened,
provided by Millar, the surgeon; Able Seaman Lionel Braden; Leading
Signalman Johnston Robertson; Sub Lieutenant Glen; the Assistant
Paymaster; and LTO Woodward.

Leading Signalman Robertson's report was typical:

Sir:

*On Friday 12 January 1917 I was Signalman of the forenoon
watch and at 10.30 am sighted a black object three points before
the Port beam 3½ miles away which I reported to the officer of
the watch. It proved to be the conning tower of a submarine and
was gradually closing and when 2½ to 3 miles off she opened fire
the shot going over. We eased to 60 revolutions and steam was
blown off. The submarine again opened fire firing two rounds at
a few minutes interval and hoisted signal FH 'Send a boat',
which we answered and she hauled down. We then stopped and a
boat manned by an officer and four hands was lowered and
pulled away from the ship. We made signal EU 'Boat is going to
you' which submarine did not acknowledge. The submarine was
still closing on Port Beam and when she was 250 to 300 yards off
we opened fire and went full speed ahead the first shot fell short,
second hit at bottom of conning tower causing an explosion
which was greater than that of a 12 pdr shell. The third also hit
the conning tower. The conning tower was completely destroyed*

only a few uprights being left. She then sank bow first the stern leaving the water as she went. We crossed over the place where she sank finding air bubbles rising and oil plentiful dropping two depth charges which exploded. As Submarine was approaching I noticed two men on the conning tower and two or more by the gun.

I am Sir your obedient servant

Johnston Robertson

Leading Seaman R. Jolley also made a written statement giving an eye-witness account of his own part in the action against the German U-boat and declared that he saw 'the conning tower was gone, and a large part of the after part blown away. The seas washed over her and she sank like a stone.' There was an amendment to his statement:

30 January 1917

Did your ensign staff and Danish ensign come down before you fired

John L Marx

Yes the ensign staff and Danish ensign came down with the rails, R Jolley

Rules of engagement meant that Q ships had to show their true national flag before opening fire. Marx wanted to make it clear that he did. Anxiously, he awaited the outcome.

In view of Marx's passionate conviction that he had sunk the German submarine, Admiralty decided reluctantly to inform him of the reasons for their implacable decision. They sent him, via Admiral Bayly, a copy of the secret telegram which had been intercepted from Berlin to the

German Embassy at Washington on 21 January 1917. The copy was wrongly dated 21 January 1916, but obviously referred to the incident of 1917.

> *On the 12th January, one of our submarines sighted a steamer in the English Channel.*

> *The Danish neutrality indications of the Danish flag and the words FAI Denmark painted in large white characters were clearly seen. The Commander of the Submarine thought he had to do with a harmless Danish steamer and approached, when suddenly the steamer dropped its mask. The boards of the aft wheel house fell down and a gun of between ten and fifteen centimetres calibre became visible over which the Danish flag remained flying. At the same time several shots were fired from guns on the steamer. The U boat succeeded in escaping from danger by quickly submerging. In the meantime it has been ascertained without doubt that the real FAI was lying in the English harbour of Sunderland up to 13th January, that we have to deal again with one of those shameless cases in which English seamen misuse the neutral flag in the most ruthless manner as U boat traps.*

However, Admiral Bayly told Marx that he had written to Admiralty and informed them that *Q 13* was alias *KAI* at the time. It looked as if there could have been some mistake in identity.

Marx's pleasure at the honour of the DSO was destroyed by Admiralty's unwillingness to acknowledge the sinking of the submarine. He determined to prove them wrong. *Q 13* had been disguised as *KAI* not *FAI* – there had been some mix-up.

Meanwhile, it was now time for *Q 13* to go into the dockyard for careening and for Marx to go home to prepare to receive his DSO at Buckingham Palace. Before he left Queenstown he called for a chat with Admiral Bethel,

Bethel, who was and is an avowed Fisherite spoke strongly about the Meux speech.[8] I held my tongue for a wonder, only observing that our Friend Fisher was senile and patted ladies hands and told them of his love affairs as a Midshipman.

On 10 March Marx went to Buckingham Palace to receive his DSO decoration. He found '...some 60 or 70 people to be decorated...King looking very seedy, quite kind and genial, asked me two or three questions...very wet at Clatford.' Again, a laconic, modest, entry.

At this time Jellicoe, in his campaign against the German U-boats, was deploying British submarines to attack German submarines and the decoying Q ships acted as bait. An account of the sinking of the *Benheather* shows what these ships were up against. At the beginning of April, *Q 13* was patrolling the North Sea with subs *E-54*, *E-32* and *HS*. On 1 April a shot struck the water 200 yards on the port beam of *Q 13*, in a heavy sea. A second shot struck, 400 yards over on the starboard beam, and a conning tower was made out at a distance of not less than 8,000 yards. A third shot fell in line with the ship 800 yards ahead. He had obviously got the range of *Q 13* who put her engines slow ahead and turned south to put her stern to the submarine and make as much smoke as possible to screen her. The engines were stopped and started but there was too much sea to go astern. The submarine appeared to approach for ten minutes then appeared to change its mind and after having veered east, then west, disappeared. Marx changed the colour of *Q 13*'s funnel and her cowls and waited for the sub to return but nothing further was seen. *E-48* had to return to Queenstown with damaged battery due to battery explosion and *HS* had to return to Berehaven to make repairs to her aerial. British subs were easily damaged and keeping up good maintenance was a constant problem.

Meanwhile a submarine had been sighted at the entrance to Berehaven Bay. She was fired on by a sloop off the entrance to the bay and dived, having failed to establish her identity by arc lamp. Establishing identity was important. Even at this time, damage by friendly fire was not uncommon. On 4 April, *Q 13* communicated visually with *E-32* and arranged a rendezvous for the next morning. Marx heard that their coxswain, Petty Officer G Saunders, had been washed overboard two days earlier, in the considerable sea of 1 April. Marx then instructed *E-32* to take station astern of *Q 13* and be prepared to dive and attack the enemy if it should succeed in torpedoing the Q-boat bait. At 10.57 the track of a torpedo was seen to pass astern and immediately afterwards a periscope was observed following the track and at a distance of 200 yards astern, steering from starboard to port. Marx then ordered *E-32* to dive and tried to drop a depth charge on the submarine's periscope but he could not pick it up again. He now observed that a steamer eight miles to the northwest had been torpedoed and went as quickly as he could towards her. He hoisted a signal for *E-32* to follow, which was taken in through her periscope. An SOS came from the damaged steamer ahead and he sighted a sub on the starboard bow, stationary on the surface about seven miles away. Easing down to eleven knots, Marx hoisted the Danish ensign and the international signal, '*I am coming to save life*' and commenced to zigzag. He saw the ship ahead again torpedoed and sighted survivors in three boats. Their ship had now disappeared and the shipwrecked men were rowing about desperately in boisterous weather in a heavy sea. The enemy sub dived about three miles to the northwest and Marx was able to pick up the Captain of the steamship, *Benheather*. Uncertain of the situation, Marx began to zigzag in the vicinity of the wreck. The Captain declared that he had been torpedoed on both sides from the same submarine, the second torpedo being fired from a range of at least 3,000 yards while the enemy was on the surface. Marx then stopped and picked up the rest of the relieved survivors. He rescued thirty-seven men from three rowing boats and survivors on rafts. *E-32* rose within half a mile in answer to a signal from *Q 13* and Marx directed her to submerge and wait for the return of the enemy. Two other sloops and a destroyer were ordered to keep clear. *E-32* continued to follow and fire at the enemy sub but the enemy eventually dived and abandoned the long and complicated chase. At the end of the account Marx pencilled into his diary, 'Bad luck. Bad shooting.'

On 21 May, Bayly gave Jolley and Robertson their medals. Flushed with success, Jolley stayed overnight in Queenstown against Vice Admiral's orders. Marx seems determined to have allowed no *lèse-majesté* and asked the Vice Admiral to court-martial Jolley. He refused and sensibly told Marx to deal with it himself. There were always niggling problems with the men, 'Muchronabie failed to announce my signal…had a disagreeable time with both Tod and Campbell at four a.m. Both rude and I got angry. I think that they are now at heel….' It is not surprising that such demanding work produced tensions in the men and irritability in the Commander. Marx was desperately unhappy about Admiralty's attitude towards the sinking of his German sub and Tod's uncertain navigation was a constant problem to him: 'Off the Fastnetts. Tod sends down that we are 4 miles from Galley Head. We are warned to keep 5 miles off all headlands. I told him not to go within 6…'

But Marx was about to be dealt another blow. The pleasure of being informed that he was to have the honour of receiving a CB at Buckingham Palace on 30 June ('I see I have to congratulate you again,' wrote Edith Bayly. 'I am so glad and hope it will go on and on…can you come out and have tea?') was quite ruined by an interview with Jellicoe the day before his investiture. It was not a happy occasion. To start with, Jellicoe told him 'to be careful and hoist my flag'. Was Jellicoe, who was always concerned for the safety of the Q-ship men, warning Marx not to leave it too late before he opened fire for his own good, or was he implying that Marx might have been dodging the rules of engagement by not showing his flag until after he had opened fire? An Old Navy captain sailing 'too close to the wind'? Be that as it may, the sting in the interview came when Jellicoe said that the submarine Marx supposed he had sunk on 12 January had, in fact, got away and returned to Germany. Marx was horrified and furious but managed to say calmly enough, '…in this we agreed to differ'. (He privately vowed again, to prove otherwise.) Jellicoe then added insult to injury by saying that there would be no base for Marx in future and he would have to become a convoy sloop.

Leaving the interview, Marx was only cheered by meeting Everett 'who was pleasant' and Casson who called him 'a brave man'. In the evening he took refuge with Lily at 40 Albert Mansions and dined with his old favourite cousins, Edith and Ethel. The Saturday brought a mixed weekend to a good end. Marx duly received his CB at the Palace and recorded modestly, '...saw the King who was highly complementary'.

Life quietened down. Bayly ordered *Q 13* to Queenstown to clean her boilers and look into a new alteration of her gun platform. For the time being it was back to the ordinary management of a Q ship. An incident on 5 July underlined just how little time a Q-ship commander had for decision. At ten a.m. Marx sighted a white painted submarine and gave chase. Four minutes later the submarine opened fire. Fortunately, the shot fell beyond him but it was followed by rapid fire. Marx altered course and threw smoke boxes overboard, several of which did not burn. He reduced speed to eight knots and sent out the mercantile SOS. He continued to pursue her. At 10.07 the submarine dived out of danger. *Q 13* continued to seek her for another hour and a half. At 1.30, a periscope passed from starboard to port at about 100 yards distant from the ship. The area was searched until 3.45 but nothing further found. The German sub was apparently chasing the *Clan Mackintosh*. In this time of considerable submarine activity there were many sightings. Marx was always concerned to find out whether his suspicions of submarines present in the area of his operations were later confirmed by events and wrote to Admiralty to establish if they had any news relating to the times when he thought he had hit a sub in *Agatha* and *Iolanda*. Often the only sign at the end of an action was 'heavy oil' as the sub got away. The secrecy of *Q 13* was well preserved throughout and resulted in some interesting newspaper articles relative to *Aubretia*'s incognito feats: 'the men had the good fortune to be rescued by a trawler'.[9]

After the interview with Jellicoe, Marx was more determined than ever to prove that *Q 13* did sink a U-boat. In desperation, he wrote to Admiral Duff in July,[10]

*I hope you will excuse me writing to you on a personal matter.
On the 12th Jan 1917, we knocked the conning tower out of a
submarine, holed her below the water line, struck her deck by the
foremost gun which must have put it out of action, hit her twice
with a three pdr, saw the big hole where the conning tower had
been before she sank, and saw her sink, after that dropped two
depth charges on her and saw a portion of her hull come up with
the gases.*

*I am afraid the First Lord still thinks that she got back to
Germany and in the January monthly chart of submarines, in no
9 track of the UB type it is supposed that after this handling she
attacked the SS Maru Hakata at 11.15 am, on 13th Jan, the SS
Toftwood at 5.10 pm, the SS Martin at 11 am on the 14th, the
Danish SS Cornwall at 12.30 pm, 15th, the Spanish SS Manuel
on the 16th at 1.35 pm, the French SV Jeune at 8 pm on 17th,
Spanish SS Valle at 5 pm, 17th.*

*The First Sea Lord told me that the relatives of the prisoners
taken by her had received letters from them on getting to
Germany, and I am so certain we sunk her I am writing to ask if
you could give me the addresses of these people that I might get
into communication with them and find out if the submarine
which sunk their ships had no conning tower or gun as I should
like to find out for certain if there is not some misapprehension
about it. I know that you are always as busy as possible but this
is important to me as I have made a statement which from this
evidence appears to be untrue and one feels a bit sore on the
subject. Owing to these ships being turned over to convoy duty I
am losing my most interesting job and if you have another
vacant ship I should much like to continue serving under you.*

Admiral Duff apparently did nothing but Marx received a reply from
the Intelligence Division of Admiralty:

In view of the decision of the Board of Admiralty with regard to this engagement, it would be quite impossible again to raise the question of the fate of the submarine, unless any fresh evidence could be adduced bearing on the matter. I am sorry to say that no such evidence is at present available, but you may be sure that every effort is made by the Intelligence Division to promote a just distribution of rewards for actions against enemy submarines.

It was not rewards Marx wanted but justice. Perhaps all this stress was affecting his health, which had always had a question mark over it. On 22 July he saw Dr Townsend who told him his blood pressure was normal. Quite a feat for an older man in this time of high activity, when the prospect of immediate death was never far away and there was mental as well as physical stress. Bayly thought Q-ship commanders did not usually last for more than a year – and most of them were young! It was a hazardous business, not only when trying to engage and sink the enemy but when involved in the considerable amount of rescue work, the ship undertook:

> We picked up the crew consisting of 16 British, 1 Greek and 44 Chinamen and proceeded to the Westward turning round so that we should arrive on the spot where the submarine had been working, when it became dark…

A ship was always in danger when picking up survivors. The rescue work alone was courageous.

It is possible that Marx became genuinely unwell at this time though he makes little of it in his diary. It is more likely that Bayly, or Marx himself, was using it as an excuse for the bombshell that Bayly dropped, perhaps out of kindness, on 19 September:

> Bayly told me he had telegraphed to Jellicoe for me to be relieved. (I suppose it was because of my being off colour) he said we had lost so many Qs he could no longer take the

responsibility of having one [me?] in command. I was sick but said nothing. He asked what I would like. I said, anything at sea and he said that he would ask that I might have a survey or something of that sort.

It seemed no time now was to be lost in removing the old Admiral from the Q ships. Marx was superseded in *Aubretia* on 24 September. A week later, on 29 September, he again saw Jellicoe. His worst fears were confirmed: 'He said he had no job and wanted to give me in shore one and sent me to Duff who was almost unfriendly and I don't see much chance of getting [anything].' With a heavy heart Marx turned over his ship on Sunday 1 October 1917 and returned to Clatford Lodge, for the moment weary and 'glad to be home'.

However, things were little better at Clatford. He found the place 'much gone to pieces'. Johnson (the gardener) had given a week's notice and was leaving his cottage. Marx turned his frustrated energies to his house. He demolished the cowhouse, which a tree had knocked down, demolished another shelter, bought galvanised iron for the bad workshop roof and spent an agreeable time mending it. He took an interest in the design and purchase of deckchair hammocks. He fixed the water pump. He sold a cow and a calf for £46. He took himself to Winchester for an *interesting* local government council meeting and to Winton for a Mental Deficiency meeting. Above all, there were the old pleasures of hunting and shooting. Son George came to visit and they enjoyed the field sports together. A complimentary letter from Bayly, saying that *Aubretia* was 'a 95 p.c. ship', and a supportive letter from Everett saying he would see what he could do to get Marx further employment, cheered him.

But the Navy had not yet done with Admiral Marx. Two months later, on 25 November 1917, Marx received notice of a final appointment. He was to hoist his flag in the escort ship, HMS *Bayano*, *ACS* and be in charge of a large mercantile convoy. Was this a final chance to fly his admiral's flag at sea? There is some confusion here as to the nature of this appointment. He had been promoted to Vice Admiral (retired) in July of 1910, and Admiral (retired) in June of 1913. He had served as temporary Captain, RNR, in the Auxiliary Patrol and the Q ship. Was he to serve as a captain in charge of convoys, or since ordered to hoist his flag, as an admiral? Throughout the first half of 1918, the Navy list shows him merely as temporary Captain, RNR. He disappears from the second half of the year's list. But *Bayano*, at 6,788 tons, was large enough to accommodate flag facilities and ACS may stand for Admiral's Cruiser Squadron, or Auxiliary Cruiser Squadron. Their Lordships' letter on Marx's retirement[11] gives indication that it may simply have been regarded as a 'one off' honorary admiral's appointment brought about by the nature of the war. Presumably, when he 'hoisted my flag' (written twice in his diary!) in *Bayano*, to command the first of several big mercantile west-coast convoys, it was the flag of a full admiral. Or was it? His last demanding work in charge of convoys casts light on this.

---

1 Rear Admiral Campbell VC, DSO, *My Mystery Ships*, 1928.

2 Ibid.

3 Vice Admiral L Bayly, commanding on the coast of Ireland, July 1915.

4 Probably Vivian R Brandon.

5 Robert F. Pitcairn?

6 Admiral Charles Dare.

7 Probably Commander M E Nasmith, notably promoted Lieutenant for five firsts in subs' exams.

8 The Hon Sir A E Bethell was the Admiral commanding Coastguard and Reserves in 1915. He, like Marx and Admiral of the Fleet, Sir H Meux, disagreed with the idea of recalling Lord Fisher to Admiralty. Meux made a trenchant and amusing speech about it in Parliament.

9 Undated, unattributed, probably local, newspaper article referring to *Benheather* rescue.

10 Rear Admiral A Duff, Admiralty war staff.

11 See letter of retirement at the close of Chapter Fifteen.

Fifteen

The Convoy Admiral – December 1917 to June 1918

'...not a bad record considering what brutes they are...'

On 1 December 1917 Rear Admiral Marx travelled to Shieldhall Wharf in Glasgow to take a look at his new ship and hoist his flag. He found the *Bayano* 'a fine ship, accommodation good. Speed about 16, 14 when loaded.' As usual, he threw himself into the new work, sending telegrams to Admiralty about getting a motorboat and increasing the number of crew. The Paymaster was away so he tackled the Deputy Paymaster. By 15 December Marx was ready to start sea preparations but was disturbed to find, again, a very disgruntled crew aboard *Bayano*. 'In the forenoon I fell the ship's company in and enquired into their grievances as I found that there was a want of discipline amongst them.'

Initial trials off Greenock were successful, including those of the paravanes (torpedo-shaped device towed at a depth regulated by its vanes or planes to cut the moorings of submerged mines) but the freezing climate of the snow-clad hills of the North took their toll on Marx. '*Cold very bad.*' Lily at the same time was writing of the ice and snow at home, but her heart seemed warmer, this time saying, '*...it would be nice to see you again, if only for one minute, I can manage* *to be charming for that length of time...and sending heaps of love, L. Marx.'*

On the 20th, the *Bayano* set off for Lamlash where it anchored and Marx found his first convoy waiting. The old problem of crew unrest was still apparent. When he went ashore in the evening, he met the Boatswain. The Boatswain took the opportunity of telling him that 'our men would not work with his'. Brookes AB, who had earlier complained about merchant men and naval men working together, 'again stepped out and said that the men objected to working with other men who get more money'.

> I told him he had made his agreement and must abide by it. I also saw Mr. Drew who was and had been drinking and told him that he was the principal cause of this and that if any more trouble occurred, I would land him and send him under arrest to his depot.

This was Marx's first experience of a big mercantile convoy. He found it was not an easy thing to manage. To start with, there was not only trouble with the discrepancy of pay between the Royal Navy and the Merchant Navy, but any number of other problems. As they prepared to leave,

> the 9 ½ knot ship had a lunatic aboard and [the Captain] is intending to leave him behind and will miss the convoy. Castle [the Master] has not got hold of the way to manage his ship and nearly fouled a buoy. The ships took 1hr to go out. We were led by the Albion. The Justinian blew out a boiler tube and delayed us half an hour...picked up the destroyers...

The *Justinian* remained a problem. Next day, by eight a.m., she was nearly out of sight. Marx sent a destroyer to tell her to slow down to six knots with the others. She made a signal saying she could only go nine knots. While the other ships kept a good station, at one p.m. the *Justinian* was one degree out in her longitude. 'God help the crew,' declared Marx. At four p.m. the escorting destroyers asked leave to go and the convoy was on its own, to start the course to Halifax. The weather became surprisingly good and on a pleasant and peaceful Christmas Day, Marx read the King's seasonal message to the men. Then the course became biting cold, the snow thick and the compass froze. When they arrived at Halifax, Drew made a mess of the sounding and they had to go to sea instead of into harbour. The fog was thick and though they thought they were steering for Halifax, they found themselves off Crops Island and twenty-seven miles from Cape Sabel. They received new orders to make for St John, New Brunswick.

The weather remained thick and they heard that the thermometer on shore stood at twenty-four degrees below zero. The ship was covered with ice. In Marx's cabin the outer walls had a quarter of an inch of ice. The pipes were all frozen and the compass solid. They could not sound, until they got the forge alight to thaw the sounding wire. Marx had to go and superintend the soundings because they were coming up false. Eventually they hit the coast ten miles south of St John, and to their relief saw the smoke of the town in the distance. Marx, surprisingly fit after such an experience, enjoyed a brief but pleasant stay at St John:

> St. John was yesterday honoured by a visit from Admiral C. Marx C.B. a retired imperial naval officer, who is at present the commander of the Canadian coast patrol service.... . He was accompanied by Commander Roberts of the naval service. Admiral Marx is one of England's distinguished naval officers...they were registered at the Royal Hotel.[1]

Then it was to Halifax to meet with Admiral Chambers[2] and discuss a conference of captains that was to be arranged. He found that there had been a terrible explosion and fire in the city. He had to have a pass for the devastated district,

> ...and devastated I found it, everything in small pieces except the wooden houses which in many cases had sides and roofs

blown out and off, quite whole. I saw a tug complete on top of the wharf, her engineer escaped. He was in the boiler room and climbed out quite dazed and was found afterwards. A man with a sleigh gave me a lift to his house where he expected to find the kitchen chairs the only thing he had left. He told me that he was away when the explosion occurred, that his son of 9 years ran back from school and rescued the baby.[3]

Calling on the Governor, Marx met a Mrs Black who had come from America to help with the relief work. She asked him 'if he had ever met a Captain Marx who had married an Australian and who had one son, a boy in the service who had died under sad circumstances. I told her that I had and he had not died. She said that she had agreed to meet Mrs Marx in England but Mrs Marx had not turned up.' Marx was the toast of the town and introduced to many other people, including bankers from Massachusetts who had come up about the explosion, and 'the good looking Mrs. Chambers'. Halifax provided a delightful but short-lived break.

On 7 January 1918 twenty convoy ships were ready to return to England. There was a force-four wind and heavy rain squalls. The ships became scattered. Marx went down to the rear of the convoy and appointed a vice commodore to keep the tail in hand. When the weather allowed it, there was firing practice and firing with the cannon tube. Not everybody appreciated Marx's handling of this, Lieutenant Ensor, Gunnery Officer, RNR, was 'exceedingly insubordinate' at target practice. There was the constant problem of keeping the ships all together. On 14 January '*Benwood* and *Norwegian Victor* miles astern, went down to them.... . Collected the convoy except *Largo Laws*.' Apart from the danger of submarines, there were always the dangers of collisions, with untried crews. On the 15th Marx felt a shock on the *Bayano* and the alarm buzzer sounded. He went to the bridge and saw 'a black mass in the considerable sea', he was told an oiler had run into their portside. Thwaites, on watch, said it had no lights and though he tried to avert the collision, porting and starboarding, it was inevitable.

Fortunately the damage was only to the deckhouse, nothing underwater, but the cabin was smashed and the after boats' derrick twisted. The oiler was later discovered to belong to the Standard Oil Company. *Benwood* continued to cause trouble by being so slow. Marx told the Captain he would have either to abandon him or tow him, because he would not endanger nineteen other ships for him. The Captain signalled that he was worth $400,000. Next day, she dropped astern with engine trouble. Three of the ships were running out of coal. Marx wired this to Admiralty. By the 19th all ships were within ten miles except *Largo Laws* who was 'some days back'. They still had 616 miles to go and a heavy gale blew up again scattering the convoy. When the gale abated, Marx could see only three ships in sight. After much signalling, he got those in front 'in a cluster' and went back to find the Commodore who was with a ship, fifteen miles astern:

> I told him to come ahead full speed, then 8th Engineer let the water out of one of our boilers and we nearly had the crowns down so I did not get back to my lot until too late to join up with the Commodore. So I wired him to go 7 while I told my lot 6½.

> And trust I may find him in the morning. I also wirelessed to destroyers. I am fortunate in having got all the 18. Largo Lawes I have given up.

One is reminded of a sheepdog desperately trying to get the flock into the fold.

The convoy was now approaching England, only 350 miles to London. Marx ordered the ships to 'get out defence' (a system of protection against torpedoes) but only two out of the eighteen could get it out. The escort destroyers Marx had signalled for arrived on 22 January. There were eight of them, including two American destroyers. The American destroyers were ordered to convoy the ships destined for Falmouth. The others escorted the ships bound for London. Marx could at last relax, his first convoy had been stressful but relatively successful.

> Thus closes the convoy: one collision, one missing, not a bad record considering what brutes they are.

Bayano sailed alone into Victoria Docks on 28 January at one in the morning, 'the whole of the river a blaze of light, no wonder the Germans find London… .' Marx went to Admiralty and saw Duff and others and then made his way home where he found Lily 'flourishing'.

No sooner had he arrived home than a most unpleasant incident occurred:

> Bucher and Bert came to shoot and at the same time Wormwold and a Police Inspector came to search the house for food none of which they found. I went to find Grahame who had gone to shoot at Redges, found him, told him how indignant I was at the Indignity.

Perhaps Marx was unaware of food restrictions. Perhaps not. Next day Marx told the goods porter to hold the food that had come with him from Canada and several days later he arranged to have it returned!

However, Marx did not remain long at home. His convoy work had not ended. He appears to have been involved with six more convoys before the war concluded and made interesting summaries as to the attacks made upon them. Perhaps his convoy management improved: he declared convoy OD 98, from Plymouth on 10 June, 'the best convoy for keeping station and for speed, that I have seen'. This too was not easy work for an old man. Conditions in the North, with often freezing temperatures and difficult weather, continued to demand the courage and endurance of which Marx seemed to have a never-ending supply. His daily diary ends in February of 1918 but his work with the convoys did not end until July.

The war itself came to an end in November and John Locke Marx was finally no longer needed. His beloved naval life could not last forever. On 16 December 1918 Admiralty wrote to him at Clatford Lodge:

Sir,

I am commanded by my Lords Commissioners of the Admiralty to acquaint you that, in view of the present position of affairs, no further opportunity of utilising your services will occur, and it will therefore be necessary for you to revert to the Retired List as from 7th January, 1919.

2:— My Lords desire me to express to you their appreciation of the manner in which you have carried out arduous, responsible and valuable service while flying your flag as Flag Officer of a Commissioned Escort Ship in charge of a large mercantile convoy passing through the areas of great enemy activity.

It marked the end of an illustrious and heroic career, acknowledged by the Royal Navy and his peers alike. Admiral Bayly paid tribute to him:

No weather daunted him, no difficulty was too great; he was always ready and nearly always smiling.[4]

---

1 Undated, unattributed cutting from St John newspaper.

2 Admiral B M Chambers was in command of the Naval College, Geelong, Australia, until May 1914.

3 A French ship, the *Mont-Blanc*, laden with explosives for the war in Europe, collided with an empty ship, the *Imo*, going to collect relief supplies for the civilians in Belgium. The collision caused the biggest man-made explosion so far seen. Two thousand people on ships and shore were killed, including a number of children. Over 9,000 were injured.

4 Admiral Lewis Bayly, *Pull Together*, p199.

Sixteen

Retirement

'A Truly Grand Old Man'

Once reluctantly retired from the Navy, Marx looked round for more opportunities to serve in civil life and he was soon involved in local affairs. On 30 June 1919, he was appointed to the Commission of the Peace for Hampshire and sat regularly on the Andover Bench, being particularly useful, so his colleagues declared, when servicemen came before the magistrates.[1] For a while he represented the Hurstbourne Tarrant electoral division on the county council and was an effective member of the Standing Joint Committee. He was interested in the British Israelite Federation and took the chair at local meetings. But his great love was the local hunt, the Tedworth. He was Honorary Secretary for a long time before the war and only relinquished it in 1914, when he rejoined the Navy. He acted again in the same capacity for the east side of the county from 1925–27. When he died, a leading member of the hunt recorded that he never missed a meeting of the committee,

> ...of which he was a very old standing member and possessed as he was of ripe experience and common sense, he was a tower of strength to the Committee and more particularly his successors whenever any difficulties arose. Up to the end of last season he hardly ever missed a meet of hounds, within

reasonable distance of his home, never sending his horse on but riding to the Meet and back himself, an example to many far younger. Although handicapped by failing eyesight and an injured leg, his nerve remained unimpaired, and he had a preference for riding a five year old to the more staid and mannerly animal which his great age would have justified. A truly Grand Old Man.[2]

As much as possible Marx involved himself in Naval Service interests. He became President of the Andover branch of the British Legion and according to his obituary,

> ...members felt a thrill when he came on parade. In fair weather or foul, he always took charge until recently, and although over eighty years of age then, one could not but envy him his smartness on parade. His breast always gleamed with the medals he had won for gallantry. Unfortunately in December, 1936, when he was away in a Nursing Home, his medals were stolen from his home, and although he recovered them eventually, they were not the same as formerly, for they had been damaged by burning.

Throughout his retirement, Marx never ceased to stress the interests of the Senior Service, especially the importance of Navy Week in his home county of Hampshire. He was behind the tour of the model of HMS *Repulse*, which with 'a crew' to explain all about it, was a familiar scene in the towns and bigger villages of the countryside. It was thought a word from Admiral Marx went a long way to inducing young men to sign on for the Navy. He served on pensions committees connected with ex-servicemen and worked in connection with King George's Fund for Sailors. As his obituarist said, 'His was a busy life, well lived, a pattern for all to emulate.'

But throughout his retirement, with its full round of civic duties and its country sports pleasures, one thing never ceased to plague retired Admiral Marx. He still believed there had been a miscarriage of justice in relation to his action of 12 January 1917. He thought that if he could only find out the truth about it, he could prove that *Q 13* had sunk a German submarine. He did not believe that the U-boat he had hit could have returned to Germany. He believed, if he could only find enough evidence, he would change Admiralty opinion. He would even take Their Lordships to court if he could find enough evidence to produce a case.

As soon as he was retired, he wrote to Admiralty from Clatford Lodge on 21 January, asking for the evidence on which they based their conclusion that *Q 13* had not sunk *UB 23* or another German U-boat. He received a reply from the Intelligence Department, dated 21 January 1919, stating that the principal points of evidence were:

> *1 A circumstantial German account of the action, published on 20th January 1917, stated that the submarine escaped by rapidly submerging.*
> *2 A reliable prisoner of war, captured in 1917, stated that U.B.23 was damaged on 12th January, 1917 by Q.13 disguised as S.S. KAI. He added that she was badly hit, but was able to submerge, and was then attacked with depth charges, none of which did any damage.*
> *3 There is no German submarine missing before May 1917 to which a case cannot definitely be assigned, whereas this action took place on 12 January.*
> *4 U. B. 23 was subsequently damaged by depth charges, and interned herself at Corunna on 29th July 1917.*

This did not satisfy Marx who now with time on his hands, prepared to defend his position. He wrote back on 2 February 1919:

> *Sir,*
>
> *I have the honour to thank you for sending me a precis of what the Admiralty evidence would be in the event of my bringing into court the case of the submarine attacked by HMS Aubretia*

on January 12th 1917. I should be grateful if in the event of any evidence coming to hand as to the correctness of my opinion that the submarine was utterly destroyed, it may be sent me.

I submit that this opinion is also that of the 70 eye witnesses of the action and also of the Naval Constructors I have consulted on the matter.

I would also submit that the account of the affair was taken to Germany by a companion of the submarine attacked, who witnessed the action and was the submarine which attacked the SS Marie [?] on 13 and the Softwood on 14th, the Danish S.S. Cornwall, on 18th, the Spanish SS Manuel on the 16th the SS Jennerton, 17th, the Spanish SS Valle. All of which attacks are attributed to the submarine attacked by HMS Aubretia, in the Admiralty submarine chart track and which it is absolutely impossible for her to have carried out without a conning tower (see sketch). The gaping hole was caused by the explosion by a Lyddite shell of at least six German bombs seen by us to be brought on deck and placed at the foot of the conning tower, ready to go on board the Aubretia, any of which would have sunk her.

I would also point out that witnesses when prisoners seldom speak the truth, especially if they are Germans.

Your obedient servant

John L Marx
Admiral

There was a brief respite as Marx settled into his new retired life at Clatford Lodge. Clatford was at Anna Valley, just south of Andover. The house had fifty acres of land, rough shooting and a stretch of the Pill Hill Brook, a tributary of the River Test. There was much to be done on the domestic front. He liked to make his own furniture. (Perhaps Lily was less pleased to be told to use it rather than buy new!) But in 1921 there was a return to the ever-present problem. How could he prove *Q 13* had sunk *UB 23* or another German sub? Was it possible to take Admiralty to court? Could he find enough additional evidence to make his case?

During 1921, Admiral Marx made his final effort to vindicate himself and the crew of *Q 13*. Letters went back and forth to Admiralty. Men who had been on *Q 13* were contacted again and new eyewitness accounts were sent to Admiralty. He wrote to Admiral Edward Charlton,[3] working at the Naval Inter-Allied Commission of Control, in Berlin and asked him to contact Admiral Reymann, the President of the German Naval Peace Conference, for information. Charlton replied on 14 March 1921:

Dear Admiral Marx,

On receipt of your letter, I wrote at once to Admiral Reymann, the President of the German Naval Peace Conference and I enclose his reply—

This was the reply:

I have the honour to inform you that according to our records here, no German Submarine was lost in the English Channel on 12th January 1917, but that a German Submarine was sunk there on 14th January 1917; it is believed that it was a victim of Q 7 (ship PENSHURST). No other German submarines were lost in the English Channel in 1917

I am, etc.

Max Reymann

Charlton continued,

I am afraid it will not be of much assistance to you but I have no reason to doubt his statement as we have exchanged similar requests before. I will endeavour to sound him on the next occasion as to whether any U boat returned that month badly damaged – But it requires careful handling, as if he knew the object, he would probably close down –

I return the Kaiser's telegram. Of course, at that time, their feelings were much hurt at being taken in by a legitimate 'ruse de guerre'. I have just noticed that the Kaiser's telegram is dated 21st January 1916 and that was the date we enquired about; your letter however, states that 'the date of the action was Jan 12th, 1917'. [How Marx's heart must have lifted at this point!] One of these dates must be incorrect. Please let me know if I can make further enquiries. All quiet here and the anti-Entente meetings yesterday were an absolute failure.
Yours sincerely Edward Charlton

Ten days later a sympathetic Charlton wrote,

I enclose a further reply from Admiral Reymann.
I gather that the date 14th January, 1917 was an assumed one as nothing more was heard of that particular German submarine after that date. Q7 must also be only an assumption but for some reason Reymann does not give the number of the last boat. I will endeavour to extract it.

*1 April 1921 – Just got it by telephone **U.B.37.** I hope this may be of use to you and except for the German's estimate of the date, it seems good confirmation of your very clear narrative. Our opposite numbers on the G.N.P.C. are fairly truculent at present but the Military ones are more so as there is rather a* *tendency to allow even further occupation of Germany to take place in preference to carrying out some of the troublesome details of the treaty. My wife's brother in law, Captain Kenneth Dewar, is living somewhere near you. Perhaps you have met?*

Yours sincerely,
Edward Charlton

On 6 April, Marx wrote to thank Charlton for all the trouble he had so kindly taken but repeated his conviction that if his 'sunk' sub had got back to Germany, it would have been a miracle. His letter continued,

You are well out of this country just at present as what with the coal strike and the threat of the Railway men and Transport workers to come out, everything is held up to say nothing of the arson that is going on. My next door neighbour has had 7 fires lately on his farm and there have been many rick fires in this neighbourhood and no-one caught — saw mills near here were burnt about 10 days ago. All men on leave have been recalled by the naval and military authorities and I do not see much signs of the Millenium or a better England just yet.

On 6 April 1921, Marx made his final appeal for justice as he saw it, to Admiralty,

Sir,

I have the honour to request that I may be informed of the U. Boat acknowledged by the German Admiralty to have been destroyed in the Channel on or about the 14th January, 1917 and if it has been accounted for and credited to Q 7 (HMS Penshurst).

I have been making enquiries and find that U 37 was destroyed about that date and I firmly believe that she was the one destroyed by Q 13 off the Casquets on Jan 12th, 1917.

I am induced to make these enquiries on finding that telegram no. 365 to the Vice Admiral Commanding at Queenstown which was forwarded to me was dated in error, Jan 21st 1916, instead of Jan 21st 1917.

Telegram no. 365 enclosed gives the following intercepted telegram from Berlin.

I have always been of the opinion that the information given in the telegram was taken to Germany by a second submarine which I think must have been present at this engagement.

In the January 1917 chart giving the depredations of the enemy's submarines, the U boat which Q 13 destroyed is given the credit for having sunk many ships before she returned to Germany. This, of course was an impossibility as when I last saw her, she had no gun or conning tower and was besides, badly holed as we could plainly see, being quite close to her.

I am etc.
John L Marx
Admiral (retd.)

I would be much obliged if the enclosures in the following list may be returned to me eventually.

List of enclosures.
1 Copy of my letter and reports of action.
2 Copy of German telegram to V.A. Queenstown, No. 365 2-1-1916, really 1917.

3 *Copy of J. Woodward's, P.O. L.T.O., statement.*
4 *Ad. Van Reymann's letter to Admiral Charlton 30.3.21.*

Their Lordships were not to be moved. Their final letter arrived on 23 April 1921,

Sir,

With reference to your letter of the 6th instant, I am commanded by my Lord Commissioners of the Admiralty to inform you that the submarine engaged by HMS Q 13 on the 12th January, 1917, although damaged, was not sunk. The submarine sunk on the 14th January 1917 has been credited to HMS Q 7.

In returning the enclosure to your letter, Their Lordships desire me to draw to your attention the extremely confidential nature of Admiralty telegram No 365 of 21st January 1917 to the Vice Admiral Commanding, Queenstown, and to request that you will treat the copy in your possession as a 'Most Secret' document.

Marx's bid to change Admiralty minds had failed. It looked as if it was the last he would hear of the affair. His day in court was not to be forthcoming.

However, there was another day in court to come for Admiral Marx, about his submarine, though not quite what he had envisaged.

In 1933 Dr Halliday's book, *The Arches of the Years*, was published. It was an autobiography written by the same doctor, Halliday Sutherland, who had visited Admiral Marx earlier. It covered a time during the war when the doctor had served with the Navy. In his book he recounts two meetings with 'a pukka R.N. Captain, aboard an armed yacht', one meeting already referred to, and another including an apparent conversation with Marx's commander, referring to the sinking of a German submarine, presumably the incident of 12 January, which in the words of *The Times*, 6 July 1934, purported to give an account of the engagement with the submarine, and…contained the statement that Admiral Marx, after ramming the submarine, had, in his enthusiasm, caused to be blown two blasts on the whistle of the ship, although the engines of the ship were being reversed at the time and two blasts of the whistle were the signal for the relief of depth charges carried at the stern.

That could only mean that Admiral Marx had needlessly imperilled the lives of those under his command.

Marx was furious upon reading this account and sued the author and publisher, Mr G Bles, for libel. The action was short-lived. Counsel for Marx stated that if the court case were to go on, witnesses would be called to prove that the account of the engagement was entirely untrue, that the submarine was sunk by gunfire and not by ramming and that Admiral Marx had always shown himself a man of the utmost coolness and resource. Dr Sutherland did not realise the implications of what he had done. He genuinely admired the heroic Admiral and apologised at once, declaring that he now realised the account was quite untrue. He expressed his deep regret for publishing what he acknowledged to be a serious libel on a most gallant officer; he had only been reporting hearsay and had believed it to be true at the time; the offending passage would be deleted in further editions of the book. Mr Bles likewise apologised and said he 'was most distressed to think he had, however, innocently, been the means of causing offence to such a distinguished officer'. Matters were settled. Marx, who had 'never wished to make a penny out of the matter', simply asked that the record be withdrawn on the terms endorsed on counsel's briefs. These included an indemnity with regard to Marx's costs and a payment of a small sum to him as token of the defendant's regret.

One might expect that that would be the final, disillusioned end to the story of the sinking of Marx's enemy submarine. But no! On one amazing day, on the anniversary twenty years later of the attack on the U-boat, Marx received a telegram from a certain Kapitan Leutnant Ziemer, apparently the Commander of *UB 23*. It informed Marx that he had been the Captain of 'the submarine which Q 13 did not sink…'![4] Why it should take so long for such a missive to arrive and what Marx thought when he received such unquestionable proof we can only guess at. However, perhaps the certainty of outcome and the ensuing friendship spoken of by family memory, helped to mollify Marx at last. Apparently friendly letters were exchanged between the two old enemy commanders as they reflected on the fact that history was about to repeat itself. Letters and telegram are no longer in Marx's papers, but a final signed photograph of the handsome, dynamic, younger German officer, complete with medals, ready to engage in new battles, was received by Marx shortly before he died in 1939. His own battles were over.

On 19 November 1930, Marx's wife Lily died. She had been ill for some time. They had been together for forty-five years and although it had perhaps not always been the happiest of marriages, Marx was bereft of a companion he had grown to value and no doubt, at the end of their lives, to love. Lily had always had to live a life of her own while her naval husband lived his. It had made her strong. Her obituary in the *Andover Advertiser* gives a good idea of the development of her uncompromising and formidable character. A correspondent wrote,

> Mrs. Marx was a born organiser and a great worker, but behind all that was a great driving force, a progressive spirit that was always directed to the right goal. She was a wonderful chairman, always ready with a jest or the right word to smooth over the awkward moment, or soothe ruffled tempers [no doubt Marx had given her practice!], but she never lost sight of the real issue nor gave way when a question of principle was involved. …her work for such movements as the Mother's Union can never be forgotten… . Her great strength lay in the fact that she was intensely religious, and that without the smallest show or parade… . During the war she gave valuable service to the V.A.D. and later was one of the County Officers of the Girl Guides…the League of Nations have lost an enthusiastic supporter.

Even at the last when months of illness had forced her to lay aside all active work, she still retained her interest in things and her sense of humour. The neighbourhood will miss her sorely.

Marx's final years – it is hard to say declining – remained as remarkable as ever. At the age of eighty-seven, the doughty old Admiral was still hunting with the Tedworth. He was almost blind at this stage and it is said that he managed to jump only because he followed a lady friend with a large grey horse, which he could see as a grey blur. He was blind in one eye and wore a watchmaker's glass in the other. His old horse was called Stilton and had as much trouble as him with age! When we last see Admiral John Locke Marx, he is constructing an air-raid bunker on the farm at Clatford Lodge ready for World War Two. No doubt he would have wangled himself into that, in some capacity or other, but on 13 August 1939, the truly 'Grand Old Man' had to leave this world – perhaps to make his mark in another!

---

1 *Andover Advertiser*, 22 November 1939.

2 Ibid.

3 Admiral E Charlton, appointed to Admiralty for special service in 1914.

4 Written on cover of photograph.

Epilogue

There is no better summary of the naval life of Admiral John Locke Marx than the verses printed in *Punch* on 4 April 1917.

Admiral Dugout

He had done with fleets and squadrons, with the restless roaming seas,
 He had found the quiet haven he desired,
And he lay there to his moorings with the dignity and ease
 Most becoming to Rear-Admirals (retired);
He was bred on 'Spit and Polish' – he was reared to 'Stick and String' –
 All the things the ultra-moderns never name;
But a storm blew up to seaward, and it meant the Real Thing,
 And he had to slip his cable when it came.

So he hied him up to London for to hang about Whitehall,
 And he sat upon the steps there soon and late,
He importuned night and morning, he bombarded great and small,
 From messengers to Ministers of State;
He was like a guilty conscience, he was like a ghost unlaid,
 He was like a debt of which you can't get rid,
Till the Powers that Be, despairing, in a fit of temper said,
 'For the Lord's sake give him something' – and they did.

They commissioned him a trawler with a high and raking bow,
 Black and workmanlike as any pirate craft,

With a crew of steady seamen very handy in a row,
And a brace of little barkers fore and aft;
And he blessed the Lord his Maker when he faced the North Sea
sprays
And exceedingly extolled his lucky star
That had given his youth renewal in the evening of his days
(With the rank of Captain Dugout, R.N.R.).

He is jolly as a sandboy, he is happier than a king,
And his trawler is the darling of his heart
(With her cuddy like a cupboard where a kitten couldn't swing,
And a smell of fish that simply won't depart);
He has found upon occasion sundry targets for his guns:
He could tell you tales of mine and submarine;
Oh, the holes he's in and out of and the glorious risks he runs
Turn his son – who's in a Super-Dreadnought – green.

He is fit as any fiddle; he is hearty, hale and tanned;
He is proof against the coldest gales that blow;
He has never felt so lively since he got his first command
(Which is rather more than forty years ago);
And of all the joyful picnics of his wild and wandering youth –
Little dust-ups from Taku to Zanzibar –
There was none to match the picnic, he declares in sober sooth,
That he has as Captain Dugout, R.N.R.

CFS